3666 Interesting, Fun And Crazy Facts You Won't Believe Are True

The Knowledge Encyclopedia To Win Trivia

Scott Matthews

Table of Contents

1144 Random, Interesting & Fun Facts You Need To Know

1. In 2013, an Egyptian city name Heracleion was discovered underwater after being lost for 1200 years in the Mediterranean Sea.

2. Malaysian based artist, Brian Lai, has the unique ability to draw in negatives.

3. In Japanese myth, there's a creature called the Asiarai Yashiki. It's a giant unwashed foot that appears before you and demands to be washed. If you don't wash it, it rampages through your house.

4. There's a dog named Faith that was born with no front legs but learned to walk on its hind legs. The dog and its owner both travel to military hospitals to demonstrate that even a dog with a severe disability can live a full life.

5. There's a 34-year-old chimpanzee named Kanzi that not only knows how to start a fire and cook food, but knows how to make omelettes for himself.

6. In 2013 in Belo Horizonte, Brazil, construction workers permanently cemented a truck into a sidewalk after the owner refused to move it.

7. The Canadian post office has assigned a postal code of "H, O, H, O, H, O" to the North Pole where anyone can send a letter to Santa Claus. Every year more than one million letters are addressed to Santa Claus, each of which are answered in the same language they were written in.

8. There's a spa called 'Bali Heritage Reflexology and Spa' in Jakarta, Indonesia that uses pythons placed on a customer's body as a form of massage treatment.

9. In 2010, a man got lost in the woods of northern Saskatchewan and chopped down power lines just to draw attention to himself in hopes that someone would rescue him. It worked.

10. Coffee was so influential in early Turkish culture that the word "breakfast" literally translates to 'before coffee' and the word "brown" translates to 'the color of coffee'.

11. The longest that anyone has ever survived in a shipwrecked raft was 133 days. Chinese man, Poon Lim survived shipwrecking in 1942 by fishing, drinking bird blood and even killing a shark with a jug of water. He lived to the age of 72, dying in 1991.

12. In order to be a London Black Cab driver, one is expected to know 25,000 roads and 50,000 points of interest in order to pass the test called 'The Knowledge'. Applicants usually need twelve appearances and 34 months of preparation to pass it.
13. In Tunisia, you can book an overnight stay at Luke Skywalker's boyhood home - a real hotel called "The Hotel Sidi Driss", for only $10.
14. There is a lake in the country of Palau called Jellyfish Lake where jellyfish have evolved without stingers. These golden jellyfish are completely harmless to humans and you can even swim with them.
15. In 1770 the British Parliament passed a law condemning lipstick stating that "any woman found guilty of seducing a man into matrimony by a cosmetic means would be tried for witchcraft."
16. A 'butt' was a medieval unit of measurement for wine. Technically, a butt-load of wine is 125 gallons (475 liters).
17. Tap water in Canada is regulated to a higher standard than bottled water.
18. In 1947, Sugar Ray Robinson, one of the greatest boxers of all time, backed out of a fight because he had a dream that he was going to kill his opponent. After being convinced to fight he went into the ring and actually killed his opponent.
19. In 2011, the Coble family lost their three children, two girls and a boy in an unfortunate car accident. A year later the mother gave birth to triplets, two girls and one boy.
20. The highest scoring soccer game in history recognized by the Guinness Book of World Records was 149 to zero between two teams in Madagascar in 2002. It happened because one of the teams began scoring on themselves in protest of a bad call by one of the referees.
21. The Sahara is only in a 'dry period' and is expected to be green again in 15,000 years.
22. In 1567 Hans Steininger who once had the longest beard in the world at 4.5 feet (1.4 meters) long, died when he broke his neck after accidentally stepping on it.
23. Deceased North Korean leader Kim Jong Il's official biography lists among his achievements a 38-shot round of golf, the ability to control the weather, the need to never have to poop, and being the creator of the hamburger.
24. David B. Leak was an American soldier from the Korean War who was given the Medal of Honor after killing five soldiers, four with his

bare hands, while giving medical attention to one of his comrades after being shot.

25. Thomas Edison taught his second wife Mina Miller Morse code so that they could communicate in secret by tapping each other's hands when their families were around.

26. Leonardo DiCaprio was named Leonardo because his pregnant mother was looking at a Leonardo da Vinci painting in Italy when he first kicked.

27. The human brain uses 20% of the bodies energy even though it's only 2% of the body's total weight.

28. In 2013, a 59-year-old man named Alan Markovitz was upset at his ex-wife for cheating on him, bought a house next to hers and installed a giant $7,000 statue of a hand giving the finger aimed at her house.

29. Kim Peek, the inspiration for the movie Rain Man, was born with significant brain damage. He's read over 12,000 books and remembers every single one of them. He's even able to read two pages at once, one with each eye and remembers everything in them.

30. In 1997, a seventeen-year-old Merino sheep named Shrek in New Zealand ran away and hid in a cave for seven years. When he was finally found in 2004, he had gone unsheared for so long that he had accumulated 60 pounds (27kg) of wool on his body, the equivalent to make 20 suits.

31. "Mike the Headless Chicken" was a famous chicken from 1945 that was beheaded by a farmer for his dinner but continued to live for another 18 full months.

32. It cost 1.5 cents to make a penny and the U.S. mint issued $46 million worth of these coins in 2018.

33. The 'Intempo' skyscraper in Spain has forty-seven floors but no elevators.

34. The Neanderthal's brain was 10% bigger than a homosapiens but they were not as intelligent as us. This is because their brains were more devoted to vision, where more of ours is devoted to reasoning, decision making, and social interaction.

35. The human body contains trillions of microorganisms i.e bacteria outnumbering human cells by 10 to 1.

36. In China, the extremely wealthy can avoid prison terms by hiring body doubles.

37. There are miniature wolves in the Middle East that only reach about 30 pounds (6kg). In comparison the largest wolves in the world found in Canada, Russia and Alaska can reach up to 175 pounds (80kg).

38. It takes 40,000 years for a photon of light to travel from the core of the sun to its surface. For the same photon to travel from the sun to Earth, it only takes eight minutes.
39. The first-ever diamonds were found in India in the fourth century BC. The next country it was discovered in Brazil in 1725.
40. In the year 2020, there will be approximately 40 billion gadgets connected to the internet.
41. The smallest country in the world is the Vatican which only has 0.22 square miles (0.44 square kilometers).
42. As of 2019, the country with the highest homicide rates in El Salvador with 82.84 homicides per 100,000 inhabitants per year. With approximately 6 million people that equates to 5,000 people per year. The extremely high homicide rate in this country is marked by the significant occurrence of gang-related crimes and juvenile delinquency.
43. The Terracotta Army is a collection of more than 8,000 clay soldiers, chariots and horses that took around 37 years to make. They were buried with the Emperor in 210 BC with the purpose of protecting him in his afterlife.
44. A person who drives 10 miles to buy a lottery ticket is three times more likely to die in a car accident than winning the lottery.
45. In only 3% of all the bird species does the male have a penis.
46. In 2017 19% of brides said they met their spouse online. This industry now brings in $3 billion a year.
47. You are not allowed to flush the toilet after 10 pm in Switzerland. Other bizarre things you can't do in this country are use a high-pressure power hose on your car, hike naked, hanging out laundry, cut your grass or recycle on Sundays. Some random things you must do in this country is pay tax on your dog if you have one and have a buddy for pets such as guinea pigs, goldfish and budgies so they have company.
48. There are no clocks in the casinos of Las Vegas so customers lose track of time and stay in the premises longer.
49. Grasshoppers have ears in the sides of their abdomen.
50. There are 350 pyramids that were built by the rulers of the ancient Kushite kingdoms now known as Sudan.
51. Situated on Sark Island in Guernsey, an island between England and France, Sark Prison is the world's smallest prison which only fits two people.

52. The average speed of a commercial airplane is 485 knots which is 560 mph (900km/h)
53. The longest recorded living animal is an Ocean Quahog Clam which was recorded at a staggering 507 years. Second place goes to a Greenland shark at 392 years followed by a bowhead whale at 211 years.
54. The largest tigers in the world live in Siberia.
55. It has only snowed in Cuba once way back on March 12, 1857.
56. Bamboo can grow up to 35 inches (91cm) in a single day.
57. There are approximately 6,500 languages spoken in the world today however 2,000 of those languages only have 1,000 speakers or less
58. Saddam Hussein, the late President of Iraq wrote several novels and a number of poems that were published anonymously.
59. The first building to have more than 100 floors was The Empire State Building.
60. The most visited city in the world is Bangkok with 20 million people in 2018 followed by London and Paris.
61. Humans only make up 48 percent of users on the internet. The other 52 percent of web traffic are bots.
62. Hitler was Time's "Man of the Year" in 1938.
63. China is home to half of the pig population on earth.
64. There are 1.2 million species documented in existence today, however, scientists estimate the number to be somewhere around 8.7 million. Due to extinction, however, we may never know the exact number.
65. You would weigh more at the poles than you would weigh at the equator however the difference would only be 0.5% approximately. You would weigh slightly more at sea level than at the top of a mountain. This is due to oblateness and gravitational pull.
66. Occasionally in the arctic, the sun can appear square when it's on the horizon.
67. On average, brunettes have less hair on their head compared to red-haired and blondes.
68. Royal tradition states that Prince Charles and Prince William cannot board the same plane together in case there is a crash and the monarch loses two heirs at once. Technically the same rule applies for Prince William and his five-year-old son, Prince George.
69. The largest organ on the body is skin.

70. It is false that you can bite through a finger as easily as a carrot. It takes 200 newtons to bite through a raw carrot and 1485 newtons just to cause a fracture to a finger.
71. It took over 22 centuries to complete the Great Wall of China. It was built, rebuilt and extended by many imperial dynasties and kingdoms. The wall exceeds 12,000 miles (20,000km).
72. The largest empire the world has ever seen was the British Empire, which covered almost a quarter of the planet in its peak in 1920.
73. Most of the camels in Saudi Arabia are imported from Australia.
74. China produces the most pollution in the world contributing 30% of all the countries total. These come from coal, oil and natural gases.
75. There are currently 1.6 billion live websites on the web right now. However 99% of these sites you cannot access through Google and is known as the Deep Web.
76. Just like all languages, sign language has different accents based on country, age, ethnicity and whether the person is deaf or not.
77. There are over 1200 different species of bats in the world and contrary to popular belief, none of them are blind. Bats can hunt in the dark using echolocation, which means they use echoes of self-produced sounds bouncing off objects to help them navigate.
78. When you're buried six feet down in soil and without a coffin, an average adult body normally takes eight to twelve years to decompose to a skeleton.
79. Pigs are physically incapable to look up into the sky.
80. The largest detonated bomb in the world was the Tsar Bomba on October 30 in 1961 by the Soviet Union. The blast was 3,000 times stronger than the bomb used on Hiroshima. The impact was enough to break windows 560 miles (900km) away.
81. The wars between the Romans and Persians lasted about 721 years, the longest conflict in human history.
82. There were at least forty-two known assassination plots against Hitler.
83. It took approximately 75 years for the telephone to reach 50 million users, the radio 38 years, 13 years for the television, 4 for the Internet, 2 for Facebook and only 19 days for Pokemon Go.
84. The biggest island in the world is Greenland, as Australia is a continent.
85. In 2018, 4 billion people have access to the internet yet 844 million people still don't have access to clean water.
86. A single teaspoon of water has eight times more atoms than there are teaspoonsful of water in the Atlantic Ocean.

87. Ancient Egyptians used headrests made of stone instead of pillows.
88. France was the first country to introduce the registration plate on August 14th, 1893.
89. The Netherlands was the first country to legalize same-sex marriage which was in 2001.
90. The average human attention span has almost halved since 2,000 decreasing from 20 seconds to 12 in 2018.
91. The oldest recorded tree in the world is reported to be 9,550 years old located in Dalarna, Sweden.
92. The oldest living system ever recorded is the Cyanobacterias, a type of bacteria that originated 2.8 billion years ago.
93. Being hungry causes serotonin levels to drop, causing a whirlwind of uncontrollable emotions including anxiety, stress, and anger.
94. On Monday, March 23, 2178, Pluto will complete its full orbit since its original discovery in 1930.
95. There are more than 150 people cryofrozen right now in the hopes that one day the technology will be invented to revive them with over 1000 people registered to do the same upon their death.
96. Under extremely powerful pressure, peanut butter can be turned into diamonds.
97. After the movie 'The Princess and the Frog' came out in 2009, more than 50 people were hospitalized with salmonella poisoning from kissing frogs.
98. Albert Einstein never wore socks.
99. A can of regular coke will sink to the bottom of water while a can of diet coke will float.

Part Two

100.   In 2010, The Technical University of Munich built slides four stories high to help their students get to class quickly instead of them having to take the stairs.

101.   Only 2% of the Earth's population has green eyes.

102.   When Jackie Chan was eighteen, he got into a street fight with bikers where shortly after he noticed a piece of bone sticking out of his knuckles. He tried spending an entire day pushing it back in until he realized that it wasn't his bone but the other guys tooth.

103.   In 1971, a man named Jean-Claude Romand lied about passing important medical exams where he continued crafting elaborate lies until everyone he knew thought he was an actual medical doctor. He got away for it for eighteen years until he eventually killed his entire family to avoid being revealed.

104.   There was an orangutan named Fu Manchu, who was repeatedly able to escape from his cage at the Henry Doorly Zoo in Nebraska. It was found that he was using a key that he fashioned out of a piece of wire. The reason was able to do it so many times and kept getting away with it was because every time the zookeeper's inspected him, he would hide the key in his mouth.

105.   In 1984 when "Air Jordans" were introduced, they were banned by the NBA. Michael Jordan wore them anyway as Nike was willing to pay the $5,000 fine each time he stepped onto the court.

106.   Zach Galifianakis was approached by Nike to be in their advertising after the success of The Hangover. During the conference call, he broke the ice by asking "So do you still have seven-year-olds making your stuff?"

107.   In France, a bakery by law has to make all of its bread that it sells from scratch in order to have the right to be called a bakery.

108.   In 2005, 110 people tied for the second prize in the Powerball Lottery. Officials suspected cheating was involved but discovered that the winners had all used the same lucky numbers off copies of the same fortune from fortune cookies.

109.   In Denmark, 'Fartkontrol' means "speed check".

110.   The Vatican City is home to the world's only ATM that gives instructions in Latin.

111.   In Australia, there are trees that grow several different types of fruits known as fruit salad trees.

112.   The shortest presidency in the history of the world was by President Pedro Paredes of Mexico, who ruled for less than one hour on February 19, 1913.

113.   A twenty-ounce bottle of Mountain Dew contains the equivalent of 22 packets of sugar.

114.   In Moscow, stray dogs have learned to commute from the suburbs to the city, scavenge for food, then catch the train home in the evening.

115.   The human brain has a negativity bias causing us to continually look for bad news. It's an evolutionary trait that stem from early humans as a survival mechanism.

116.   The smallest known reptile in the world is the "Brookesia micra" which is so small it can stand on the head of a match.

117.   In 2011, a 99 year old Italian named Antonio C. divorced his 96 year old wide Rosa C. after finding secret love letters revealing that she had an affair in the 1940s.

118.   We're technically living about 80 milliseconds in the past because that's how long it takes our brain to process information.

119.   In 2008, a nineteen-year-old from Somerset, England named George Garrett officially changed his name to 'Captain Fantastic Faster Than Superman Batman Wolverine The Hulk And The Flash Combined'.

120.   In 1993, Dave Thomas, who was known for founding popular chain "Wendy's" went back to high school to earn his GED decades after dropping out, because he was worried kids may see his success as an excuse to also drop out of school.

121.   There was a billionaire named Paul Getty who refused to pay a seventeen million dollar ransom for his kidnapped grandson. When the teenager's severed ear arrived, he agreed to pay three million but only actually paid 2.2 because that was the maximum he would be able to write off as tax.

122.   Pogonophobia is the fear of beards.

123.   The average "Game Of Thrones" episode costs $2-$3 million to produce. That's two to three times what a typical network or cable show costs per episode.

124.   Baboons in the wild have been known to kidnap puppies and raise them as pets.

125.   In 2005, a man named "Ronald McDonald" robbed a Wendy's in Manchester, England.

126.   In 1977, we received a radio signal from space that lasted 72 seconds and was dubbed 'the wow signal'. To this day we still don't know where it came from.

127.   Socialist Karl Marx's' final words before he died in 1883 were "Go away, last words are for fools who haven't said enough".

128.   Oona Chaplin, the actress who plays Talisa in "Game of Thrones" is actually Charlie Chaplin's granddaughter.

129.   A wolf will respond with a howl if a human imitates a howl.

130.   The moon is capable of having 'moonquakes'. They are less frequent and intense as the ones on Earth however.

131.   It is estimated that only 8% of the world's total money is real. The rest exists electronically on computer hard drives and bank accounts.

132.   Elephant grass can grow upto 10 feet (3 meters) tall that even elephants can hide in.

133.   A single factory in Ireland makes more than 90% of the worlds botox.

134.   Most airplane crashes happen either three minutes after taking off or eight minutes before landing.

135.   Carl Gugasian is serving 17 years in jail after robbing 50 banks over a 30 year period stealing $2 million.

136.   Twenty four women have made accusations that Donald Trump has elicited inappropriate sexual behavior over the previous thirty years.

137.   A group of camels is called a caravan.

138.   In 2013, Scottish scientists created a pizza that has 30% of your daily recommended nutrients.

139.   There are still 30 million people living in caves in China.

140.   There is a skywalk on Tianmen Mountain in China, which is 200 feet (61 meters) long with 8.2 feet (2.5 meter) deep with thick glass. The bridge is so high up that it allows visitors to look down on the peaks of smaller mountains below.

141.   The lighter was invented before the matchstick.

142.   In 2009, a 10 year old British girl named Zoe Pemberton tried to sell her grandmother on eBay because the little girl found her annoying and wanted to get rid of her.

143.   One in five people in Singapore are millionaires.

144.   Cockroaches were here 120 million years before the dinosaurs.

145. The most popular animal for a pet is freshwater fish. Next comes the cat followed by a dog.

146. One hundred acres of pizza are cut every day in the US alone.

147. In 2006, artist Kim Graham and a group of 25 volunteers spent 15 days using entirely non-toxic recycled paper products to create a 12 foot (3.7 meter) tall paper mache tree doll.

148. Lightning strikes are not as rare as you think. Approximately 100 strikes hit the earth per second! Each bolt can have upto a billion volts of electricity.

149. Mark Zuckerberg has signed the 'Giving Pledge' campaign created by Warren Buffet and Bill Gates which encourages wealthy people to contribute a majority of their wealth to philanthropic causes.

150. In Japan, it's considered to be good luck if a sumo-wrestler makes your baby cry.

151. Carrots used to be purple in colour.

152. Over 99% of all species (equal to five billion species in total)l that ever been on Earth have died out.

153. Jeff Bezos, the owner of Amazon.com, is also the owner of the Washington Post.

154. Google rents goats to replace lawn mowers at their Mountain View headquarters.

155. When you get blackout drunk, you don't actually forget anything because your brain isn't recording in the first place.

156. Nintendo has banked so much money that they could run a deficit of $250 million every year and still survive until 2052.

157. Taiwan has become the first country to offer free Wi-Fi to all tourists using over 4,000 hotspots located over the island.

158. There's a fruit called black sapote which is nicknamed the "chocolate pudding fruit" as when the fruit is at the right ripeness, it tastes like chocolate pudding. As well as this, it is low in fat and has about four times as much vitamin C as an orange.

159. In North Korea, citizens are forced to choose from one of twenty eight government approved haircuts.

160. It's estimated that there are approximately three million shipwrecks on the ocean floor, worth billions in value and treasure.

161. A seven year old second grader was suspended for biting a pop tart into the shape of a mountain which school officials mistook for a gun.

162. In 2013, a company called "Limite Zero" created a 2300 foot (720 meter) international zipline between Spain and Portugal.

163. All of the air in potato chip bags that people complain about isn't air at all. It's actually nitrogen which serves the purpose to keep chips crisp and to provide a cushion during shipping.

164. In 2005, a documentary was filmed called "Reversal of Fortune" where filmmakers gave a homeless man named Ted Rodrigue $100,000 in cash and followed him around to see what he would do with the money. Less than six months later he was completely broke and back in the same place he was before it all started.

165. The infinite monkey theorem states that a monkey hitting keys at random on a typewriter for an infinite amount of time will eventually type out any given text including the complete works of William Shakespeare.

166. If you don't identify as an extrovert or introvert, you may be an ambivert. This is a person moderately comfortable with groups and social interactions, but also relishes time alone away from crowds.

167. In 2007, a twin was born 34 minutes after her brother but, because of daylight savings time, adjustment was actually born 26 minutes before her brother.

168. In a study to improve hospital design for children, researchers from the University of Sheffield polled 250 children regarding their opinions of clowns. Every single one reported disliking or fearing them.

169. The most expensive thing ever created is the International Space Station at a cost of $160 billion and rising as new sections are added.

170. In a study conducted by the Bay State Medical Center in Springfield, approximately 68% of people experience phantom vibration syndrome, a sensory hallucination where you mistakenly think your phone is buzzing in your pocket.

171. In 2013, a man named Harrison Okene survived for three days at the bottom of the ocean in a sunken ship by finding a pocket of air.

172. In North Korea, it is currently the year 109 because their calendar is based on the birth of Kim Il-Sung, the founder of North Korea.

173.   Teddy Roosevelt was shot in 1912 right before giving a speech. Noticing that it missed his lungs since he wasn't coughing up blood, he proceeded to give the full ninety minute speech.

174.   In Armenia, all children age six and up are taught chess in school as a mandatory part of their curriculum.

175.   Schools that ditch schoolyard rules are actually seeing a decrease in bullying, serious injuries and vandalism, while concentration levels in class are increasing. This is because fewer rules requires critical thinking whereas simply obeying instructions requires very little critical thinking.

176.   Sand from the Sahara is blown by the wind all the way to the Amazon recharging it's minerals. The desert literally fertilizes the rainforest.

177.   As a child, Muhammad Ali was refused an autograph from his boxing idol Sugar Ray Robinson. When Ali became a prized fighter he vowed to never deny an autograph request which he honored throughout his entire career.

178.   President JFK purchased over a thousand Cuban cigars just hours before he ordered the Cuban trade embargo in 1962.

179.   In 1976, a Greek war veteran named Stamatis Moraitis was diagnosed with cancer and told he only had six months to live. He went back to the doctors ten years later to tell them he was still alive only to discover that all of the doctors who had diagnosed him were dead. He lived to be 102 years old.

180.   An Indiana state prison allows murderers to adopt cats in their cells to help teach them love and compassion for other living things.

181.   The Gatling gun was invented by DR Richard Gatling, who noticed that the majority of soldiers during the Civil War who died were due to disease, not gunshot wounds. By inventing a machine that could replace hundreds of soldiers, the need for large armies would be reduced thus diminishing exposure to battle and disease.

182.   If New York City was its own country and the NYPD was its army, it would be the 20th best funded army in the world just behind Greece and ahead of North Korea.

183.   The WWOOF or the Worldwide Opportunities on Organic Farms is an international program that allows you to travel the world with free food and accommodation in exchange for volunteer work.

184.   Brass door knobs automatically disinfect themselves in eight hours which is known as the "oligodynamic effect"

185.   In 2014, a man in China bought a first class ticket on China Eastern Airlines, where he went to the airport and ate free food for almost an entire year in the VIP lounge. Astoundingly he cancelled and re-booked his flight an incredible 300 times over the course of the year and then cancelled his ticket for a full refund once the airline became wise of his scam.

186.   Until its demolition in 2012, 1% of Greenland's entire population lived in one apartment building called Blok P.

187.   German used to be the second most widely spoken language in the United States before it was forcibly repressed during World War One.

188.   In the 1960's, the US did an experiment where two people without nuclear training had to design a nuke with only access to publicly available documents. They succeeded.

189.   By the time Donald Trump was 27, he owned 14,000 apartments.

190.   The "Challenger Deep" found in the Mariana Trench is the deepest point in Earth's oceans that we know of at 10994 meters.

191.   Chaology is the study of chaos or chaos theory.

192.   Hitler collected Jewish artifacts for a museum of what he hoped to be an extinct race after the second world war.

193.   Male puppies will let female puppies win when they play even though they are physically more powerful to encourage them to play more.

194.   The Antonov An-225 is the largest aircraft ever made and was initially created for the task of transporting spaceplanes. It weighs 285 tonnes, has a wingspan of 288 feet (88 meters) and cost $250 million.

195.   One quick kick from a giraffe can kill a lion.

196.   The youngest Pope to ever be elected was Pope Benedict IX born in 1012 who was 12 years old.

197.   Xylography is the art of engraving on wood.

198.   It took 410 days for the Empire State Building to be made.

199.   There is a superman somewhere in every scene of Seinfeld.

200.   The average Boeing 747 plane has 160 miles (260km) of wiring inside of it.

201.   There are still several unexplored hidden passages in the pyramids of Giza.

202.   J.K. Rowling is the first author to reach billionaire status. She also holds the status of losing her billionaire status due to giving away most of her money.

203.   During the 1600's, there was "Tulip mania" in Holland, a time where tulips were more valuable than gold. This is the first reported economic bubble. When people came to their senses the bubble burst and caused the market to crash.

204.   In ancient Egypt, the Egyptians shaved off their eyebrows to show grief from the death of their cat.

205.   Lake Chagan is the only lake artificially created by a nuclear test. Even though the nuclear test was fired in 1965 it's still unsafe for swimming due to radiation.

206.   Before the renaissance era, three quarters of all books in the world were in Chinese.

207.   The human eye can see a candle flickering upto 30 miles (48km) away on a dark night.

208.   Due to a genetic mutation, the first blue eyed humans only began to appear six to ten thousand years ago.

209.   For less than the cost of a Ferrari, you can buy a renovated Boeing 737.

210.   There are approximately 250,000 active patents applicable to the smartphone.

211.   Sugar was first invented in India, where extraction and purification techniques were developed in 510 BC. Before that, the most popular sweetener was honey.

212.   The typical American spends $1,200 on fast food every year.

213.   A camel can drink 53 gallons (200 litres) of water in three minutes.

214.   The amount of water on Earth is constant, however a billion years from now, the Sun will be ten percent brighter, increasing the Earth's heat, leading to total water loss on Earth.

215.   You cannot invent faces in your dream, which means you've encountered every face you've seen in your dream in real life.

216. Crabs are able to regenerate their legs and claws to 95% of their original size.

217. The largest living creature on Earth is the Great Barrier Reef, which measures at 1200 miles (2,000km) long.

218. The Old Testament was written over the course of 1000 years, whereas the New Testament was written within 75 years.

219. Astronauts would weigh one sixth of their weight if they were in space compared to on Earth.

220. If two rats were left alone in an enclosed area with enough room, they can multiply to a million within 18 months.

221. It's impossible to taste food without saliva. This is because chemicals from the food must first dissolve in saliva. Once dissolved chemicals can be detected by receptors on taste buds.

222. The heaviest drinkers in the world are in Belarus, with 17.5 litres consumed per capita every year.

223. Polar bears evolved from brown bears, somewhere in the vicinity of Britain and Ireland 150,000 years ago.

224. The fastest land animal is the Cheetah, which has a recorded speed of between 75.0 mph (120 km/h) . The Peregrine Falcon is the fastest bird with a diving speed of 242 mph (389 km/h).

225. A jellyfish has no ears, eyes, nose, brain or heart.

226. The largest earthquake recorded was in Chile in 1960. It was placed in at 9.4–9.6 on the magnitude scale and lasted for 10 minutes.

227. There are 2.32 billion monthly active users on Facebook as of 31st December, 2018.

228. The African driver ants can produce 3 to 4 million eggs every 25 days.

229. The average IQ rate has been declining over recent decades. This is because smarter people are having less children.

230. The most popular sport in the world is Football. Second place goes to Cricket followed by Field Hockey.

231. Each sperm contains about 3 billion bases of genetic information, representing 750 Megabytes of digital information.

232. One out of every 4 cranes in the world is located in Dubai. The countries artificial Palm Islands also used enough sand to fill 2.5 Empire State Buildings.

233. Humans can have anywhere from 12 to 60 thousand thoughts per day, with 80 percent of these thoughts being negative.

234. The human brain has 100 billion brain cells.

235.   The top ten cheese eating countries are all in Europe with French being number one. The average French person consumes 57 pounds (25kg) of cheese per year.

236.   The highest temperature ever recorded on Earth was El Azizia on 13th September, 1922, at 136 degrees Fahrenheit (58 degrees Celsius).

237.   There are more living organisms in a teaspoon of soil than there are humans in the world.

238.   Oranges are not even in the top ten list of common foods when it comes to vitamin C levels.

239.   There are 100 to 400 billion stars in the Milky Way, and more than 100 billion galaxies in the Universe.

240.   Astronomers have found what appears to be one of the oldest known stars in the universe, which is located about 6,000 light-years away from Earth. The ancient star formed not long after the Big Bang 13.8 billion years ago.

241.   A penguin can hold its breath for 20 minutes.

242.   According to scientists, the weight of the average cloud is the same as 100 elephants.

243.   95% of the decisions you make have already been made up by your subconscious mind.

244.   By the time you are 2, your brain is already 80% the size of an adults.

245.   The reason birds fly in a 'V' formation is to save energy due to wind resistance. The birds take turns being in the front and fall to the back when they're tired.

246.   The average person has 10,000 taste buds, which are replaced every 2 weeks or so.

247.   If all the stored batteries in the world were used for consumption, they would be flat in 10 minutes.

248.   The Burj Khalifa is the tallest building in the world standing at 2700 feet (830 meters). Construction started in 2004 and took 4 years to complete.

249.   Almost a tenth of all Chinese have the last name 'Wang', which translates to king.

250.   Humans take in 11 million bits of information every second, however we're only aware of about 40 of these things.

251.   Russia has 1.8 times the landmass of the U.S.

252.   The pollution is Beijing is so bad they have come up with a term called the 'Beijing Cough'.

253.	In 1967 the Prime Minister of Australia went missing. It was only four decades after he went missing that it was confirmed that he had accidentally drowned.

254.	Jackie Chan's mother was a drug smuggler while his father was a spy. This is in fact how they met, when his father arrested his mother for smuggling opium.

255.	George Lucas wanted the role of Mace Windu to originally go to Tupac, however he died before he could give an audition and the role went to Samuel L. Jackson instead.

256.	Many murder cases in Japan are declared suicides in order for Police Officers to save face and to keep crime statistics low.

257.	A scorpion can hold its breath underwater for up to six days.

258.	Ethiopia is currently in the year 2006 because it has thirteen months in its year.

259.	The City of New York paid $5 million in 1853 for the land that is Central park, which is now worth $530 billion.

260.	The oldest instruments date back 43,000 years ago. They were equivalent to flutes but were made out of bones from birds and mammoth.

261.	A flame is round and blue when in zero gravity.

262.	Studies have shown that people with creative minds find it harder to fall asleep at night and prefer to stay up later.

263.	Patients in an insane mental asylum in the 1950's, have the same stress as the average current day high school student.

264.	A group of lemurs is called a conspiracy.

265.	The longest prison sentence was 320,000 years to a man named Gabriel Grandos for failing to deliver over 70,000 letters.

266.	There is a city being created in the Arab Emirates right now that will be entirely reliant on renewable energy sources with a zero waste ecology.

267.	A study done by the Bureau of Economic Research concluded that first born children have higher IQ's than their younger siblings.

268.	The smallest poisonous frog is only 10 millimeters in length and secretes a toxic poison from its skin as a defense mechanism.

269.	There's a natural gas vent in Iraq known as the Eternal Fire that's been burning for over 4,000 years.

270.	Farting helps to reduce blood pressure and is good for overall health.

271.   The artificial sweetener Splenda was discovered when a researcher misheard the command to test this chemical as 'taste this chemical'.

272.   Before Sylvester Stallone sold the script for Rocky, he was broke and had to sell his dog for $50. A week later he sold the script and bought his dog back for $3,000.

273.   Chinese soldiers stick needles in their shirt collars in order to keep a straight posture during military parades.

274.   There are 36 armed dolphins trained by the US Navy to kill terrorists which have been missing in the Gulf of Mexico since Hurricane Katrina in 2005. They carry toxic dart guns capable of killing a person with one shot.

275.   A Dutch artist discovered a way to create clouds in the middle of a room by carefully balancing humidity, lighting and temperature. He uses this regularly in his artwork.

276.   The largest cemetery in the world is the Wadi Al-Salaam Cemetery, located in Iraq. It's 2 miles (6km) squared and is so big that it's unknown how many bodies are in there. It's estimated to be in the millions and half a million more get added each year.

277.   Before "Scar" got the scar on his face in The Lion King, his name was "Taka" which means 'garbage' in Swahili.

278.   Benjamin Franklin wasn't trusted to write the US declaration of Independence, because it was feared he would conceal a joke in it.

279.   The app Candy Crush was making $956,000 a day in its prime.

280.   Bill Gates, Steve Jobs, Albert Einstein, Walt Disney and Mark Zuckerberg all dropped out of school.

281.   The deepest indoor pool is located in Belgium, Brussels, named Nemo 33 at 108 feet (32 meters) deep.

282.   The famous torrent site Pirate Bay once tried to buy it's own island to make their own country with no copyright laws.

283.   Prairie dogs say hello with kisses.

284.   All humans have the ability to see ultraviolet light, however it's passively filtered through our lens. People who get surgery done to remove the lens can see ultraviolet light.

285.   The Filipino flag is flown with its Red stripe up in times of war, and blue side up in times of peace.

286.   License plates in the Canadian Northwest territories are shaped like polar bears.

287.   Crows have the ability to recognise human faces and even hold grudges against ones they don't like.

288.   Jaguars in the wild are known for frequently getting high eating hallucinogenic roots, which also increases their senses for hunting.

289.   The reason "Harry Potter and the Goblet of Fire" is longer than the first three books is because author J.K. Rowling made a plot hole half way through and had to go back and fix it.

290.   Cherries contain 2 compounds inhibiting tumor growth, and even cause cancer cells to self-destruct without damaging healthy cells.

291.   On the planet Venus, it snows metal.

292.   The U.N. has deemed access to the internet a human right.

293.   Crocodiles don't have sweat glands. In order to cool themselves down they keep their jaws open.

294.   It takes a sloth two weeks to digest their food.

295.   On Valentine's Day 2014, a group of single men in Shanghai bought every odd-numbered seat for a theater showing of Beijing Love Story. They did this to prevent couples from sitting together as a show of support for single people.

296.   In 2014, the Department of Transportation in Colorado was forced to change their mile marker from 420 to 419.99 just to get people to stop stealing their sign.

297.   Naked mole rats are one of the only animals to not get cancer.

298.   LSD has been known to help aid in treatment of Post Traumatic Stress Disorder, such as in the case of Yehiel De-Nur, a Holocaust survivor who, after taking the drug, was able to sleep for the first time in 30 years without nightmares.

299.   In 1983 a 61 year old potato farmer named Cliff Young who was not an athlete, won the 544 mile (875 km) Sydney to Melbourne Ultra Marathon, simply because he ran while the other runners slept.

300.   Penguin's legs are actually longer than they appear. They only look short because of the amount of feathers covering them.

301.   Queen Elizabeth does not have a passport. Since the British Passport is issued in her name, she does not need to possess one however the other members of the Royal Family do.

302.   Adam Rainer, an Australian man is the only person in medical history to have been classified as both a dwarf and a giant in his lifetime. He stood at 3.8 feet (1.17 meters) on his 21st birthday and was classified as a dwarf, but by the time he died at the age of 51, stood at 7 foot 6 (2.34 meters) tall, due to a growth spurt.

303.   During World War Two, two Japanese officers named Tokiashi Mukai and Tsuyoshi Noda had a race to see who could kill 100 people first, using only a sword. Disturbingly, it was covered like a sporting event in Japanese newspapers, with regular updates on the score.

304.   In 2006, the FBI planted a spy in a southern California mosque and disguised him as a radical muslim, in order to root out potential threats. The plan backfired when Muslims in the mosque ended up reporting him to the FBI for being a potentially dangerous extremist.

305.   On the first day of school, children in Germany, Austria and the Czech Republic are given a cardboard cone filled with toys and sweets known as a 'Schultute'.

306.   Coal power stations put out 100 times more radiation into the air than nuclear power plants producing the same amount of energy.

307.   A group of owls is called a parliament.

308.   In 1987, a German Shepherd dog named Gabby in a Belgrade Zoo once saved a zoo employee by fighting and defeating an escaped jaguar. For this, a monument was erected in her honor.

309.   In 1951, a woman named Henrietta Lacks died of cervical cancer, but her tumor cells were removed and later discovered to be the first ever human cells that could thrive in a lab. Her cells have been the subject of more than 74,000 studies, many of which have yielded profound insights into cell biology, cancer, vaccine and cloning.

310.   Sigmund Freud, Austrian neurologist and Father of Psychoanalysis, loved cocaine so much that he used to give it away to friends and family as gifts.

311. There is an insect called the 'tree lobster' which is almost the size of a human hand. They can only be found in one place, on the huge mountainous remains of an old volcano called Ball's an Island off the coast of Australia.

312. In Mexico, artists like painters, sculptors and graphic artists can pay their taxes by donating pieces of artwork that they create to the government.

313. Despite having billions of dollars and being one of the wealthiest businessmen in the world, Ikea founder Ingvar Kamprad is notoriously cheap. He lives in a small home, eats at Ikea, takes the bus and only flies economy class.

314. The stickers that you find on fruit are actually made of edible paper and the glue used to stick them on is actually food grade, so even if you eat one you'll be completely fine.

315. When ants die, they secrete a chemical that tells other ants to move the body to a sort of burial ground. If this chemical is sprayed on a live ants, other ants will treat it as a dead ant, regardless of what it does.

316. Australia is home to the 'golden silk orb weave' spiders, arachnids that are so big that they can eat entire foot and a half (half a meter) long snakes.

317. A group of giraffes is called a tower.

318. There was a goat in Utah named Freckles that was implanted with spider genes as an embryo that is now known as the Spider Goat. She produces spider silk proteins in her milk, which is used to make bio-steel, a material stronger than Kevlar.

319. Richard Klinkhamer, a Dutch crime writer wrote a suspicious book on seven ways to kill your spouse, one year after his wife disappeared. He became a celebrity and spent the next decade hinting that he murdered her, and in 2000 it turned out that he really had, after her skeleton was discovered at his former residence.

320. In Siberia, there's a toilet located 8500 feet (2591 meters) above sea level at the top of the Altai Mountains. It serves the workers of an isolated weather station and is known as the world's loneliest toilet.

321. When Shakira was in the second grade, she was rejected from the school choir because her music teacher didn't think she could sing, and thought she sounded like a goat.

322. Cats are one of the only animals that domesticate themselves and approach humans on their own terms.

323.   Journalist Sara Bongiorni and her family attempted to live without Chinese-made goods for an entire year and found it almost impossible. They documented their experience in a book called "A year without 'made in China'".

324.   In Japan, there are owl cafes where you can play with live owls while enjoying a drink or meal.

325.   In 1954, a man named John Thomas Doyle committed suicide by jumping off the Golden Gate Bridge. His suicide note read absolutely no reason other than "I have a toothache".

326.   Between the 1600's and 1800's lobsters were known as the cockroaches of the sea. They were fed to prisoners and servants and were used as fish bait.

327.   There is a super tiny species of antelope called the Dick-Dick, named after the sound they make when alarmed.

328.   Termites are currently being researched by scientists at UConn and Caltech as possible renewable energy sources. They can produce up to half a gallon (two liters) of hydrogen by ingesting a single sheet of paper, making them one of the planets most efficient bio-reactors.

329.   The first ever ticket purchase to the first ever 'Comic Con' in New York was by George RR Martin in 1964. He was the first of only thirty people there that day.

330.   Today there are more people suffering from obesity than there are suffering from hunger.

331.   In 2007, a man named Mike Warren-Madden designed a device called the Aquatic Pram, that allows you to take your fish for a walk.

332.   In Quebec, Sweden and Norway, it's illegal to advertise directly to children. This is to prevent companies from encouraging children to beg their parents to buy them stuff.

333.   Smokers are four times more likely to get gray hair in their lives than non-smokers.

334.   Marshmallows exist because of sore throats. For centuries juice from the marshmallow plant has been used for pain relief. In the 1800s it was mixed with egg whites and sugar for children with sore throats, and the recipe was so tasty that people turned it into a treat called marshmallow.

335.   Skunks have muscles next to their scent glands that allows them to spray their fluids accurately upto 10 foot (3 meters) away.

336.   Gorillas are known to sleep upto 12-14 hours a day.

337.   The length of human vessels in the body equate to 60,000 miles (96,000 km) if you lay them out from beginning to end.

338.   There are 50 different types of kangaroos.

339.   Depending on the species of sharks, they can either give birth to live young or lay eggs.

340.   A man in Wisconsin took a photo containing three albino deer in the woods. The chances of this happening is one in seventy nine billion.

341.   A cockroach can live up to several weeks without its head. It only dies due to hunger.

342.   Humans can only live without oxygen for three minutes, water for three days and food for three weeks.

343.   An elephant drinks 34 gallons (130 litres) of water a day.

344.   If you wear headphones for an hour, it will increase the amount of bacteria you have in your ear by 700 times!

345.   Camels have three eyelids that protects them from the rough winds in deserts.

346.   Due to the placement of a donkey's eyes, it can see all four of its feet at all times.

347.   Slugs have tentacles, blowholes, and thousands of teeth.

348.   In praying mantises, 25% of all sexual encounters result in the death of the male due to the female ripping the male's head off.

349.   Flamingos are not born pink, but eventually turn this color from their diet of brine shrimp and blue-green algae.

350.   The loneliest animal in the world is a male whale in the North Pacific, who can't find a mate due to the way it communicates. The whales frequency is on another level and can't be heard by other whales.

351.   The largest organism in the known world today is a fungus that lives in the mountains of Oregon. It spans across 2.4 miles (3.8km).

352.   Like fingerprints, our tongues all have unique prints.

353.   You are born with 270 bones when you're born, which form into 206 by the time you're an adult. A quarter of these are in your hands and wrists.

354.   During the lifespan of a human, enough saliva can be created to fill up two swimming pools.

355.   A group of parrots is called a pandemonium.

356.   Sterling Silver is not completely made out of silver. A little copper is added as pure silver is too soft and would bend otherwise.

357.   Chewing gum when cutting onions prevents you from tearing up as it forces you to breathe through your mouth.
358.   Honey is the only food that doesn't spoil.
359.   Coca-Cola only sold 25 bottles its first year. Today, it sells 1.8 billion bottles a day.
360.   There are no genuinely blue foods. Foods that appear blue such as blueberries are often a shade of purple.
361.   It takes 12 bees a lifetime of work to create a teaspoon of honey.
362.   There used to be a horse sized duck called 'dromornithidae' roaming present day Australia 50,000 years ago.
363.   There are gold glitter pills you can buy for $400 online that promise to turn your poop gold.
364.   The fear of being away from your phone is called nomophobia.
365.   The first ever modern toilet was created by Thomas Crapper, hence the phrase 'to take a crap'.
366.   In the University of Victoria in British Columbia, Canada you can take a course in the science of Batman. It uses the caped crusader to explain the human condition and the limitations of the human mind and body.
367.   The Philippine island of Luzon contains a lake that contains an island that contains a lake that contains another island.
368.   Hudson Bar in Canada has less gravity than the rest of the earth. It's unsure exactly why but scientists hypothesise that it has something to do with the convection occuring in the earth's mantle.
369.   Only 1-2% of the total world population are redheads.
370.   There is real life sport called Banzai skydiving which involves throwing your parachute out of the plane and jumping out after it.
371.   There is a swing at the edge of a cliff in Ecuador that has no safety measures. It hangs from a tree house overlooking an active volcano, and has been called the "Swing at the End of the World."
372.   Sunflowers can be used to clean up radioactive waste. Their stems and leaves absorb and store pollutants. It's also why the sunflower is the international symbol for nuclear disarmament.
373.   Doctors with messy handwriting kills more than 7,000 people and injures over a million people each year due to receiving the wrong medication.
374.   Adding sugar to a wound will greatly reduce the pain and speed up the healing process.

375. Real diamonds don't show up in x-rays.

376. Germans were the first country to realise the link between smoking and lung cancer. Hitler was one of the first ones to lead the anti-smoking campaign.

377. The creator of Pringles, Fredric Baur, had his ashes stored in a Pringles can after he died.

378. In 1996, DC and Marvel Comics published a crossover series where Wolverine and Batman were made into one character called Dark Claw or Logan Wayne.

379. There are roses that exist that are all black, but can only be found in Halfeti, Turkey.

380. Sweden recycles so well that it actually has to import garbage from Norway in order to fuel its waste to power energy plants.

381. There are actually seven different types of twins. They are: Identical, fraternal, half-identical, mirror image, mixed chromosome, superfetation and superfecundation.

382. Pluto is smaller than Russia.

383. There is a Pizza Hut perfume that smells like a fresh box of Pizza Hut pizza when you spray it.

384. The tongue of a blue whale weighs more than an elephant, and its heart weighs more than a car.

385. Labeorphilist is the collection and study of beer bottle labels.

386. Dolphins don't drink as seawater makes them ill, and could even potentially kill them. Instead they get all their liquids from the food that they eat.

387. There are giant hornets in Japan with venom so strong it can melt human skin.

388. According to researchers at the University of Helsinki, running in shoes that are highly cushioned make your legs stiffer and increase impact loading. The reason behind this is because the extra cushioned shoes alter spring-like mechanisms of running.

389. Diet soda ruins your tooth enamel just as badly as cocaine and methamphetamines.

390. The Okinawa island in Japan has over four hundred people living above the age of 100 and is known as the healthiest place on earth.

391. Skittles and jelly beans contain insect cocoons, which are used to coat the candies. This coating gives them that special shine, known as shellac.

392.   Coco leaves are still used by Coca-Cola to this day. A company in New Jersey first extracts the cocaine from the leaves, giving the spent leaves to Coca-Cola to put in their drinks.

393.   The skin of a honey badger is so thick that it can withstand machete blows, arrows and spears. The only sure way to kill one is to use a club or a gun.

394.   If the sun was scaled down to the size of a cell, the Milky Way would be the size of the United States.

395.   'Grammatical Pedantry Syndrome' is a form of OCD in which sufferers feel the need to correct every grammatical error they see.

396.   Every year, the Netherlands sends 20,000 tulip bulbs to Canada to thank them for their help in the second world war.

397.   There is a flower called the chocolate cosmos that smells like chocolate, but isn't edible.

398.   There is a house sized shoe box in Amsterdam that is an Adidas store.

399.   Ben and Jerry's has a cemetery where they bury all their discontinued flavors.

400.   Donald Duck comics were banned from Finland because he isn't wearing any pants.

401.   If the 1st of January on a leap year falls on a Sunday, the months of January, April and July will each have a Friday the 13th. In the 20th century, this happened in 1928, 1956 and 1984. And in the 21st century this will happen four times in 2012, 2040, 2068, 2096.

402.   The average commuter wastes around 42 hours waiting in traffic each year.

403.   Even though the Eiffel Tower is stable on its four legs, it is known to move. The 900 foot (320 meter) structure can sway if the wind is strong enough or expand 7 inches if the sun is hot enough.

404.   The set used in the 2009 Sherlock Holmes film was reused as the house of Sirius Black in Harry Potter and the Order of the Phoenix.

405.   The 'Santa Rita Do Sapucai' prison in Brazil allows its inmates to pedal exercise bikes to power lights in a nearby town in exchange for reduced sentences. For every sixteen hours that they pedal one day is reduced from their sentence.

406.   In 2012, a man in China named Zao Phen had 9,999 red roses sewn into a dress for his girlfriend, before asking for her hand in marriage.

407.   The code of Hammurabi is a well preserved Babylonian law that dates all the way back to 1772 BC. It describes progressive laws in it such as minimum wage and the right to be a free man. It was written well before the Bible.

408.   In the novel Forrest Gump was based upon, Forrest goes into space with NASA but upon returning crash lands on an island full of cannibals and only manages to survive by beating the head cannibal every day at chess.

409.   There is a secret McDonald's menu item that you can order which is a McChicken in the middle of a double cheeseburger.

410.   A hacker group named UGNazi once took down Papa John's website because the company was two hours later than expected in delivering their food.

411.   The world's largest privately constructed nuclear fallout shelter is the 'Ark Two'. It began being built in the 1980's by Bruce Beach, just north of Toronto. It's ten thousand square feet and is composed of 42 school buses mixed with concrete, runs on internal

generators and has its own chapel, decontamination room and radio station.

412.	Lamborghinis, Bentleys, Aston Martins are all used as police cars in Dubai.

413.	A prince in Abu Dhabi spent $2.5 million to create a Mercedes Benz with a V10 engine with 1600 horsepower that goes 0 to 100 in less than two seconds running on biofuel.

414.	Instead of using spray cans, some artists create semi-permanent images on walls or other services by removing dirt from a surface known as reverse graffiti or clean tagging.

415.	There's a Turkish artist named Esref Armagan who is blind, yet taught himself to write and paint and has been doing so on his own for the last 35 years.

416.	Aerogel, also known as frozen smoke, is one of the world's lowest density solids being made up of anywhere from 95-99 percent air. It's almost impossible to see or feel but can support 4000 times its own weight.

417.	There was a golden haired Tibetan Mastiff puppy which was sold for twelve million yuan or two million dollars making it the most expensive dog in the world.

418.	Unlike many other members of the cat family, tigers actually enjoy water and can swim well. They often soak in streams or pools of water to cool off.

419.	'Oriole O's' are a type of cereal that's exclusively available in South Korea.

420.	It was discovered in 2008 that a fifty six year old crime reporter named Vlado Taneski, who was reporting on gruesome murders, was in fact the serial killer himself.

421.	When a person lies, they experience an increase in temperature around the nose known as the 'Pinocchio effect.'

422.	In 1980s, a man known only as George who had severe OCD, shot himself in the head in an attempt to commit suicide. Instead of the bullet killing him, it destroyed the part of the brain that was causing the OCD and he went on to get straight A's in college five years later.

423.	Henry Ford was the first Industrial giant to give his workers both Saturday and Sunday off, in hopes that it would encourage more leisure use of vehicles, hence popularizing the concept of the weekend.

424.   Contrary to popular belief, cracking your bones doesn't hurt your bones or cause you arthritis. It's simply the gas bubbles bursting that you hear, however doing it too much does cause tissue damage.

425.   The reason Lego heads have holes in them is so air can pass through them if a child ever swallows one.

426.   If one of your eyes were a digital camera, it would have 576 megapixels within it..

427.   Scientists have discovered a planet using the Hubble telescope, a deep azure blue planet sixty three light years away that rains glass sideways.

428.   Tourists throw over a million euros into the Trevi fountain in Rome each year. The city uses this money to fund a supermarket for the poor.

429.   There's a mattress invented for cuddling, it has a place to put your arm while you cuddle.

430.   A 'leopon' is a hybrid animal cross between a male leopard and a lioness.

431.   Sand tiger shark embryos fight each other to the death in the mother's womb until there's one survivor which is the one that gets to be born.

432.   There is an insect called the assassin bug which wears its victims corpse as armor.

433.   Veronica Seider holds the Guiness World Record for the best sight in the world. She can see 20 times better than the average person being able to identify someone's face from one mile (1.6 km) away.

434.   A tablespoon of cake frosting has less fat, calories and sugar than a tablespoon of Nutella.

435.   The word font only refers to things like italics, size and boldness. The style of the lettering is called a typeface.

436.   A grizzly bear's jaw strength is so powerful that it could crush a bowling bowl with it.

437.   The original script of "Lord of the Rings" was originally one long saga, but was eventually split into three books for the publishers to make more money.

438.   In Churchill Manitoba, Canada, it's illegal to lock your car in case someone needs to hide from one of the 900 polar bears in the area.

439.   The Baobab tree, native to Madagascar, can hold upto 31,000 gallons (120,000 litres) of water.

440.   Pandas are the national animals of China. They are also only found in this country and if you happen to see one in another country they're on loan there.

441.   Using a paper towel after washing your hands decrease bacteria by 40%, while using an air dryer increases the bacteria by upto 220%. This is because bacteria grow quickly in moist, warm environments.

442.   There's a company named Neurowear that sells a headphone that can read your brainwaves and selects music based off your state of mind.

443.   Before Nazis used the salute we now know as Hitler's salute, it was called the Bellamy salute which was used by Americans to salute the flag, until it was replaced in 1942 by the hand over heart salute.

444.   'Fire whirls', also known as fire tornadoes, are whirlwinds of flame that occur in countries where it's sufficiently hot enough, such as Australia.

445.   The nose is connected to the memory center of your brain, hence why smell triggers some of the most powerful memories.

446.   Climonia is the excessive desire to stay in bed all day.

447.   Blind people who have never seen before will still smile despite never having seen anyone else do it before, because it's a natural human reaction.

448.   Norway allows any student from anywhere in the world to study at their public universities, completely free of charge.

449.   In the state of Nevada, public intoxication is not only explicitly 'legal', however, it is illegal for any city or town to pass a law making it illegal.

450.   There's a company called 'True Mirror' that makes non reversing mirrors that show you how you actually appear to other people.

451.   Over 90% of the Australian population live within 50kms of its coastline.

452.   The four ghosts in Pacman are all programmed to do certain things. Blinky (the red ghost) chases you, Pinky (the pink ghost) simply tries to position herself in front of pacman, Inky (the blue ghost) tries to position himself in the same way and Clyve (the orange ghost) moves randomly.

453.	The smallest cat in the world was a Himalayan persian cat named Tinkertoy. At seven years old she measured 3 inches (7cm) tall and 7 inches (19cm) long.

454.	There are tiny eight legged creatures that are closely related to spiders living in the pores of your facial skin called 'demodex'.

455.	Iceland has no army, and has been recognised as the most peaceful country in the world for the last six years. In comparison the UK is 44 and the US sits at 100.

456.	The human hearing range is from 20 to 20,000 herts. If it was any lower than 20 we'd be able to hear our muscles move.

457.	Contrary to popular belief, washing your hands in warm water doesn't kill any more bacteria than washing them in cold water. This is because bacteria only die when water is boiling.

458.	The term for forgetting something after walking through a doorway is called an 'event boundary'.

459.	There's a flower located in Central and South America that looks like hookers lips that are named 'Hooker's Lips.'

460.	The English word orange was the name of the fruit for a few hundred years before the color was later named after the fruit. Before that what we now know as orange was known as yee-o-ler-eed

461.	In the early versions of the Little Red Riding Hood, the girl cannibalizes her own grandmother and then gets eaten by the wolf after getting into bed with him.

462.	In Egypt, actors were once not allowed to testify in court as they were seen as professional liars.

463.	In 2010, Johnny Depp responded to a letter from a nine year old girl named Beatrice Delap by actually showing up at her school in costume as Captain Jack Sparrow after she wrote asking that pirates help her stage a mutiny against her teachers.

464.	Bob Marley was buried with his red Bison guitar, a bible opened to Psalm 23 and a bud of marijuana.

465.	Papaphobia is the fear of the pope.

466.	In the original version of 'The Little Mermaid' by Hans Christian Anderson, Ariel doesn't marry the prince. He actually marries someone else and she dies.

467.	Tigers, Jaguars and Cheetahs are attracted to the cologne 'Obsession' by Calvin Klein.

468.	In 2012, a sixty-three year old man named Wallace Weatherhold from Florida, had his hand bitten off by an alligator and he was charged with illegally feeding the animal.

469.   Jackie Chan's son will receive none of his $130 million fortune, as he's quoted saying "If he's capable he can make his own money. If he's not, then he'll just be wasting my money.

470.   Bruce Lee could perform one handed push ups using only his index finger and thumb. He was also known for his famous one inch punch where he was capable of knocking back an opponent from a distance of just one inch.

471.   In 2013, Vietnam unveiled a steel bridge that's shaped like a dragon that literally shoots fire out of its mouth that's called the 'Dragon bridge'.

472.   Manel Torres, a Spanish fashion designer, invented the world's first spray on clothing which can be worn, washed and worn again.

473.   In 1983, Marvel published a comic called 'Your Friendly Neighborhood Spider Ham'. He was a spider pig named Peter Porker.

474.   Bed bugs survive longer in beds that are made, so scientists actually suggest that you leave your bed unmade once in a while as it ends up being healthier for you.

475.   The British submarine HMS Trident had a fully grown reindeer onboard as a pet for six weeks during WWII.

476.   Democracy was invented in Greece 2500 years ago.

477.   Romans used urine to clean and whiten their teeth. They were actually onto something as urine contains ammonia which has a cleaning substance that results into clearing out everything.

478.   There is a city called 'Rome' in each continent

479.   The driest place on Earth is Antarctica, where some parts haven't seen precipitation for years.

480.   There are zero rivers in Saudi Arabia.

481.   There's a movie from 2010 called 'Rubber', about a murderous car tire named Robert that rolls around killing people and blowing things up.

482.   There's an alarm clock named 'Clocky' that has wheels and runs away and hides if you don't get out of bed on time.

483.   You can make your own Gatorade at home by simply adding salt to some Kool-aid. It's not the exact recipe but it's got just as many electrolytes.

484.   On Good Friday in 1930, the BBC announced there is no news followed by piano music.

485.	Volvo invented the three point seat belt, but opened up the patent to any car manufacturer who wanted to use it as they felt it had more value as a life saving tool than something to profit from.

486.	The most successful interrogator of World War Two was Hanns Scharff, who instead of using torture would befriend the prisoner. He would gain their trust by taking them to a cinema on camp and sharing a coffee or tea with them.

487.	In the Curve Gallery at the Barbican Center in London, there's something called the 'rain room', where through the use of sensors, rain falls everywhere in the room except for where you're walking.

488.	At the Crocosaurus Cove Aquarium in Australia, there's a popular tourist attraction called the 'Cage of Death' which allows you to get up close and personal with giant crocodiles.

489.	There's a Canadian toy company called' Child's Own Studios' that turns children's drawings into stuffed animals.

490.	All humans have lines on our bodies called 'Blaschko's lines' which can only be seen under certain conditions such as UV light.

491.	At the end of the 1990's, BMW actually had to recall their GPS systems because male German drivers didn't want to take directions from a female driver.

492.	In 2010, a black Nigerian couple living in the UK gave birth to a blond white baby with blue eyes that they called the miracle baby.

493.	The dot over the 'j' or 'i' is called a 'tittle'.

494.	Atelophobia is the fear of not being good enough or having imperfections.

495.	The letter 'u' was first used as a substitute for the word 'you' by William Shakespeare in his comedy Love's Labour's Lost around 1595.

496.	The actor who plays Mr. Bean, Rowan Atkinson once saved a plane from crashing after the pilot passed out despite never having piloted a plane before.

497.	In the summer of 1932, while sitting in a restaurant, Adolf Hitler designed the prototype for what would become the first Volkswagen Beetle.

498.	In March 2013, a man got a tattoo of the word Netflix on his side for which after tweeting a picture of it to the company gave him a free year of service.

499.	In order to drink, giraffes have to spread there almost two meter long legs apart, just to get close enough to the water.

500.   The offspring of two identical sets of twins are legally cousins, but genetically siblings.

501.   Doritos can be made without the powder and taste exactly the same, but the company intentionally adds it because they believe it "adds to the Doritos experience."

502.   Ryan Gosling was casted for the role of Noah in the movie 'The Notebook' because the director wanted someone 'not handsome'.

503.   When Charles Darwin first discovered the huge tortoises on the Galapagos Islands, he tried to ride them.

504.   Since 1945, all British tanks have come equipped with tea making facilities.

505.   Falling in love produces the same high as taking cocaine.

506.   In 1945, a man named Tsutomu Yamaguchi survived the atomic blast at Hiroshima, only to catch the morning train so that he could arrive at his job on time in Nagasaki, where he survived another atomic blast.

507.   There is a metal called 'gallium' that melts in your hand.

508.   Bruce Lee's reflexes were so fast that he could snatch a quarter off of a person's open palm and replace it with a penny before the person could close their fist.

509.   In the late 90's, there was a Russian TV show called 'The Intercept' where contestants had to steal a car. If they didn't get caught by police in 35 minutes they got to keep the car, otherwise they were arrested.

510.   Turophobia is a fear of cheese.

511.   According to a study done by Mekuin University in Canada, playing video games before bedtime actually gives a person the ability to control their dreams. It also suggests that gamers are more likely to have lucid dreams as opposed to non gamers.

512.   The small pocket in your large pocket of your jeans was originally meant for your pocket watch.

513.   Watermelons contain an ingredient called citrulline that can trigger production of a compound that helps relax the body's blood vessels, just like Viagra.

514.   Crocodiles can not stick out their tongues or chew.

515.	Marvel Comics once created a superhero named 'Throg' who was a frog that has the power of Thor and is in a group called the 'Pet Avengers.'

516.	The largest natural bridge in the world is the Ferry Bridge in China, and was virtually unknown to the rest of the world until it was observed on Google Maps.

517.	It took a whole month for Erno Rubik, the inventor of the Rubik's cube to solve his own creation.

518.	In Switzerland, if you fail your practical drivers license three times, you are required to consult an official psychologist to assess the reason for your previous failures before you're allowed to retake the exam.

519.	In 2011, a man named Richard James Verone robbed a bank for $1 so that he could be sent to jail to receive free medical health care.

520.	A software company called PC Pitstop once hid a $1000 prize in their terms of service just to see if anyone would read it. After five months and three thousand sales later, someone finally did.

521.	Crying is actually very healthy for you. It helps emotionally, lubricates your eyes, removes toxins and irritants and reduces stress.

522.	In the US, April 2nd is National Peanut Butter and Jelly Day.

523.	There is a Russian published a novel called "The Last Ringbearer" which retells "The Lord of The Rings" from the perspective of Sauron.

524.	If you rearrange the first letters of the main characters names in the movie 'Inception', they spell "dreams" (Names inc. Dom, Robert, Eames, Arthur, Mal and Saito)

525.	Verne Troyer, the actor who plays Mini-me in the Austin Powers movies, has to do all of his own stunts because at 2.7 feet (81 cm) tall, there's no stunt double his size that can fill in for him.

526.	In 2006 a rare grizzly and polar bear hybrid species was confirmed in Canada called 'pizzly bears' or 'grolar bears'. Global warming is causing polar bears habitats to melt, so they find shelter elsewhere and end up mating with grizzlies.

527.	In 1993, a Chinese man named Hu Songwen was diagnosed with Kidney failure. In 1999 after no longer being able to afford the hospital bills, he built his own dialysis machine which kept him alive for another 13 years.

528.	When he was a freshman in 1987, a man named Mike Hayes got a friend who works at the Chicago Tribune to write him an article asking the millions who read it to donate one penny each towards his tuition. Immediately, pennies, nickels and even larger donations came pouring in from all over the world. After accumulating the equivalent of 2.9 million pennies he graduated and paid for his degree in Food Science.

529.   After being eliminated from the show Hell's Kitchen, the contestants are immediately taken to get psychiatric evaluations and then to a house where they are pampered with back rubs, haircuts and manicures. This is because the experience on the show is so draining that the producers don't want the eliminated contestants to kill themselves or someone else.

530.   Bhumibol Adulyadej, the king of Thailand was actually born in Cambridge, Massachusetts in the United States in 1927. When he was born the hospital room that he was delivered, it was briefly declared Thai territory so he could be born on Thai soil.

531.   Switzerland has enough nuclear shelters to accommodate 114% of its population. It's a legal requirement for the Swiss to have a protected place that can be reached quickly from their place of residence.

532.   A study conducted by Loma Linda University in 2010 concluded that laughter not only reduces stress, but increases the production of antibodies and kills the activity of tumor cells.

533.   There's a chimpanzee in a Russian zoo named Zhora that became addicted to booze and smoking after too many visitors began giving him alcoholic treats and cigarettes. In 2001, the chimp actually had to be sent to rehab to be treated for his addictions.

534.   Ioannis Ikonomou, the Chief Translator in the European Commission can speak 32 different languages. His native language is Greek and he's the only in-house translator in the European Commission who's trusted to translate classified Chinese documents.

535.   In 1860, Abraham Lincoln grew his famous beard because he got a letter from an 11 year old girl named Grace Bedell who said that all ladies liked the whiskers and they would convince their husbands to vote for him for President.

536.   In 2013, Sean Conway became the first man ever to swim the entire length of Great Britain. The 900 miles (1400km) trek took him 135 days to complete. Ninety were spent in water while the rest were spent avoiding bad weather and resting.

537.   There's a syndrome called the 'Tetris Effect' that occurs when people dedicate so much time and attention to an activity that it starts to pattern their thoughts, mental images and dreams.

538.   Experts believe that New York is home to as many as 800 languages, making it the most linguistically-diverse city in the world.

539.   The red mushrooms featured in Nintendo's Mario games are based on a real species of a fungi called 'amanita muscaria.' They're known for their hallucinogenic properties and can distort the size of perceived objects. This is also the same mushroom that is referenced in Alice in Wonderland.

540.   In 2013, France banned child beauty pageants because they promote the hypersexualizations of minors. Anyone who organises such a pageant could face jail time for upto 2 years and a fine of up to 30,000 euros.

541.   Before he was Iron Man, actor Robert Downey Junior was a notorious drug addict. He credits his sobriety to the fast food chain Burger King. In an interview with Empire magazine, he revealed that in 2003 he was driving a car full of drugs when he ordered a burger from Burger King that was so disgusting that he felt compelled to pull over, get out and dump all of his drugs into the ocean.

542.   During World War Two, prisoners in Canadian War camps were so well treated that they were given games and entertainment, held soccer tournaments and created musical groups. When the war ended many of them didn't want to leave Canada.

543.   The rules of most airlines require that the pilot and co-pilot of a plane eat different meals. This is just in case one of the meals causes food poisoning.

544.   In 1938, Walt Disney was awarded an honorary Oscar for Snow White. The statuette that he received came with seven mini-statuettes on a stepped base.

545.   In 2014, Budapest broke the world record for the tallest Lego tower ever built. Made of 450,000 colorful bricks, topped with a large Hungarian Rubik's cube, the structure stands at 114 feet (34 meters) tall in front of Saint Stephen's Basilica.

546.   In 2013, Google sent a lone employee to an abandoned Japanese island called Gunkanjima to map it for Google Street View. The island was once the most densely-populated island in the world, but is now completely abandoned.

547.   Eccrinology is the study of excretion.

548.   In the early 1930's, a social movement became popular, although it eventually died out which proposed replacing politicians and business people with scientists and engineers that could manage the economy.

549.   There is a side effect of sleep deprivation called microsleep, in which a person will fall asleep for a few seconds or even a few minutes without realizing it. It's extremely dangerous and is one of the largest contributors to accidents on the road.

550.   In 2014, a competitive eater named Molly Schuyler, who weighs only 126 pounds (57kg), won four eating contests in only three days. She ate a total of 363 chicken wings, 59 pancakes, 5 pounds of bacon and 5 pounds of barbecued meat.

551.   The Centennial Light Bulb in Livermore, California, has been burning since 1901 and is the world's longest lasting light bulb according to the Guiness Book of World Records. The bulb is at least 113 years old and has only been turned off a handful of times.

552.   There is a sixteen story office building in Osaka, Japan called the 'Gate Tower Building' that has an entire highway that passes through the fifth, sixth and seventh floors of the structure.

553.   We miss 10% of everything we see due to blinking.

554.   There are 1000 gigabytes in a terabyte and most neuroscientists estimate that the human brain can hold between 10 and 100 terabytes of information.

555.   Half the world has never made or received a phone call.

556.   Roughly a third of all food produced in the world for human consumption every year goes to waste. This is approximately 1.3 billion tonnes, equating to roughly a billion dollars down the drain.

557.   In Iceland, it's forbidden to give your child a name that hasn't been approved by the Icelandic naming committee.

558.   A tribe in West Africa known as 'The Matami Tribe' play a version of football, which consists of using a human skull as the ball.

559.   The first country where a woman was allowed to vote was New Zealand in 1893.

560.   The World Health Organisation states that from the one billion smokers in the world more than 600,000 people die every year from secondhand smoke.

561.   Until the 1930's, the letter 'E' was used to represent a failing grade. However, in the US, that was changed to F as professors began to worry that their students would mistake 'E' for excellent.

562.	There's a school called Ordinary Miracle in Yoshkar-Ola, Russia that looks like a fairy-tale castle. A man named Sergey Mamaev had built it for his wife, who wanted to teach at a school that children would actually want to go to.

563.	In April of 2014, the Danish government built an exact replica of their country in the online game 'Minecraft' using four trillion Minecraft building blocks. It was intended for educational purposes, but within weeks, American players had invaded the game, planting American flags everywhere and blowing things up.

564.	In 1975, professor Jack Hetherington from Michigan State University added his cat as a co-author to a theoretical paper that he had been working on. He did this because he mistakenly used words like 'we' and 'our' in the paper and didn't feel like revising it.

565.	In Finland, when you earn your PhD, you're given a doctoral hat that looks like a top hat as well as a doctoral sword.

566.	A man named Sogen Kato was thought to be the oldest man in Tokyo, until 2010, when officials arrived at his home to wish him a happy 111th birthday, only to find his mummified remains. It turns out he had been dead for 30 years and his family had been collecting his pension money.

567.	Sound can travel quicker through solids. This is because the molecules in a solid medium are much closer together than those in a liquid or gas, allowing sound waves to travel more quickly through it.

568.	A solid glass ball can bounce higher than a rubber ball when dropped from the same height. A solid steel ball can bounce even higher than a solid glass ball.

569.	Antibiotics are actually ineffective against fighting viruses. They are only effective against bacterial infections.

570.	Oil expands with the rise of temperature, hence if you're filling your car up it's best in the morning or late at night when it's not hot to get the most bang for your buck.

571.	The founders Bill Hewlett and David Packard flipped a coin to decide whether the company they created would be called Hewlett-Packard or Packard-Hewlett.

572.	1,000 selfies are posted to Instagram every 10 seconds. This is 93 million selfies a day.

573.	97% of all emails sent are spam.

574.	Digital storage doesn't go up in measurements of thousands. 1024 bits make a byte, 1024 bytes make up a kilobyte followed by megabyte, gigabyte, terabyte, and petabyte.

575.   A group of ravens is called an unkindness.

576.   Some estimates report that 1 in 8 babies are given to the wrong parents at some point during their hospital stay.

577.   Besides the crocodile's belly and top of its head, the rest of the skin is bulletproof.

578.   The filtration technology used in airplanes is the same technology they use to filter air in hospitals.

579.   Even after 6 hours of dying, a person's muscles continue to spasm periodically.

580.   As of 2016, about 280 climbers have died on Everest. Their bodies are so well preserved that they are used as markers.

581.   The arteries of a blue whale is so large that an adult human could crawl through it.

582.   The nicotine from one puff of a cigarette reaches your brain in seven seconds. Alcohol takes approximately 6 minutes.

583.   Humans have the largest brain in terms of brain to body ratio. The animal with the biggest brain overall is a sperm whale weighing in at 17 pounds (7 kgs).

584.   The country with the most millionaires in the US. The country with the most billionaires in China.

585.   The country with the longest coastline on Earth is Canada.

586.   When the silk of a spider is stored in its abdomen, it is actually liquid which only hardens to a solid when it leaves the spider's glands and comes into contact with the air.

587.   The first email was sent in 1971. The email was sent to the computer right next to it as a test.

588.   Humans are capable of feeling the effects of a broken heart. This is known as 'stress cardiomyopathy' in medical terms. If you're suffering from a broken heart, your blood can have 3 times the amount of adrenaline than someone suffering from a heart attack.

589.   The tin can was invented in 1810. The can opener was invented 48 years later. People used hammers and chisels between this time.

590.   The average adult has eight pounds (3.6 kilograms) or about 22 square feet (2 square meters) of skin.

591.   The first hard drive was invented in 1956 and weighed over a ton.

592.   Although the brain is physically developed by the age of 5, the rational part of the brain isn't fully developed and won't be until age 25.

593.   From the poll of 2500 participants, the average person spends 42 minutes a week or almost 92 days over a lifetime on the toilet.

594.   The Pyramid of Giza was built from 2 million stone bricks with stones weighing more than two tonnes each. It was built over the course of 85 years.

595.   Lions have the loudest roar of any animal, reaching 114 decibels at a distance of about 1 meter. It can be heard from over 2 miles (3km) away.

596.   Sloths can live up to 30 years and spend 15-18 hours a day sleeping.

597.   Only 30% of the Earth is covered by land.

598.   The Black Death in the 14th century is estimated to have killed 30–60% of Europe's total population.

599.   It would take 1.2 million mosquitoes sucking once each to completely drain the blood in a human adult.

600.   Anything that melts can be made into glass, however, there will be molten residue stuck to it.

601.   Written language was invented by the Mayans, Egyptians, Chinese and Sumerians independently.

602.   There's a phenomenon that occurs in the Mekong River in Thailand where red fireballs called "Naga Fireballs" randomly shoot into the air and nobody knows why it happens.

603.   If you search 'askew' in Google, the screen will tilt slightly clockwise.

604.   Mosquitoes don't just bite you and suck your blood, they urinate on you before flying off.

605.   The reason people traditionally put wedding rings on the left ring finger is because before medical science figured out how the circulatory system functioned, people believed that there was a vein that ran directly from the fourth finger of the left hand to the heart.

606.   Vodka in Russian translates to 'little water' in English.

607.   Your mobile phone carries 10 times more bacteria than your toilet seat.

608.   Half of the DNA in a banana is identical to what makes up you.

609.   A giraffes tongue is 8 inches (21cm) long.

610.   Today's gold medals are only 1.3% gold. The last time a pure gold medal was given out was in the 1912 Stockholm Olympics.

611.   It would take over fifty million balloons to lift the average house off the ground like in the movie 'Up'.

612.   There's a book that exists called 'Everything Men know about Woman' that has 100 pages, all of which are blank.

613.   A male honeybee's orgasm is so powerful that its sex organs explode shortly after climax, causing the bee to die.

614.   The Kevlar bulletproof vest was invented by a pizza delivery guy after being shot twice on the job.

615.   If you left Tokyo by plane at 7 am, you would arrive at Honolulu at approximately 8 pm the previous day due to the nineteen-hour difference in time zone.

616.   There is a condition called 'hyperthymesia' that causes the person to remember every single detail of their lives. Only twelve people on Earth have this condition.

617.   All the characters in Toy Story only blink one eye at a time.

618.   Both the companies Louis Vuitton and Chanel burn their products at the end of the year, preventing them from being sold at a discount.

619.   It's possible to see a rainbow as a complete circle from an airplane.

620.   The brothers Adolf Dassler and Rudolf Dassler, who started Puma and Adidas, were part of the Nazi party.

621.   The youngest mother in medical history was Lina Medina from Peru who gave birth when she was 5 years of age.

622.   Ants go to war just like humans and can strategize by doing things like sending out the weaker ants out to fight first.

623.   If you're taller than 6 foot 2, you can't become an astronaut.

624.   As well as an actor, Jackie Chan is a well known pop star in Asia, releasing 20 albums since 1984. He also sings the theme songs to his own movies.

625.   Coca-Cola was invented by an American pharmacist named John Pemberton, who advertised it as a nerve tonic that could cure headaches and fatigue.

626.   The highest-grossing stop motion animation film is Chicken Run from the year 2000 starring Mel Gibson.

627.   We know more about the surface of the moon than we do about our own oceans.

628.   The word 'checkmate' in chess comes from the Arabic 'Shah Mat' which means' the king is dead'.

629.   Voldemort in French translates to 'flight of death'.

630.   Russia and Japan have still not signed a peace treaty to end World War Two.

631.   Potatoes have more chromosomes than a human.

632.   In the United Kingdom, the Queen cannot be arrested no matter what crime she commits. This is because the crown itself is the prosecuting force in the UK and hence, the Crown cannot verse the Crown itself. The other members of the Royal family do not share the same immunity.

633.   In 2011, Barack Obama became the first president to have ever brewed beer in the White House, which is named 'White House Honey Ale'.

634.   The pinky swear came from Japan and indicated that if someone broke the promise they must cut off their pinky.

635.   "Twilight" was rejected fourteen times before it was accepted.

636.   The term 'Googol' is actually a mathematical term for a very large number which is one followed by one hundred zeroes.

637.   There's a phobia called the 'Jonah complex' which causes a person to fear their own success, preventing them from reaching their full potential.

638.   Arnold Schwarzenegger was paid $15 million in the second "Terminator" - a film in which he only said 700 words of dialogue. At a cost by word basis his famous line 'Hasta la vista baby' cost over $85,000.

639.   There are now snuggery services where you can hire someone to snuggle with you for $60 per hour.

640.   The 'China National Highway 110' traffic jam was considered the longest traffic jam in history. It was 100 km long and lasted 11 days.

641.   If you removed all the empty space from the atoms that make every human on earth, all humans on Earth could fit into an apple.

642.   If we somehow discovered a way to extract gold from the Earth's core, we would be able to cover all the land in gold up to our knees.

643.   It rains diamonds on the planets Uranus and Neptune.

644.   Jousting is the official sport in the state of Maryland.

645.   A Blue Whale can consume 480 million calories of food in a single dive.

646.   There are only two parts on the human body that never stop growing: the ears and the nose.

647.   The clothing store H&M stands for Hennes & Mauritz.

648.   The longest human jump is further than the longest horse jump. In the 1968 Olympics, the world record was set at 8.9m while the record for a horse is 8.4m (28 feet)

649.   The entire Pixar staff had to take a graduate class in marine biology before making Finding Nemo.

650.   In Bern, Switzerland, there's a 500-year-old statue of a man-eating a sack of babies and nobody is sure why.

651.   Koi fish can live for centuries. The oldest Koi to have ever lived, named Hanako, lived for 225 years before it died.

652.   "Space Jam" is the highest-grossing basketball movie of all time.

653.   The Beast from "Beauty and the Beast" is a creature called a 'Chimera' which has features from seven different animals.

654. Bubble wrap was originally invented in 1957 to be sold as wallpaper.

655. If you Google 'Zerg rush', Google will begin to eat the search page.

656. "The Prince Charles Cinema" in London has volunteer ninjas that sneak up and hush anyone in the theater that is making noise or throwing things.

657. An employee at Pixar accidentally deleted a sequence of Toy Story 2 during production. It would've taken a year to remake what was gone but luckily another employee had the whole thing backed up on a personal computer.

658. The first commercial flight only lasted 23 minutes and cost $8500 in today's currency. It was between St. Petersburg, Florida and Tampa, Florida.

659. The French-language Scrabble World Champion doesn't actually speak French. Nigel Richards memorized the whole French Scrabble dictionary which contains 386,000 words in nine weeks.

660. Women have been using pregnancy tests since 1350 BC. They used to pee on wheat and barley seeds to determine if they were pregnant or not. If wheat grew, it predicted a female baby and if barley grew it predicted a male. The woman was not pregnant if nothing grew. This theory was tested and proved accurate 70% of the time.

661. Martin Luther King Jr. got a C grade in public speaking.

662. The temperature of tennis balls affects how a ball can bounce. Wimbledon go through over fifty thousand tennis balls a year that are kept at 68 degrees Fahrenheit to make sure only the best are used.

663. Adult cats don't have enough lactase enzyme to digest the lactose from milk, making them lactose intolerant.

664. Campanology is the art of bell ringing.

665. Popes cannot be organ donors because their entire body has to be buried intact as it belongs to the universal Catholic Church.

666. You can create 170 thousand pencils from the average tree.

667. 90% of Earth's ice is in Antarctica

668. In Italy, the richest business is the mafia that turns over $178 billion a year, which is 7% of the country's GDP

669. The words Tokyo, Beijing and Seoul all translate to 'capital' in English.

670.　　　The sound you hear when you put a seashell next to your ear isn't the sea, but the blood running through your veins.

671.　　　The information travelling inside your brain is moving at 268 miles per hour (430 km/h)

672.　　　In 1936, the Russians created a computer that ran on water.

673.　　　Google, Amazon, Microsoft and Facebook alone have 1.2 million terabytes of information stored on the internet.

674.　　　Cats can't taste sweet food.

675.　　　The human brain can compute over a thousand processes per second making it quicker than any computer.

676.　　　Only 15% of all plants are on land.

677.　　　People have been eating potatoes since 7000 years ago.

678.　　　The largest ocean on Earth is the Pacific Ocean, covering 30% of the globe.

679.　　　The country Brazil is named after a tree.

680.　　　You are 14% more likely to die on your birthday than any other day.

681.　　　There are more vegetarians in India than any other country.

682.　　　Beaver eyelids are transparent which allows them to see whilst blinking as they swim underwater.

683.　　　Indonesia has more than 17,000 islands.

684.　　　Mandarin is the most spoken language in the world, with a total 1.1 billion speakers.

685.　　　Diamonds are actually not that rare. A company called De Beers owns 95% of the market and suppresses supply to keep the prices high.

686.　　　Over 50% of the oxygen supply we breathe comes from the Amazon rainforest.

687.　　　Burger King in Japan has released two black hamburgers called the 'Kure Diamond' and the 'Kuro Pearl' with everything including the bun, the sauce and cheese colored black with squid ink.

688.　　　There's an artist named Scott Wade who is famous for creating dust art on dirty cars using only his fingers and a brush.

689.　　　When tractor owner Ferruccio Lamborghini voiced his frustration over his clutch in the Ferrari to car's founder Enzo Ferrari, Enzo insulted him telling him that the problem was with the driver, not the car. Ferruccio decided to start his own car company and thus the Lamborghini was born.

690.　　　Putting dry tea bags in smelly shoes or gym bags is an easy and quick way to absorb any unpleasant odors.

691.   The creator of Peter Pan, J. M. Barrie gave away the rights to the franchise to the Great Ormond Street Children's Hospital so that they could always collect royalties and fund the hospital.

692.   A woman from Michigan named Barbara Soper gave birth on 8/8/8, 9/9/9 and 10/10/10: the odds of which are 50 million to 1.

693.   The largest indoor water park in the world is the Seagaia Ocean Dome in Japan. It measures at 900 feet (300 meters) long and 328 feet (100 meters) wide.

694.   There is a tribe in India called the War Khasi that has been passed down for generations

695.   In addition to Neanderthals, humans interbred with another species called Denisovans. A 90,000-year-old skeleton of a girl was discovered who was a hybrid between the two species.

696.   In 2005, Johan Eliasch a Swedish Millionaire bought a plot of land almost half a million acres big in the Amazon rainforest, just so he could preserve it.

697.   There is a town in Alaska called Talkeetna that has had a cat named Stubbs as its honorary mayor since 1997.

698.   In 2011 a 46 year old man named Mark Bradford hunted down and choked a 13 year old boy who killed him several times in Call of Duty.

699.   The original founders and owners of Macy's, Isidor and Ida Straus both died on the Titanic. This was replicated by an old couple in the movie, who went to sleep as the ship went down, which is what actually happened.

700.   A 102 year old man named Alan Swift from Connecticut, drove the same 1928 Rolls Royce Phantom 1 for close to 77 years before he died in 2005.

701.   Astronauts aboard the International Space Station see 15 sunrises and 15 sunsets a day, averaging one every forty-five minutes, due to the station's proximity to the Earth and the speed of its orbit.

702.   A study by the University of Westminster in the UK, determined that watching horror movies can burn up to almost 200 calories, the same as a half hour walk.

703.   It would cost approximately $42,000 a year to attend Hogwarts if it were real.

704.   In the Despicable Me movies, the gibberish that the minions speak is actually a functioning language written by the directors called 'Minionese.'

705.   In 2012, a woman from New York named Deborah Stevens donated a kidney to her boss and was fired almost immediately after.

706.   Jesse James, a notorious outlaw from the 1800's, gave a widow who housed him enough money to pay off her debt collector and then robbed the debt collector as the man left the widow's home.

707.   Every factory employee at Ben and Jerry's gets to take home three pints of ice cream every day.

708.   In the ancient Persian empire, men used to debate ideas twice, once sober and once drunk, as they believed an idea had to sound good in both states in order to be considered a good idea.

709.   Brazil's prisons offer their prisoners the chance to reduce their prison sentences by up to 48 days a year for every book they read and write a report on.

710.   Honey badgers have been known to eat porcupines and poisonous snakes, raid bee hives for honey, kidnap baby cheetahs and steal food from hungry lions.

711.   Over 90% of mobile phone sales in Japan are for waterproof devices because the Japanese are so fond of their mobile phones, they even use them in the shower.

712.   A California couple named Helen and Les Brown, who were both born on December 31st, 1918, were married for 75 years, before dying one day apart at the age of 94 in 2013.

713.   In 1939, the New York Times predicted that the television would fail because the average American family wouldn't have enough time to sit around watching it.

714.   Former billionaire Chuck Feeney has given away over 99% of his $6.3 billion to help underprivileged kids go to college, resulting in him having $2 million left.

715.   Before alarm clocks were invented, there was a profession called a 'knocker up', which involved going from client to client and tapping on their windows or banging on their doors with long sticks until they were awake. This lasted till the 1920's.

716.   Dalhousie University in Halifax, Nova Scotia, has opened a puppy room where students can go play with puppies to relieve stress.

717.   There is a man named Tim Harris with down syndrome who owns and runs a restaurant in Albuquerque, New Mexico called "Tim's Place", where they serve breakfast, lunch and hugs. It's the only known restaurant owned by a person with down syndrome and is known as the world's friendliest restaurant.

718.   Scientists from ATR Computational Neuroscience Laboratories in Tokyo, Japan has successfully developed a technology that can put thoughts on a computer screen.

719.   Sixty-three year old former math professor Joan Ginther, who has a PhD in statistics from Stanford University, has one scratch and win lottery four separate times for a grand total of $20.4 million. She never revealed how she did it but the odds of accomplishing what she did is one in 18 septillion.

720.   In the early 1990's, Michael Jackson tried to buy Marvel comics so that he could play Spider Man in his own self-produced movie.

721.   In 2013, the Netherlands closed eight prisons due to the lack of criminals.

722.   There is a luxury hotel in Fiji called "Poseidon Resort" where, for $15,000 a week, you can sleep on the ocean floor and you even get a button to feed the fish right outside your window.

723.   'Percussive maintenance' is the technical term for hitting something until it works.

724.   In 2005, there was a reality show that piloted in Germany called "Sperm Race" in which 12 contestants donated their sperm to a lab, where doctors observed their seed race toward an egg. The winner of the sperm race got a Porsche.

725.	In 1967, a magazine called Berkeley Barb published a fake story about extracting hallucinogenic chemical from bananas to raise moral questions about banning drugs. Unfortunately, people didn't realize it was a hoax and began smoking banana peels to try and get high.
726.	Buses can replace forty cars if people made the switch.
727.	Four American presidents have been killed by gunshot.
728.	The first-ever web page to go live was on August 6, 1991.
729.	Zenography is the study of the planet Jupiter.
730.	Although the Holy Bible is available for free at many places of worship, it is the most stolen book in the world.
731.	Extremely shy people are more likely to experience anxiety when they're hungover than their extroverted counterparts. The term is called hangxiety.
732.	The word "Lord" occurs 7836 times in 6,668 verses in the Bible.
733.	If you combine the sales of McDonald's, Kellogg's and Microsoft together, Cocaine would still exceed the three combined.
734.	Portuguese navigator Ferdinand Magellan named the Pacific Ocean due to the calmness of the ocean. Pacific translates to peaceful.
735.	Angel Falls is a waterfall in Venezuela that is the world's highest uninterrupted waterfall, at a height of 3,200 feet (979 meters).
736.	The World's Biggest Flower Garden Sits in the Middle of a Desert in Dubai, which has over 500,000 fresh flowers.
737.	You're not allowed to take Mercury onto a commercial passenger plane as it can damage the aluminium the plane is made out of.
738.	If you put an apple in the sea it will float because it's less dense than water.
739.	A newborn baby has about one cup of blood in their entire body.
740.	Big Ben in London is not the tower, but the bell inside.
741.	99.8% of Cubans can read and write, making it one of the most literate countries in the world.
742.	As a person dies, hearing is the last of the five senses to stop.
743.	Sharks kill about twelve people a year. People kill about eleven thousand sharks an hour.

744. More people die from attempting selfies than from shark attacks.
745. Approximately 1 in every 6 Jewish people killed in the Holocaust died at Auschwitz.
746. Pirates used to wear eye patches on one eye during the day so they could see better at night with that same eye.
747. Astatine is the most rare element on Earth, with only 30 grams total existing in the Earth's crust.
748. The most powerful organism is the Gonorrhea bacteria, which can pull up to 100,000 times their size.
749. Humans have 23 pairs of chromosomes, while Great Apes have 24.
750. The Queen of England legally owns one third of the Earth's surface.
751. The biggest moon in our solar system is called Ganymede, which is bigger than the planet Mercury.
752. Antarctica is considered a desert as it only receives 2 inches (50 millimeters) of precipitation a year.
753. By land mass, Canada is only 2% smaller than Europe.
754. The hippocampus, a part of the brain which is responsible for memory, is notably larger in the female brain compared to male.
755. 'Amazon' is the first company to ever hit a trillion dollars.
756. The highest divorce rate in the world by country is Luxembourg at 87%. The lowest is India with 1%.
757. Cats have been around since 3600 BC
758. A penguin has the ability to jump six feet (1.8 meters) out of the water with no aid.
759. Cuba has the highest doctor to patient ratio in the world.
760. 300 hours of video are uploaded to YouTube every minute, and almost 5 billion videos are watched on Youtube every single day.
761. A quarter of the world's prisoners are locked up in the US.
762. There is a spa in India dedicated for Elephants only.
763. You would lose a third of your body weight on Mars due to lower gravity.
764. There are more artificial Christmas trees sold in the world than real ones.
765. There are currently 147 million ounces of gold in Fort Knox. At the price of about $1776 per ounce that's worth $261.6 billion.
766. The traffic in London is as slow as transporting carriages from a century ago.

767.   Most of the vitamins you get from eating a potato are in the skin.

768.   The Kuwaiti Dinar is the strongest currency in the world, with one Dinar equating to $3.29 USD.

769.   You're shorter in the evenings than you are in the mornings.

770.   The oldest living person on Earth, whose age has been verified, is Japan's Misao Okawa, who is 116 years old.

771.   Snails have the ability to regrow an eye if it's cut off.

772.   The crime rate in Iceland is so low that the police there don't carry guns.

773.   Cats don't meow to each other, they meow to get the attention of humans.

774.   The richest man in history was Emperor Mansa Musa's, whose wealth is believed to have been around $400 billion when taking into account inflation.

775.   The Witwatsrand Basin was the densest area containing gold in the world. More than 40% of all of the gold ever mined has come out of the Basin.

776.   Trypophobia is the fear of holes.

777.   The average lifespan of a Redwood tree is 500-700 years old. Coastal redwoods have been known to live to over 2,000 years. They can grow to over 360 feet in height (109 meters).

778.   Grizzly bears can hibernate up to 7 ½ months. This means no eating, drinking, urinating, or defecating.

779.   At the university of Oaksterdam, you can graduate with a degree in Cannabis Cultivation.

780.   The average strawberry has 200 seeds on the outside. It's also not considered a fruit.

781.   Hitler planned on invading Switzerland, but gave in as it was too difficult with the surrounding mountains.

782.   A group of ferrets is called a business.

783.   During the Cold War the US's passcode to nuclear missiles was eight zeroes, so they could fire them as quick as possible.

784.   Only .1% of an atom is matter. The rest is air.

785.   There are over 4 million apps available for download, on both the Android and Apple app store.

786.   There are now 22 countries worldwide that have no army, navy or airforce.

787.   There is an ancient book called "The Voynich" from the Italian Renaissance that no one can read.

788. The longest street in the world is Yonge Street in Canada, which is 1178 miles (1896 km).

789. There is no explanation as to why there are no mosquitoes in Iceland.

790. Stephen Hawking was diagnosed with ALS at 21 and was expected to die at 25. He lived till 70.

791. During an emergency landing, a plane has the ability to dump its fuel from the wings to prevent it from exploding if it crashes.

792. ``Sir, I demand, I am a maid named Iris' is the longest palindrome, i.e. it makes the same sentence if you say it backwards.

793. Cows have best friends, and can experience stress when separated from them.

794. A baby octopus can be as small as your finger tip.

795. There's a restaurant in New Jersey owned by Bon Jovi, where there are no fixed prices. Instead customers donate money or volunteer to pay for their meals.

796. Internet addiction disorder ,also known as IAD, is a real mental disorder in which somebody engages in addictive, compulsive or pathological internet use.

797. Cameron Diaz and Snoop Dogg both went to school together. Cameron even bought some weed off of Snoop once.

798. In 1961, Mel Blanc, the voice of Bugs Bunny, was in a serious car accident that put him in a coma that he could not wake up from. Doctors began speaking directly to the characters that he voiced from which he would actually respond in their voices and three weeks later, he actually woke up.

799. The first ever occurrence of the name 'Wendy' was in Peter Pan. This name had never been registered before the book's publication.

800.   Pineapple isn't a fruit, it's actually a berry.

801.   There are several words that don't rhyme in the English language, besides orange and purple. They include silver, month, ninth, pint, wolf, opus, dangerous, marathon and discombobulate.

802.   Rhythm is the longest word without any vowels.

803.   The companies Audi, Bentley, Bugadi, Ducati, Lamborghini and Porsche are all owned by Volkswagen.

804.   'Almost' is the longest English word in alphabetical order.

805.   'Uncopyrightable' is the longest common word you can use that doesn't contain repeat letters. 'Subdermatoglyphic' is longer, however is only used by dermatologists.

806.   'I am' is the shortest English sentence.

807.   In World War Two, Jacklyn Lucas lied his way into the military and became the youngest marine ever to earn a medal of honor. When he was 17, he threw himself on two live grenades to protect his squad members and survived.

808.   144 successful prisoners escaped Auschwitz

809.   It is estimated that malaria has been responsible for half of the deaths of everyone who has ever lived.

810.   Apples, peaches and raspberries are all members of the rose family.

811.   The pygmy monkey marmoset is the smallest monkey in the world, with an average length of only 5 inches (13 cm) and an average weight of 3.5 ounces (100 grams).

812.   All US presidents pay for their own food while staying at the White House.

813.   'Overmorrow' is a word that means the day after tomorrow.

814.   Jose Mujica is the president of Uruguay and is the poorest president in the world, as he gives away most of his income to charity.

815.   In Cambodia, they sell 'Happy Pizza', which is a cheese pizza garnished with weed on top.

816.   Snoop Dogg has a book published called "Rolling Words" that has lyrics of all his songs that you can later rip out and use as rolling papers.

817.   Jellyfish and lobsters are biologically immortal.

818.   There's a fish in Spongebob Squarepants that's been shown in multiple episodes with a clearly shown penis.

819. The strongest beer in the world is called "Snake Venom" and it contains 67.5% alcohol.

820. International 'Have a Bad Day' day is November 19th.

821. The human brain cell, the universe and the internet all have similar structures.

822. The Indonesian Ministry of Marine Affairs and Fisheries determined that a single manta ray, if caught and killed, is worth anywhere from $40-$500. They also determined, however, that if kept alive, they're worth up to a million dollars in tourism revenue, so they created the largest manta ray sanctuary in the world.

823. A group of turkeys is called a rafter.

824. The person who did the voice of Minnie Mouse, Russi Taylor was married to Wayne Allowing, the voice of Mickey Mouse.

825. There's a vending machine in Singapore that dispenses a Coke to anybody that hugs it.

826. Jim Cummings, the voice of Winnie the Pooh ,would call up children's hospitals and talk to them in his Winnie voice to make them feel better.

827. Walt Disney was fired from Kansas City Star in 1919 because his editor said that he lacked imagination and had no good ideas.

828. Black tomatoes can be grown without any genetic engineering. They are full of beneficial anthocyanins which are believed to help with obesity, cancer and diabetes.

829. Most cats don't like to drink water if it's too close to their food source. Always keep your cat's water and food supply separate so they don't get dehydrated.

830. The best selling book in history is the Bible, with 5 billion copies in sales.

831. DC comics published an alternate universe where Bruce Wayne died instead of his parents. In it, Thomas Wayne becomes Batman and Martha Wayne goes crazy and becomes the Joker.

832. The average iPhone only costs $200 to make.

833. Watson, IBM's artificially intelligent computer, learned how to swear from the urban dictionary. Because of this, it began talking sassy, so scientists had to remove the entire urban dictionary database from its memory.

834. The children's book 'Where the Wild Things Are' was originally titled 'Where the Wild Horses Are' however the author and illustrator Maurice Sendak ended up changing the name of it after he realized he had no idea how to draw horses.

835. An Indonesian boy named Aldi Rizal began chain smoking when he was just 18 months old and continued smoking over 40 cigarettes a day, until he was five years old before he was sent to rehab.

836. The state of Illinois has banned exfoliating face washes because the microbeads in them are so small that they actually slip through the water treatment facilities and end up back in the water supply.

837. The first recorded human flight with artificial wings in history was in the 6th century in China. Emperor Kao Yang would strap prisoners to kites and throw them off buildings to see if they could fly.

838. A psychologist named Timothy Leary was sent to jail in 1970 and given a series of tests to determine which jail he should be placed in. Since he designed many of the tests himself, he manipulated his answers so that he would be placed in a low security prison as a gardener and ended up escaping only eight months later.

839. Noah Webster, the creator of the first ever American dictionary, learned 26 languages so that he could understand and research the origins of his own country's tongue in order to write it.

840. The word 'jay' used to be used as slang for a dull or stupid person, so when anyone who ignored traffic regulations and crossed roads illegally was called a jay walker.

841. Walt Disney used to visit his parks in disguise and test ride operators to make sure that they weren't rushing guests.

842. Barcode scanners actually read the spaces between the black bars, not the black bars themselves.

843. Dressed up Disneyland characters never ever break character. They're even given special autograph training sessions so that they can always sign autographs in the style of the cartoon character they're playing.

844. A study conducted in 2011 by Angela Duckworth, proved that IQ tests can be affected by motivation. By promising subjects monetary rewards, she found that the higher the reward, the higher they scored on the IQ test.

845. Before Will Smith starred in the Fresh Prince of Bel-Air, he was on the verge of bankruptcy, owing the government $2.8 million. For the first three seasons of the show he had to pay 70% of his income.

846.	There's a lake in Australia called "Lake Disappointment" that was named and found by Frank Hann in 1897, who was hoping to find fresh water but instead found salt water.

847.	National Geographic star Casey Anderson has a pet grizzly bear named Brutus. The bear was adopted in 2002 when he was a newborn cub and, in 2008 served as Casey's best man at his wedding.

848.	Philani Dladla is a homeless man from Johannesburg, South Africa, who's known as the pavement bookworm. He survives by reviewing books for people passing on the street and sells them the book if they like it.

849.	Chiune Sugihara was a famous Japanese diplomat that operated in Lithuania during World War 2. He helped more than 6,000 Jewish refugees escape to Japanese territory by issuing them transit visas, risking his life and his family's life in the process.

850.	Lotso the bear from Toy Story 3 was originally supposed to be in the first movie, but the technology needed to create his fur wasn't available at the time, so he got pushed back to the third film.

851.	Insurance companies have blacklisted Jackie Chan and anyone else who works on his stunt team. This means that if anyone gets injured while on the set of a Jackie Chan movie, he has to pay for their recovery treatment.

852.	The oldest hotel in the world is the 'Nishiyama Onsen Keiunkan' in Japan. It was founded in 705 AD and has had 52 generations of the same family operating it since it was founded.

853.	Halieutics is the study of fishing.

854.	Every spring a set of 21 swings is set up near a bus stop in Montreal's entertainment district. Every one of them acts as a musical instrument and as people swing, pre recorded sounds fill the air.

855.	The pizza Louis XIII is the most expensive pizza in the world, costing $12,000. Created by Chef Renato Viola, he prepares the entire dish at your house. The toppings include three types of caviar, Mediterranean lobster and red prawns. The size of the pizza is only 8 inches (20 cm) in diameter.

856.	Citizens of Norway pay half taxes in November, so they can have more money for Christmas.

857.	The world's largest tree house is located in Tennessee and is 10 stories, 10,000 square feet (900 square meters), took eleven years to make but cost only $12,000 since it was made of mostly recycled materials.

858.   Sea otters hold hands when they sleep so they don't drift away from each other.

859.   It's estimated that the world's helium supply will run out within the next twenty to thirty years.

860.   The Pallas's cat is the oldest living species of modern cat that first appeared 12 million years ago.

861.   Anuptaphobia is the fear of either remaining unmarried or marrying the wrong person.

862.   The famous painter Salvador Dali would avoid paying the bill at restaurants by drawing on the back of his checks, as he knew the owner would not want to cash the check because the drawings would be much too valuable.

863.   The 'Eucalyptus deglupta' or more commonly known as the 'rainbow tree' is a tree that sheds its outer bark to reveal a bright green inner bark that turns blue, purple, orange and maroon as it matures.

864.   The word 'muggle' was added to the English dictionary and is defined as a person lacking a particular skill.

865.   In the UK, people that reach their 100th birthday or their 60th wedding anniversary are sent a personalised card from the Queen.

866.   In China there is a 71 meter tall stone statue built of buddha that was constructed over 1,200 years ago.

867.   If you were to see a solid form of oxygen, it would be a sky-blue color.

868.   Woodpeckers are able to peck 20 times per second, or around 8 to 12,000 pecks per day, without ever getting a headache.

869.   There is an island off the coast of Brazil in the Atlantic Ocean known as 'Snake Island', named so as there are upto five snakes per 10 square feet (square meter) on the island.

870.   Geographically, China covers 5 different times zones, however only uses one standard time zone within the country.

871.   Since the beginning of communication, it has been estimated that 31,000 languages have existed.

872.   The black Mamba is regarded as one of the deadliest snakes in the world. It can move up to speeds of 18 feet per second (5.5 meters per second) and its bite can kill a human in less than an hour.

873.   It was known that after examining the animals, Charles Darwin used to eat them too.

874.   The longest someone has stayed awake continuously is 265 hours, done by a high school student in 1964.

875.   The longest someone has been in a coma and come out of it is 37 years. A six year old went to the hospital for a routine appendectomy, where she went under general anesthetic, and didn't come out for reasons doctors can't explain.

876.   The surface area in South America is greater than that of Pluto's.

877.   Fleas can jump over 80 times their own height.

878.   Rhinoceros beetles can carry 850 times their weight, which is the equivalent of an average human carrying 65 tons.

879.   A group of donkeys is called a drove.

880.   McDonald's has more than 37,000 stores around the world, making it the largest fast food chain globally.

881.   There is enough carbon in your body to make over 9,000 pencils.

882.   France was the first country that banned supermarkets from throwing out or destroying food that wasn't sold.

883.   Koalas can sleep upto 18-22 hours a day, whereas a giraffe only needs about two.

884.   Author J. K. Rowling wrote the final chapter of the last Harry Potter book in 1990, 7 years before the release of the first book.

885.   The Cookie Monster revealed in 2004 during a song that, before he started eating cookies and became known as the "Cookie Monster", he was called Sid.

886.   There has only been 240 years of peace in the last 3,000 years.

887.   Ostriches have eyes bigger than their head.

888.   If Gorillas were to take human birth control pills, it would have the same effects on them.

889.   When Jadav Payeng was sixteen, he began planting trees because he was concerned for the disappearing habit for the local animals. He continued doing this for over thirty five years. Today he has single handedly restored more than 1360 acres of forest.

890.   The scent that lingers after it rains is defined as 'petrichor'.

891.   Jeff Bezos net worth is so high that it wouldn't be worth him picking up a $100 bill if he dropped it. In fact he has to spend $28 million a day just to stop getting richer.

892.   There are now digital pens that can record everything you write, draw or sketch on any surface.

893.   Some Japanese companies such as Sony, Toshiba and Panasonic have banishment rooms, where they transfer surplus

employees and give them useless/nothing tasks to do until they become disheartened or depressed enough to quit on their own, thus avoiding paying them full benefits.

894.   In 1886 a man named HH. Holmes built a three-story hotel in Chicago, specifically to kill people in it. Its design included stairways to nowhere and a maze of over 100 windowless rooms, which he used to kill over 200 people.

895.   In Finland there is a giant rock named Kummakivi, sitting perfectly on a seemingly curved mound. The name translates to 'strange rock' since nobody knows how it got there.

896.   There is a device known as a ventricular assist device, or VAD, that can permanently replace the function of your heart. The only side effect is you have no pulse.

897.   Country singer Dolly Parton once anonymously entered a Dolly Parton lookalike contest and lost to a drag queen.

898.   Bangkok University in Thailand makes their students wear anti-cheating helmets during exams.

899.   Created in Germany, ESSLack is the world's first edible spray paint that comes in gold, silver, red and blue.

900.   In 2011, archaeologists at the ground zero 9/11 terrorist attack site in New York City uncovered half of an 18th century ship, believed to have once been used by merchants.

901.   It's possible to hire an evil clown to terrorize your son or daughter for an entire week before their birthday. For a fee, artist Dominic Deville will increasingly pursue your child and leave scary notes, texts and phone calls and ultimately 'attack' your child on their birthday by smashing a cake in their face.

902.   In the city of Mackinac Island Michigan, all motor vehicles including cars have been banned since 1898.

903.   In 2004, Volvo introduced a concept car called the YYC that was built specifically for women - it was a design without a hood and dent resistant bumpers.

904.   In the early years of the twentieth century, horses were causing so much pollution with their waste that automobiles were seen as the green alternative.

905.   Animal Planet aired a fake documentary about the existence of mermaids that convinced thousands of viewers in this belief. They aired the episode in 2012 and did it once again in 2013.

906.   'Futureme.org' is a website where you can send e-letters to yourself at any time in the future.

907.   In 2008, The North Face clothing company sued a clothing company called The South Butt.

908.   In 2007 in Louisiana, a pink albino bottlenose dolphin was discovered and photographed by a man named Eric Rue.

909.   When the elephant whisperer Lawrence Anthony died in March of 2012, an entire herd of elephants arrived at his home to mourn him.

910.   The pollution in China is so bad in some parts that just being in that area for one day is the equivalent of smoking 21 cigarettes.

911.   In 2012, a Russian scientist regenerated an arctic flower known as 'Silene Stenophylla' that has been extinct for over 32,000 years from a seed that was buried by an ice-age squirrel.

912.   The age of fish can be determined in a similar way to trees. Fish scales have one growth ring for each year of age.

913.   In 1985, a New Orleans man named Jerome Moody drowned at a party attended by 100 life guards who were celebrating making it through the summer without a single drowning at a city pool.

914. In 1976, an underachieving Princeton student named John Aristotle Phillips wrote a term paper, describing how to build a nuclear bomb. He received an A but never got his paper returned, as it was seized by the FBI.

915. According to a study conducted by Brock University in Ontario Canada, racism and homophobia are linked to having lower IQ, as those with lower intelligence tend to gravitate toward socially conservative ideologies.

916. There's a resort in Japan called the Tomamu Resort that's located on top of a mountain peak. It allows patrons to view a sea of fluffy white clouds beneath them.

917. Michael Birch, the founder of the social networking site 'Bebo' sold its site to 'AOL' for $850 million in 2008, only to later buy it back for a million dollars in 2013.

918. In 1961, Italian artist Piero Manzoni filled ninety tin cans of his own feces and called them Artist's sh*t and sold them according to their equivalent weight in gold.

919. Nomophobia is the fear of being without mobile phone coverage.

920. Newman's Own Food has donated 100% of its post-tax profits to charity since 1982, totaling over $400 million.

921. In 2013, over 200 strangers responded to a Facebook invitation to attend a funeral for British veteran James McConnel, who had no friends or family members to attend otherwise.

922. In Russia, wealthy citizens often hire fake ambulances that beat the city traffic which are known as 'ambulance taxis'. They can cost as much as $200/hour, have luxurious interiors, refreshments and include caviar and champagne.

923. Reed Hastings, the founder of "Netflix" got the idea to start the site when he received a late fine of $40 on a VHS copy of Apollo 13. Reed also approached Blockbuster in 2005, offering to sell the company for $50 million, which was turned down at the time. Today the company is worth over $9 billion.

924. Airports had to standardise their names in the 1930's with airport codes, so those with two letter names simply added an 'x', hence names such as LAX.

925. A quarter of the world's hazelnuts each year go towards making nutella. That's 100,000 tons of hazelnuts per year.

926. The line on Earth that separates day from night is called the Terminator, but is also known as the fray line and the twilight zone.

927.   North Korea is the biggest counterfeiter of US currency.

928.   Cats used to be sacred in Egypt and if you killed one you could be sentenced to death.

929.   The Coca-Cola made in the Maldives used to be made from ocean water.

930.   The biggest family in the world is from Baktawng, India, where father Ziona Chana has 94 children by 39 different wives.

931.   The one click option was invented by Amazon, who have a patent on it, and Apple pays them a licensing fee to use it.

932.   Brad Pitt was banned from China for 20 years after his role in the film 'Seven Years In Tibet'.

933.   More than half of the world's population is under the age of 30.

934.   The electric chair to execute people was created by a dentist.

935.   If you went through 17 tons of gold ore and one tonne of personal computers, you'd find more gold from the personal computers.

936.   Two thousand five hundred and twenty is the smallest number that can be divided by all numbers between 1 and 10.

937.   There are 158 verses in the national anthem of Greece, making it the longest in the world. In comparison the Canadian anthem only has four verses.

938.   The Maldive coconut is the largest growing seed in the world.

939.   In one night, a mole can dig a tunnel 300 feet (1km) long in soil.

940.   The average lead pencil can draw a line that will be 35 miles (56km) long.

941.   You would be a few centimeters taller in space due to gravity.

942.   If you were to take out someone's lungs and flatten it out it would have the same surface area as one half of a tennis court.

943.   Elephants are constantly tip toeing around, This is because the back of their foot has no bone and is all fat.

944.   An octopus has 9 brains, blue blood and three hearts.

945.   Polar bears hair is actually clear and it's the light they reflect that makes them appear to look white.

946.   A chameleon can move its eyes in two different directions at the same time.

947.   The whole country of England is smaller than the state of Florida by over 10,000 square miles (26,000 square km).

948.   The Mona Lisa has no eyelashes or eyebrows.

949. As of 2019, the largest yacht in the world named Azzam, is 590 feet long (the length of two football fields) and cost $600 million to build. It was created in 2013, taking four years to construct and beat the previous world record by a full 57 feet. It has 94,000 horsepower and can go upto 37 miles (60km) per hour, the fastest speed for a yacht longer than 300 feet.

950. Fully grown giraffes only have 7 vertebrae in their necks, the same number as humans.

951. Butter milk contains zero butter.

952. Disneyland does not sell any chewing gum. This is because Walt Disney didn't want people stepping in gum as they walked around the park.

953. Giraffes can last longer without water than camels can..

954. Ruth Wakefield, who invented the chocolate chip cookie around 1938, sold the idea to Nestle Toll House in exchange for a lifetime supply of chocolate.

955. In 2011, 'Lego' produced 381 million tires, making them the world's largest rubber tire manufacturer by number of units produced.

956. In 2009, 'Wikipedia' permanently banned the Church of Scientology from editing any articles.

957. In the country of Turkmenistan, water, gas and electricity have all been free from the government since 1993.

958. The largest numerical denomination bill ever made was the one million Hungarian pengo in 1946. It's value was one sextillion. That's one with 21 zeros behind it, yet it was still only worth 20 cents US.

959. France is the only country in Europe to be completely self-sufficient in basic food production.

960. When dying in 1955, Einstein refused surgery, saying, "I want to go when I want, it's tasteless to prolong life artificially, I've done my share, it's time to go, I will do it elegantly".

961. Many animal shelters will not allow black cats to be adopted around Halloween time because most people buy them as impulse during the holiday.

962. 'The Singing Tree' is a wind powered sound sculpture located in Burnley, England and was designed by architects Mike Tonkin and Anna Liu. Each time you sit under it you'll hear a melody played, depending on the wind for that day.

963. In 2011, archaeologists discovered the skeletal remains of a Roman couple who had been holding hands for over 1,500 years.

964. The Shangri-La hotel in China captured a record for the largest ball pit ever created, measuring 82 by 41 feet (25 by 12.6 meters) and contained over a million balls.

965. Starbuck is a famous Canadian bull, whose genome is so desirable that his sperm has sold for over 25 million dollars over his lifetime. In this time he has sired over 200,000 daughters.

966. The Burj Al Arab hotel in Dubai offers their guests a 24 karat gold iPad for the duration of their stay.

967. Poveglia Island in Italy is considered one of the most haunted places in the world, as it was the site of wars, a dumping ground for plague victims, and an insane asylum. In fact, it's so haunted that the Italian government has forbidden public access to it.

968. In the Victorian era, they had special tea cups that protected your mustache from getting dunked in your tea.

969. Around 350 to 420 million years ago, before trees were common, the Earth was covered in giant mushroom stalks.

970. The Lion King was considered a small B movie during productions, as all the top Disney animators were working on Pocahontas, which they considered an A movie.

971. The Pythagorean cup, also known as a Greedy cup is a cup designed to spill it's contents if too much wine is poured in, encouraging moderation.

972. In 1955, a six hundred year old plaster Buddhist statue was dropped when it was being moved locations, only to reveal that the plaster was covering another Buddhist statue made of solid gold inside.

973. Self-made millionaire Harris Rosen adopted a Florida neighborhood called "Tangelo Park". He cut the crime rate in half, increased high school graduation rates from 25% to 100% by giving everyone free day care and all high school graduates scholarships.

974. In ancient Athens, the world's first democracy, they had a process called ostracism where once a year the people could vote on the politician that they felt was the most destructive to the democratic process and that person was banished from Athens for ten years.

975. China is building a car free city called "The Great City" that will house 80,000 people. It'll use 48% less energy, 58% less water, produce 89% less landfill waste and 60% less carbon dioxide than a conventional city of the same size.

976. The Vystavochnaya subway station in Moscow accepts 30 squats as payment for a metro ticket as an incentive to exercise more.

977. In 2022, the World Cup will be played in Lusail, Qatar, a city that doesn't even exist yet.

978. In 1949, the Prince motor company in Japan developed an electric car that could travel 124 miles (200 km) on a single charge.

979. There's a mushroom in the wild called' Laetiporus' that tastes like fried chicken.

980. Saturn's largest moon named 'Titan' has an atmosphere so thick and gravity so low that you can actually fly through it by flapping any sort of wings attached to your arms.

981. There's a village in the Netherlands named Giethoorn that has no roads and can only be accessed by boats, earning itself the nickname 'Venice of the Netherlands'.

982. Christmas Island is a small Australian Island, located in the Indian ocean, that every year sees 50 million adult crabs migrate from the forest to breed. This is known as the annual red crab migration.

983. In 1979, debris from NASA's Space Station Skylab crash landed in the town of Esperance, Western Australia, for which the town fined NASA $400 for littering. They actually paid it.

984. There are completely black chickens in Indonesia known as 'Ayam Cemani'. They have black plumage, black legs and nails, black beak and tongue, black comb and wattle, black meat and bones as well as dark organs.

985. In 2007, Joshua Bell, an award winning violinist and conductor, conducted an experiment where he pretended to be a street violinist and had over a thousand people pass him without stopping. He only collected $31 that day, yet two days previously, sold out to a theatre where each seat cost $100. The violin he was playing with on the street was worth $3.5 million.

986. Due to the aging population in Japan, adult diaper sales are about to surpass baby diaper sales.

987. For years, an Indian named Rajesh Kumar Sharma has been teaching slum children who live under a local metro bridge. Five days a week for two hours a day he leaves his job at the general store to teach over 140 kids who would otherwise not be able to learn.

988. There is a method of art called tree shaping where living trees are manipulated to create forms of art.

989. The average person will fall asleep in just seven minutes.

990. The majority of lipsticks contain fish scales.

991. Ischaemic heart disease and stroke are the world's biggest killers. Ischaemic means an inadequate blood supply to an organ.

992. Vending machines kill about 13 people a year.
993. It is estimated that about 100 billion people have died since Homosapiens appeared over 200,000 years ago.
994. The world's largest gold bar is 551 lb (250kg)
995. In 1998, Larry Page and Sergey Brin, the founders of Google, offered to sell their little startup to AltaVista for $1 million so they could resume their studies at Stanford. They were rejected and decided to grow the company instead, which is now an empire worth $101 billion as of 2019.
996. There was a third apple founder named Ronald Wayne, who once owned 10% of the whole company. He decided to sell that 10% steak for $800 in 1976.
997. The fear of clowns is called Coulrophobia.
998. There is a hole in the ozone layer sitting right above Antarctica that is twice the size of Europe.
999. There are fewer than fifty of the original Apple 1 computers in existence ,with some of them selling for over $50,000.

1000.   Snails can sleep for up to three years.

1001.   The average shark has 15 rows of teeth in each jaw. They can replace a tooth in a single day and lose over 30,000 teeth in their lifetime.

1002.   Fifty nine days on earth is the equivalent of one on Mercury.

1003.   The reason a whip creates a whipping sound is because the spinning rope is moving quicker than the speed of sound, creating a small sonic boom.

1004.   Hippos sweat is the colour red because it contains a pigment that acts as a natural sunscreen.

1005.   Cows methane creates just as much pollution as cars do.

1006.   Dolphins only fall asleep with half their brain at a time, so they're only half conscious, which helps them from accidentally drowning.

1007.   When you see an advertisement of a watch, it's almost always ten past ten.

1008.   Most of the dust you'll find in your house will be your dead skin.

1009.   One-third of the Earth's surface is partially or total desert.

1010.   The word 'Sahara' in Arabic means desert, so it reads as 'desert desert' in Arabic. It also once snowed in the Sahara back in 1979.

1011.   Columbia's underground drug cartel trades as much as $10 billion, which is more than the country's legal exports.

1012.   Only a third of the snakes you see in the movie 'Snakes on a Plane' were real.

1013.   One third of the world's polar bear population lives in Canada.

1014.   Quebec only finished paying off its 1976 Summer Olympics debt 30 years later, in 2006.

1015.   Lady Gaga stars in the Guinness World Records twelve times. One of them is for including the most product placements in a video.

1016.   In 2005, a Nepalese couple climbed Everest and got married on its peak. The youngest person to ever climb Everest was young Jordan Romero at the age of 13.

1017.   If Police in Thailand misbehave, they're punished by being made to wear bright pink Hello Kitty armbands.

1018. The man who designed Saddam Hussein's secret bunker was the grandson of the woman who designed the bunker for Adolf Hitler.

1019. Facebook tracks and records your IP address, as well as the URL of every website that you visit that uses social plugins - such as the Like button on Facebook.

1020. In 2009, Burger King launched a campaign that if you unfriended ten of your Facebook friends you would receive a free Whopper. Using the Whopper Sacrifice application, your friend would receive a message telling them that their friendship was less valuable than a Whopper.

1021. Yale has a rare book and manuscript library that has no windows, but instead has walls made entirely of translucent marble that prevents the books from being exposed to direct sunlight.

1022. During the early 1900s, French gangsters used a weapon called an 'Apache Revolver', a device that functioned as a revolver, a knife, and brass knuckles.

1023. A Mexican artist created an underwater sculpture series that double as art and an artificial reef.

1024. Queen Elizabeth the second has someone to wear her shoes before she wears them to make sure they're comfortable.

1025. If a Google employee dies, their spouse gets half their salary for the next ten years as well as their existing stock benefits, while their children get $1000/month until they're nineteen.

1026. 'Backpfeifengesicht' is a German word that means 'a face that badly needs a punch.'

1027. The cheapest gas prices in the world belong to Venezuela, at just over a penny a litre.

1028. In London, there's a public toilet encased in a glass cube that's made entirely of one-way glass, allowing you to see passersby, but they can't see you.

1029. Leonardo da Vinci loved animals so much that he'd buy caged birds being sold in Italy at the time just to set them free.

1030. Sternutaphobia is the fear of sneezing.

1031. There is an island shaped like a heart in Fiji called Tavarua.

1032. It's possible for a cat to be its own fraternal twin. These cats, known as Chimera cats, are an oddity that occur when two fertilized eggs fuse together.

1033. If you inhale a pea, it is possible to sprout and grow in your lungs.

1034. There's a lake in Western Australia called 'Lake Hillier' that is filled with water that's naturally pink.

1035. The 'Orca', also known as the killer whale, is actually from the dolphin family.

1036. The Appian Way in Rome is a road that was built in 312 BC that is still used to this day.

1037. Cherophobia is the fear of being happy or joyful with the expectation that something bad will happen.

1038. The country of Niue, an island north of New Zealand, put various Pokemon on its one dollar coins in 2001. They included Pikachu, Squirtle, Meowth, Bulbasaur and Charmander.

1039. One of the oldest living creatures on Earth was believed to be Adwaita, a giant tortoise from India who was believed to be 255 years old before passing away in 2006.

1040. There are at least 7 apps on the App store that are priced $999.99, which is the maximum price you can charge on the app store.

1041. In real life, a roadrunner can only reach speeds of about 32 km/hr, while a coyote can reach speeds of upto 69 km/hr.

1042. Johnny Depp has a passion for playing guitar, playing with artists such as Marilyn Manson, Oasis, Aerosmith and Eddie Vedder.

1043. There's a religion called Christian Atheism, where practitioners believe in essentially the same things as traditional Christians, except that the bible is completely metaphorical and that God is an allegory for human morality rather than a real being.

1044. Carmen Dell'Orefice is the world's oldest working model. She started modelling at the age of 15 and is still an active model to this day at the age of 83.

1045. There is a cruise ship named 'The World' where residents permanently live as it travels around the globe. An apartment on board costs $2 million while you fork out $270,000 a year for maintenance costs.

1046. The distance between Africa and Europe is only 23 km. There are talks of constructing a bridge between the two continents called the Strait of Gibraltar Crossing.

1047. The Lego-Brucke is a concrete bridge in Germany that has become famous for being painted to look like a giant bridge made of lego blocks.

1048. Deltiology is the collection and study of picture postcards.

1049.   Justin Timberlake's mother was Ryan Gosling's legal guardian when he was a child.

1050.   Macklemore once worked at a juvenile detention center to help detainees express themselves through writing and helping them create rap lyrics.

1051.   One of the iTunes user agreement policies explicitly states that you're not allowed to use the program to build nuclear, chemical or biological weapons.

1052.   The Bingham Canyon Copper Mine in Utah is the largest man made hole, at half a mile (1km) deep, 2 miles (4km) wide and covers 770 hectares.

1053.   Nemo makes an appearance in the movie 'Monsters Inc' as a toy that Boo gives to Sully a full two years before the movie ``Finding Nemo' came out. Pixar movies are infamous for being full of Easter eggs like this.

1054.   There are Wizard of Oz-inspired shoes that get you home when clicking your heels together using a GPS system. Side note: the author of the novel created part of the name of the book when he was looking at a filing cabinet and saw the letters o-z.

1055.   There are three books in the Harvard University that are bound in human skin.

1056.   The largest cave in the world is in Vietnam called the Son Doong Cave. It's just under nine kilometers long, and its interior is so big that it has its own clouds and forests. In fact its ceiling is so high that you can fit an entire 40-story skyscraper inside.

1057.   Bob Marley's last words to his son were "Money can't buy you life".

1058.   There is a term known as a 'friend paradox' where the average person has fewer friends than his friend.

1059.   Mobile phones emit electromagnetic frequencies that heat body tissue and can affect over a hundred proteins in the brain.

1060.   Turbulence on an airplane cannot be predicted. It can occur even on a cloudless, clear day.

1061.   Ancient Rome was eight times more densely populated than modern New York.

1062.   Getting hit by lightning heats up your skin to 50,000 degrees fahrenheit (27,000 degrees celsius), a temperature which is hotter than the surface of the sun.

1063.   The Hawaiian alphabet only has 12 letters. They are a, e, i ,o ,u, h, k, l, m, n, p, and w.

1064. The only bird that can fly backwards is the hummingbird.

1065. A flamingo can only eat when its head is upside down.

1066. A study done in 1915 by the Chicago University concluded that the easiest colour to see from a distance was the color yellow, hence the most popular taxi color.

1067. The song 'Happy Birthday' is 120 years old and has a copyright to it. It's owned by Warner Chappell Music and insists that no one uses it, the reason you rarely hear it on T.V. shows or movies.

1068. In the 1980's, the infamous kingpin Pablo Escobar was making so much money off of his drug cartel that he was he was spending $2,500 ($7,200 in today's money) every single month on rubber bands just to hold all of the cash.

1069. The chances of an American being killed by lightning is the same chance a person in Japan has being shot and killed by a gun.

1070. In Victorian London, mail used to be delivered 12 times per day.

1071. There used to be sheep that grazed in Central park up until 1934. They were moved during the Great Depression as it was feared they'd be eaten.

1072. One of the clauses in the 1781 U.S. articles of Confederation states that if Canada wants to be admitted into the U.S., it'll be automatically accepted.

1073. The scientific term for pins and needles is paresthesia.

1074. The mother of Matt Groening, the creator of 'The Simpsons', was named Marge Wiggum.

1075. Ancient Roman Charioteers earned more money than international sports stars get paid today.

1076. Reciprocal liking is a psychological term used to describe when you start liking someone after you find out that they like you. It's a phenomenon that reflects the way people feel better about themselves and enjoy the company of those that provide them with positive feelings.

1077. A group of stingrays is called a fever.

1078. Contrary to popular belief, white spots on fingernails are not a sign of a deficiency of calcium, zinc or other vitamins in the diet. They're actually called leukonychia and are not only completely harmless but are most commonly caused by minor injuries that occur while the nail is growing.

1079. Since Venus is not tilted on an axis like Earth, it experiences no seasons.

1080.   If an astronaut got out of his space suit on the moon he would explode before he suffocated.

1081.   Earth is the only planet not named after a God.

1082.   The largest volcano in our Solar System is also the largest mountain in the Solar System. It is Olympus Mons on Mars which is 3 times the height of Mt. Everest.

1083.   The word twyndyllyngs, which means twins or twinlings, is the longest word in the English language.

1084.   Hot water freezes faster than cold water. This is called the 'Mpemba effect', named after a Tanzanian student who discovered it.

1085.   Light doesn't actually move at the speed of light. The full quote is actually 'the speed of light in a vacuum' which is 186,282 miles (299,792 kilometers) per second. If you were able to move at this speed you could go around Earth seven and a half times in a second.

1086.   The first man made element was Technetium created in 1937. It is used for medical diagnostic studies and as a corrosion inhibitor for steel.

1087.   Steven Spielberg waited over ten years after being given the story of Schindler's list to make the film as he felt he wasn't mature enough to take on the subject.

1088.   Shigeru Miyamoto, the creator of the famous games Mario, Zelda and Donkey Kong was banned from riding a bicycle. This is because he became so valuable to Nintendo that they didn't want to risk anything happening to him, forcing him to drive a car instead.

1089.   One lightning bolt has enough energy to toast one hundred thousand slices of bread.

1090.   Over 50% of all lottery tickets sold are bought by only 5% of people who buy lottery tickets.

1091.   The regular use of a sauna was associated with a lower risk of death from cardiovascular disease in men and women who are over 50 years old, according to BMC Medicine. The study also showed that saunas lower blood pressure.

1092.   The life expectancy in Ancient Rome was only 20 to 30 years.

1093.   Yu Youhzen, a 53 year old Chinese millionaire, works as a street cleaner for $228 per month. She does so to set a good example for her children.

1094.   A false awakening is the term used for a vivid or convincing dream about awakening from sleep, when in reality you're still sleeping.

1095.   A group of zebras is called a zeal.

1096.   The Savannah is the largest domestic breed of cat, which resembles a small leopard, but behaves like a dog. They can grow upto 40 pounds (18 kg), have an 8 foot vertical jump and be trained to walk on a leash and play fetch.

1097.   The Curiosity Rover sang Happy Birthday to itself on Mars to commemorate the 1 year anniversary of landing on the planet in 2013.

1098.   Walt Disney holds the record for the most Oscars won by any one person, with a total of 22.

1099.   In the 1960's, Alcatraz was the only federal prison at the time to offer hot water showers for its inmates. The logic behind it was that prisoners who were acclimated to hot water would not be able to withstand the freezing waters of the San Francisco Bay during an escape attempt.

Part Twelve

1100.   A man named Jonathan Lee Riches got into the Guiness Book of World Records for having filed the highest number of lawsuits in the world, with a total of over 2,600.

1101.   A stock exchange system exists with Pirates in Somalia. Locals can invest in a pirate group and after a successful heist, will receive a reward. In one instance ,a woman gave an RPG 7 to a pirate group and ended up receiving $75,000.

1102.   At the 1912 Olympics, a Japanese Marathon Runner named Shizo Kanakuri quit and went home without telling officials and was considered a missing person in Sweden for 50 years. In 1966, he was invited back to complete the marathon, finishing with a final time of 54 years, 8 months, 6 days and 5 hours.

1103.   Graphene is pure carbon in the form of a very thin, nearly transparent sheet, only one atom thick and is the world's strongest material. It's one million times thinner than paper but is 200 times stronger than steel.

1104.   In 2011, a New Zealand trucker named Steven McCormack fell on a high-pressure valve, which lodged in his butt and inflated him to twice his size nearly killing him. He did survive, but it took a full three days to burp and fart out excess air.

1105.   When Stephen Hawking was asked what his IQ was, he responded "I have no idea, but people who boast about their IQ are losers".

1106.   The creator of Sherlock Holmes, Sir Arthur Conan Doyle helped to get two falsely accused men out of prison after solving their already closed cases.

1107.   Oikology is the science of housekeeping.

1108.   In 1988, a woman named Jean Terese Keating disappeared while awaiting trial for drunkenly killing a woman in a car crash. She was arrested 15 years later after bragging at a bar about having gotten away with the crime.

1109.   Intel employs a futuris named Brian David Johnson whose job it is, is to determine what life would be like to live ten to fifteen years in the future.

1110.   Yang Yuanquing, Levino's CEO received a $3 million bonus as a reward due to record profits in 2012 which he re-distributed to 10,000 of Lenovo's employees. He did the exact same thing in 2013.

1111. Thailand celebrates a festival each year named 'Loy Krathong', where they release thousands upon thousands of sky lanterns filling up the night sky as tradition.

1112. There is a condition called Math anxiety, which causes people to perform poorly in mathematics, not because they're ungifted in math, but because the condition causes their brain to enter such a state where they simply cannot perform math.

1113. Ramon Artagaveytia once survived a sinking ship in 1871. He was so scared from this experience he didn't get on another ship until 41 years later. Unfortunately for him that ship was Titanic.

1114. In 2013, a man named Rogelio Andaverde was abducted from his home right in front of his wife, by two masked men with guns. Luckily he returned two days later, unharmed. It was later discovered that he staged his own kidnapping just so he could go out and party with his friends.

1115. When they made 'Breakout' for Atari, Steve Jobs and Steve Wozniak agreed to split the pay 50/50. Atari gave Jobs $5,000, but Jobs told Wozniak he only received $700, therefore only giving him $350.

1116. Stalin's guards were so afraid of him that no one called a doctor for over ten hours after he had originally had a stroke resulting in his death. They feared that he might recover and execute anyone who acted outside of his orders.

1117. Russia trained and deployed 40,000 anti-tank dogs in World War Two. The dogs were loaded with explosives and trained to run under tanks where they would be detonated, except many of the dogs became scared and ran back to their owners trenches, where they killed their own people.

1118. The 'over 9,000' meme that was popularized from Dragon Ball Z was a translation error. The power level was actually over 8,000.

1119. The Solvay Hut is the world's most dangerously placed mountain hut, located 13,000 feet (3962 meters) above ground level in Switzerland.

1120. An ancient Persian poet recorded the Fable of a King that challenged wise men to make him a ring that made him happy when he was sad when he was happy. They succeeded by giving him a ring etched with the phrase "This too shall pass".

1121.   Workers of Amazon's distribution centers can be expected to walk up to 11 miles (17km) per shift, picking up an order once every 33 seconds.

1122.   Triskaidekaphobia is the fear of the number 13.

1123.   In Cuba it's legally mandated that government vehicles must pick up any hitchhikers that they see.

1124.   In 2000, the KKK adopted a stretch of highway near St. Louis, so the Missouri government responded by renaming the road Rosa Parks Highway.

1125.   The longest possible uninterrupted train ride in the world is over 10,000 miles (17,000km) long, which goes from Vietnam to Portugal.

1126.   Studies have shown that smoking Hookah is no safer than smoking cigarettes and, in fact, may cause the smoker to absorb more toxic substances than cigarettes.

1127.   There's a museum in Europe called "The Museum of Broken Relationships" that exclusively displays objects that were meaningful to heartbroken exes.

1128.   Inventor, Nikola Tesla and Author, Mark Twain were best friends and mutual fans of each others work.

1129.   The sun and the moon appear to be the same size in our sky because of the amazing coincidence that the moon is 400 times smaller, but also 400 times closer.

1130.   In 2008, a Japanese man noticed that food in his home was disappearing, so he set up a webcam and came to discover that a 58 year old homeless woman had been living in his closet for an entire year.

1131.   There's a building in London called the "Walkie Talkie building" that's shaped in such a way that it reflects sunlight like a giant magnifying glass, literally melting cars on the street below.

1132.   Luis Garavito, one of the world's most dangerous serial killers; with 140 victims, had his sentence reduced to only 22 years and could be out as early as 2021.

1133.   If you open your eyes in a pitch-black room, the color you'll see is defined as 'eigengrau'.

1134.   The Pentagon spends over $250,000 each year to study the body language of world leaders such as Vladimir Putin.

1135.   The average tree is made up of about 1% of living cells at any given time.

1136.   Humans are not appropriate prey for Great White Sharks because their digestion is too slow to cope with the ratio of bone to muscle and fat.

1137.   A study conducted by the University of Oxford found that, for every person that you fall in love with and accommodate into your life, you lose two close friends.

1138.   There's a travel agency in Tokyo called 'Unagi Travel', that for a fee, will take your stuffed animal on vacation around the world while taking photos of it.

1139.   The unbroken seal on Tutankhamun's Tomb went untouched for 3245 years, until 1942.

1140.   Colonel Sanders disliked what the KFC Franchise had done to the food so much that he described it as the worst fried chicken he had ever had, and the gravy was like wall paper paste.

1141.   In 2008, a businessman from Abu Dhabi spent $14.3 million at an auction to buy a license plate labelled '1', making it the world's most expensive license plate.

1142.   In 2013, it was discovered that some bears in Russia have become addicted to sniffing jet fuel out of discarded barrels. They even go to the lengths of stalking helicopters for the drops of fuel that they leave behind.

1143.   The modern handshake dates all the way back to the 5th century BC, where swordsmen would greet each other with their weapon hand free, showing no sign of a fight.

1144.   85% of Chinese share only 100 surnames. Li and Zhang in face cover 13% of the entire Chinese population.

If you enjoyed this book and learned anything it would mean the world to me if you could please leave a review so others can easily find this book and itch their curiosity!

2222 Interesting, Wacky & Crazy Facts

Part 1

1.   A multi-millionaire named Forrest Fenn has hidden a treasure valued between one to three million dollars in the Rocky Mountains, and in order to find it, you must solve his riddle. So far, no one has done it or found the treasure.

2.   The director of the 1980 horror film 'Cannibal Holocaust' had to prove in court that the actors were still alive and didn't get killed during the movie.

3.   At the age of 15, Anne Mackosinski managed to invent a flashlight that is powered solely by the hands body heat. She later created a headlamp that's also powered by body heat.

4.   Ninjas didn't actually wear black. According to the ninja museums in Japan, the best color to wear during the night time for ninjas was actually dark navy blue.

5.   Red pandas use their long bushy tails to balance whenever they're in trees. Their tails were also used to cover themselves for warmth in the winter.

6.   During job interviews google doesn't ask for GPA or test scores from their candidates, because they don't correlate at all with success at the company.

7.   Only 5% of Norway's financial transactions are done in cash. In fact it's possible that by 2020 Norway could be completely cash free.

8.   In the movie the Matrix, Neo's passport expires on September 11th, 2001.

9.   The Ben Franklin effect is a psychological phenomenon where someone who has done a favor for someone else is more likely to do another favor for that person than they would be if they had received a favor from that person.

10.   You can actually reshape some babies' ears. Some of them have a condition called lidling, where the top part of the cartilage in the ear is basically folded over so the top ridge is kind of rounded over. However there's actually a mold, called EarWell, that can change the shape of your baby's ear in approximately six weeks.

11.   There are more bicycles than people in Copenhagen, and five times as many bicycles as cars. Over 50% of city dwellers commute by bicycle, and over 41% arrive at their place of work or study by bike.

12.   In the United States, the government can legally read any emails that you have that are over 180 days old without a warrant. The Electronic Communications Privacy Act was enacted long before everybody had email and the law still allows them to do this.

13.   India-based Graviky Labs has found a way to use pigment from carbon soot-polluted air to make pens, oil-based paints, and spray paint. A single Air Ink pen contains 30 to 40 minutes of carbon emissions from a single car.

14.   As of 2019, Apple has sold over one billion iPhones.

15.   NASA's robotic spacecraft, Juno, traveled a total distance of 1.74 billion miles (2.9 billion kms) to arrive on the planet Jupiter. It launched from Cape Canaveral on August 5th, 2011, and arrived on Jupiter on July 4th, 2016.

16.   In California, on July 30th, 2016, 42-year-old paratrooper Luke Aikens became the first person to jump from an airplane without a parachute or wingsuit. He jumped 25,000 feet (7,620 meters) to Earth, setting a world record for the highest jump. He landed safely in a 100-square-foot (9 square meter) net. That's about one third the size of a football field.

17.   According to a study done in 2008, smells can influence our dreams. Subjects of the study where the scent of roses were infused when they were dreaming gave nearly all of them pleasant dreams. However, when the air around those subjects was infused with the smell of rotten eggs while they were dreaming, they had negative dreams.

18.   There's an inn in Idaho called the Dog Bark Park Inn, where guests can stay in the world's largest beagle. You enter the body of the beagle from a second-story deck. Up another level into the head of the dog is a loft, and there's an additional sleeping space and a cozy alcove in the muzzle.

19.   In 1958, Robert Lane from New York City named his son Winner, and later another son, Loser. Winner ended up as a criminal with a lengthy arrest record, and his son loser went on to prep school on a scholarship, graduated from college, and joined the New York Police Department.

20.   The crew of Apollo 15 placed a small aluminum sculpture on the moon to memorialize the fallen astronauts. In 1971, that number was 14. There's also a plaque bearing their names.

21.   Squirrels have actually been known to adopt another squirrel's baby if the parent dies.

22.   Monkey brains are considered a delicacy in parts of South Asia, Africa, and China.They're considered an easily digestible substance often given to children, and there are even entire cookbooks dedicated on how to cook them.

23.   The Satere-Mawe Indians initiate their boys at the age of 13 by making them wear gloves made of bullet ants for 10 minutes. They are repeatedly bitten, which is incredibly painful, but must not cry out if they want to be declared a man.

24.   Octopuses will actually break off a limb as part of a fight to impress a mate or to get away from a predator. They will also eat their own arms once in a while, which some scientists believe may be due to a disease of some sort.

25.   When flying in a flock, Flamingos can fly as fast as 35 miles (55 km) per hour. They may seem clumsy in flight, however, because this is because their long necks stretch out in front of their bodies, and their long legs dangle well past their short tails.

26.   In California, there's a law that prohibits a vehicle without a driver to exceed 60 miles (97 km) per hour. Companies like Google who make autonomous cars have the technology to make them go much faster but must limit them based on this law.

27.   There is an app that exists called Photo Math that solves any math equation you can point your phone at.

28.   Lobsters have some really weird anatomy. Their brains are in their throats, their nervous systems are in their abdomens, their teeth are in their stomachs, and their kidneys are in their heads.

29.   The Carrot House in Warsaw is the world's tiniest house measuring only 92 centimeters at its narrowest point and 152 centimeters at its widest.

30.   Africam is a website that brings you live, 24/7 video feed of protected areas of southern Africa. You can watch elephants, giraffes, zebras, hyenas and all kinds of species of wildlife living there.

31.   There is a 1966 Volvo with more than 3 million miles on it.

32.   Horror movie sound tracks sometimes include infrasound, which is sound below the range of human hearing. Even though we can't hear it, we can still feel it, and infrasound has been shown to induce anxiety, heart palpitations and even shivering.

33.   In Japan, you can hire a handsome man to show up at your office and watch sad videos with you until you cry and then wipe away your tears for you.

34.   Charles Baldwin, designer of the international biohazard symbol, said regarding his design, we wanted to create something that was memorable but meaningless, so that we could educate people as to what it means.

35.   The total cost of climbing Mount Everest, to pay for 'Sherpas', supplies and permits, is between $60,000 and $120,000.

36.   According to the Guinness World Records, as of 2015, the world record for long distance archery is held by a paralympic, armless archer, Matt Stutzman.

37.   There is a ten-year-old girl named Esther Okade who is already enrolled in university, and has the highest exam scores in her class. She mastered algebra at the age of four.

38.   The rarest wild cat in the world is the Bornean Bay Cat. Only 12 have ever been captured and studied between the years of 1874 and 2002. That's one every 10 years.

39.   Shani Shingnapur is a small village in India with 300 buildings, all of which have no doors in their doorways. These people leave their homes, businesses, and schools open at all times under the belief that if anyone does anything dishonest, that they will face seven years bad luck.

40.   In 1883, the body of a bear and a man named Frank Devereaux were found dead side-by-side with the ground around them thrashed. It's believed that the man and bear fought to the death.

41.   There are over 500 hundred different ways to cook potatoes. In fact, a recipe book on it was put together by former Soviet leader Mikhail Gorbachev's wife, and was gifted to Britain. It now sits in the British foreign office.

42.   There is a bottle of vodka that costs 3.75 million U.S. dollars, and it's filtered through sand made from crushed diamonds and gems.

43.   A study concluded by the Journal of Positive Psychology concluded that two thirds of humans have no idea what they're good at and what their strengths are.

44.   In 2014, Beyonce made about $3.65 U.S. every second.

45.   The Pixar team came up with the concepts of "Wall-E", "A Bug's Life", "Monsters Inc.", and 'Finding Nemo' all over a lunch-break in 1994.

46.   There is a floating stage in Singapore that sits above the water that can bear the weight of 9,000 people. It's used as a soccer field, concert stage, and place of celebration.

47.   The world's tallest man, Bao Xishun, used his long arms reaching 1.06 meters to remove plastic from the stomachs of two dolphins, which ultimately saved their lives after trainers tried numerous other methods.

48.   When Julius Caesar first discovered giraffes, he named them camelopards, since they reminded him of both camels and leopards.

49.   British banking giant HSBC admitted to laundering billions of dollars for Colombian and Mexican drug cartels and violating a host of important

banking laws. But, somehow, there were no criminal charges and no one went to jail.

50.   You can't usually smell your own house or perfume because of the survival instinct called "olfactory adaptation". The brain is always looking for new, unusual, or changing smells as a sign of possible danger. So, it ignores smells that it has become familiar with.

51.   There is a company called Hoxton Street Monster Supplies that sells salt made from real human tears, and disturbingly there are four kinds, harvested from different moments. Sneezing, chopping onions, laughter and anger.

52.   An Australian man named Don Ritchie lives across the street from the most famous suicide spot in Australia; a cliff known as The Gap. He, alone, has prevented around 160 suicides in his 50 years of living there by striking up a conversation with people contemplating suicide by inviting them into his house for tea.

53.   For the past 15 years, a Bulgarian man named Dobri Dobrev has walked up to 25 kilometers every single day to beg for money for orphanages that are unable to pay their bills. He turned 101 in July of this year.

54.   An adopted man in Michigan named Steve Flaig searched for his birth mother for four years before finally discovering in 2007 that she worked at the same Lowe's store that he worked at. Amazingly neither of them knew.

55.   A moment is actually a medieval unit of time equal to 90 seconds. There are 40 moments in an hour.

56.   The Queen of England's portrait has been on enough International money to make a progressive timeline of her aging.

57.   An Abu-dhabi oil sheik named Hamad Bin Hamdan Al Nahyan carved his name in the desert in letters that are over 1,000 meters long.

58.   Istanbul has a vending machine that releases food and water for stray dogs in exchange for recyclable bottles.

59.   The first animal to ever ask an existential question was from a parrot named Alex. He asked what color he was, and learned that he was gray.

60.   In January 1961 the U.S. Air Force accidentally dropped two nuclear bombs in Goldsboro North Carolina when a bomber broke in half in the air. Fortunately the bomb didn't go off but if it did it would've caused more destruction than Hiroshima and Nagasaki.

61.   People who are in love can actually synchronize their heartbeats just by gazing into each others eyes.

62.   Exercising increases productivity. Having a regular exercise routine can make you happier, smarter and more energetic and thus last longer throughout the day.

63.   In 2009 archaeologist discovered the fossils of a primitive species of crocodiles that actually galloped. They lived 100 million years ago, walked with the dinosaurs and sometimes even ate them.

64.   Approximately 50% of Asians have trouble metabolizing alcohol because they're missing a liver enzyme that's needed to process it.

65.   England's Big Ben is actually leaning to the northwest by .26 degrees, putting it out of alignment at its highest point by 1.6 feet. It was discovered when Transport for London commissioned a report, that the London clay on which the tower was built on is drying out, causing the lean.

66.   In 1930, the planet Pluto was named by an 11 year old named Venetia Burney. She suggested the name Pluto to her grandfather, who in turn suggested it to a friend who happened to be an astronomy professor at Oxford University. He was also one of the leaders in the worldwide effort to produce an astrographic chart.

67.   According to a study done in 2001 by Diane Reese of the Osborn Laboratory of Marine Sciences at the New York Aquarium, dolphins actually recognize themselves and notice changes in their appearance when looking in a mirror. Prior to this research, only higher primates, such as humans and chimpanzees had demonstrated self-recognition in mirrors.

68.   Researchers at the University of Montreal have concluded that everyone has the potential ability to be a good singer. It's a developed skill that gets better with practice and worse by lack of use.

69.   There's an infrared device that exists that detects the locations of medical patients' veins and projects them onto the skin.

70.   The Keikyu Aburatsubo Marine Park in Japan has tiny holes in the otter enclosure which allows visitors to shake hands with these animals.

71.   A group of pandas is known as an embarrassment.

72.   In 1948 the committee responsible for awarding the Nobel Peace Prize chose no one, stating there was no suitable living candidate, mostly as a tribute to Mahatma Gandhi who was assassinated earlier that year.

73.   The word "BAE" which is popular in North American society is actually the Danish word for poop.

74.   You can tell identical twin babies apart by their navels since the navel is a scar and isn't caused by genetics.

75.   Allen Gans holds the world record for the longest person as an ice-cream man. He's been serving ice cream since 1947 in the greater Boston area and knows 90 % of his customers by name.

76.   The Nasir Almoque Mosque in Iran is known for its incredible stained glass windows. When the morning sunlight shines through the windows, the interior of the mosque reflects the windows like a kaleidoscope.

77.   In 1995 NASA scientists experimented on spiders to see how drugs like LSD, marijuana, caffeine and peyote would affect them. The results showed that spiders would spin webs differently depending on the type of drug that they were given. The more toxic the drug, the less organised their webs were.

78.   Soviet diplomat Vyacheslav Molotov is thought to be the only man to ever shake hands with Stalin, Lenin, Hitler, Himmler, Goering, Roosevelt, and Churchill and is also the inspiration behind the term Molotov cocktail.

79.   The Wright brothers only ever flew together once, in 1910. This is because their father feared losing both sons in an airplane accident, so he gave them special permission just that one time.

80.   Psychopaths are only capable of perceiving the positive consequences for their actions as opposed to any negative ones.

81.   When you yawn and stretch at the time, you are "pandiculating."

82.   Tupac danced ballet in high school and ended up portraying the Mouse King in a production of The Nutcracker.

83.   Babies are born without kneecaps. They don't appear until the child reaches 2-6 years of age.

84.   Arnold Schonberg suffered from triskaidekaphobia, the fear of the number 13. He died at 13 minutes from midnight on Friday the 13th.

85.   Actor Sean Bean is so terrified of flying that during the filming of Lord of the Rings, while shooting in remote mountain locations, he traveled via sky lift and walked the remainder of the journey all in full costume.

86.   There are fireworks that can be set off in daylight by using colored smoke.

87.   That dark band that you can see between the primary and secondary bows of a rainbow has a name. It's been referred to as Alexander's band or Alexander's dark band, after Alexander of Aphrodisiacs first described it in 200 AD.

88.   The Chinese giant salamander is the world's largest living amphibian and can grow up to six feet (1.8 meters) long and can weigh as much as 110 pounds (500 kg).

89.   Watermelon is made up of 92% water. It's actually an excellent choice to stay hydrated and is low in calories.

90.   It's possible for a poisonous snake, after being decapitated for hours, to bite and inject venom and still kill you. According to Steven Beaupre, a biology professor at the University of Arkansas, snakes are well-known for retaining reflexes after death. For venomous snakes like cobras and rattlesnakes, biting is one of those reflexes.

91.   In the 15 and 1600s, women who were seen gossiping, riotous, or troublesome were made to wear scold's bridle, also known as branks, as punishment. Disturbingly, it was made of an iron frame that encased the head, and at the front was a bridle or bit, like a horse, that extended into the mouth and held down the tongue with a spiked plate. It literally made it impossible to speak, so it was basically a muzzle for a woman.

92.   After Abraham Lincoln was assassinated his body was taken on a two-week, 1,600-mile (2500 km) tour via train. He was accompanied by the body of his son, William Wallace Lincoln, who had died of typhoid fever at the age of only 11, and buried in the DC area of 1862. The train made a tour through 400 train stations, and viewings were arranged where his body was on display for mourners.

93.   In 2006, Michigan woman Lynn Sterling tried to sell a mummified human skeleton on eBay. eBay removed the posting because it violated their policy against selling human remains.

94.   It's possible for cats and dogs to be allergic to human dander. Dander is made up of tiny cells shed from hair, fur, or feathers. And though you mostly hear it in relation to pets, humans produce it too.

95.   The mantis shrimp can punch with a speed equal to a bullet, fifty times that of a blink of an eye. In fact, a blow from a mantis shrimp can easily break through the shell of a crab or mollusk.

96.   Until 1987, all surgeries performed on infants were done without anesthesia, under the belief that infants were not capable of feeling pain.

97.   In 2012 a man sued Pepsi after he found a mouse in his Mountain Dew. However, Pepsi fought and won the case, proving that any mouse would have dissolved inside a can of Mountain Dew after 30 days, and that this can was purchased 74 days after being manufactured.

98.   Railroad tycoon George Pullman's family were so worried that former employees would desecrate his corpse after death that they buried him at night in a pit 2.4 meters deep under layers of steel reinforced concrete in a lead-lined casket.

99.   Elephants can use the skin folds on their backs to crush mosquitos.

100.   There is a doctor in Nepal named Sanduk Ruit who has restored vision to over 100,000 people in the developing world.

101.   In the average lifetime, a person will walk the equivalent of 5 times around the equator.

102.   A research paper from 2013 concluded that Harry Potter fans tend to be more open to diversity, politically tolerant, less authoritarian, and less likely to support the use of deadly force or torture.

103. You can be criminally prosecuted for making death threats written entirely in emoji.

104. If you were to commit suicide in Japan by either jumping in front of a train or killing yourself in your apartment building, the train or building company will actually sue your family for clean-up fees, loss of income, and negative publicity brought upon them by your suicide.

105. James Cameron was actually homeless when he wrote 'The Terminator' and sold the rights to it for only one dollar on the condition that he could direct it.

106. -40 Celsius and -40 Fahrenheit are the same temperature.

107. A company by the name of Vestergaard Frandsen, in Europe, launched a LifeStraw in 2006, which makes contaminated water safe to drink. Users simply just have to suck up the contaminated water through it as if they were any other regular straw. Without using batteries or chemicals, it removes 99.9% of parasites, 99.9999% of viruses and provides one person with an entire year's worth of drinking water for only $20.00.

108. One of the ingredients needed to make dynamite is peanuts.

109. In Dubai there's a weight loss competition called 'Your Child In Gold'. The campaign is aimed at early obesity and winners get 90 pounds (40 kilograms) in gold.

110. The pet rock became so popular when it came out that within the first six months of its release, Gary Doll the inventor earned $15 million.

111. While you sleep you can't smell anything, even really bad or potent smells.

112. In 1963 Alfred Heineken designed the 'Heineken World Bottle', a brick that holds beer that can be used to build houses. Unfortunately the project never came into fruition and the Heineken estate and museum are the only two places in the entire world with a beer brick wall.

113. The Gippsland lakes in Victoria, Australia glows in the dark. The light is created by a chemical reaction called bioluminescence when naturally occurring microorganisms in the water are disturbed.

114. In 2012, Healthpoint Biotherapeutics, of Fort Worth, Texas, developed a portable, spray on skin, that can heal severe wounds much faster. The spray on skin is actually made up of skin cells and suspended in a mixture of different types of proteins.

115. Andre the Giant died on the night of January 27th, 1993 in a hotel room in Paris. Coincidentally, he was in Paris to attend his own father's funeral.

116. The longest mathematical proof in history is 15,000 pages long, involved more than 100 mathematicians, and took over 30 years to complete.

117. Some of the largest spider webs in the world are built by the Anelosimus Eximius; a breed of social spider that works together in a community. Over 50,000 spiders can live on one web until they eventually outgrow it and have to form new colonies.

118. Apples originated in Kazakhstan, and wild apples can taste like roses, strawberries, popcorn, anise and many other flavors. In fact, in 90% of modern apples can be traced back to two trees.

119. Rotterdam, in the Netherlands, is getting a floating forest. They're taking 20 trees that have been removed for development and placing them in boats throughout the waterfront.

120. Yellow snow isn't the only snow you shouldn't eat. According to a new study published in the Journal of Environmental Science Processes and Impacts, all snow can be harmful because it attracts particles from car exhaust fumes like a magnet.

121. Instead of its Gross National Product, Bhutan measures its development and prosperity by its Gross National Happiness. It's been doing this since 1971 and is the only country to do so.

122. There is an English law called right to light that allows long-standing owners of buildings that receive natural daylight for at least 20 years, to forbid any construction that would block the windows and deprive them of that light.

123. Greek statues aren't actually white like we thought they were. Ultraviolet light has revealed that they were once originally brightly painted, but after thousands of years the paint's wore away to show the statues as we know them today.

124. Vikings never actually wore horned helmets. The only helmet that was discovered to be a Viking heritage shows a rounded iron cap and no horns whatsoever.

125. In 1950, almost the entire Soviet hockey team died in a plane crash. The team's manager was Vasily Stalin, son of Joseph Stalin. He was afraid of his father's reaction to the crash and recruited a whole team immediately and surprisingly, his father never knew the difference.

126. You can rent the entire country of Liechtenstein for 70,000 dollars a night. In fact, Snoop Dogg once tried to do that in 2011 for a video shoot but the country said no primarily because he just didn't give them enough notice.

127. Australia, literally, lost a prime minister Harold Holt, on December 17th of 1967, who went for a swim and just never came back.

128. High atmospheric pressure affects the bubbles in your coffee. Therefore, if bubbles are closer to the center, you can expect it to rain or have other stormy weather.

129.   Elephants remember and mourn their loved ones like us, sometimes years after their death.

130.   In 1999 a woman named Penny Brown saved a little boy, Kevin Stefan's life by giving him CPR after he was hit in the chest with a baseball bat. However, just seven years later, he ended up saving her from choking to death by giving her the Heimlich maneuver.

131.   There is a cryptid that's believed to exist in the Gobi Desert called the Mongolian Death Worm. It can grow up to 1.5 meters long and kills its prey with electric shocks from its eyes.

132.   In 2013 a bank worker in Germany fell asleep on his keyboard's number-two button causing him to transfer 222,222,222 euros on a transfer that should have been worth only 62 euros. Interestingly his coworker was the one fired for not spotting the error.

133.   Users upload an average of 350 million photos to Facebook every day and in total have uploaded more than 250 billion photos to date.

134.   The role of Captain Jack Sparrow was originally offered to Jim Carrey but he turned it down for the role of Bruce Almighty.

135.   According to neuroscientist Glen Jeffrey, who investigates vision at the University College London, the eye color of reindeer changes depending on the time of year. In the summer, they actually turn golden, reflecting more light through the retina, which helps them deal with the almost continuous Arctic summer daylight. In the winter however, they turn a deep blue to help them deal with the almost continuous winter darkness.

136.   There's a Sign Post Forest just outside of Watson Lake, Yukon. It was started in 1942 when a soldier named Carl K. Lindley was injured while working on the Alcan Highway. He was taken to the Army air station in Watson Lake to recuperate. While he was there he was homesick, so he decided to put up a sign of Danville, Illinois, his hometown. Tourists continued the tradition, and there are currently 72,000 signs from around the world.

137.   Since the first nuclear test explosion on July 16th, 1945, at least eight nations have detonated 2,054 nuclear test explosions at dozens of test sites around the world.

138.   There's something that exists called elimination communication where, instead of using diapers, the parent learns to use timing, signals, and cues to know when their baby needs to pee or poo.

139.   Jackrabbits are actually hares, not rabbits. They can reach speeds of 40 miles (64 km) per hour and jump as high as 10 feet (3 metres) in the air.

140.   The Lehe Ledu Wildlife Zoo in Chongqing, China, put the people visiting the zoo in cages instead of the animals. The cages are stalked by lions

and tigers, so the guests are warned to keep their fingers and hands inside the cage at all times.

141.   The unborn babies of a female sea louse actually chew their way out of the mother's insides to be born.

142.   A 63-year-old Tasmanian woman gave birth to her first baby in August of 2016, making her Australia's oldest new mother.

143.   According to a report from the Center for Disease Control and Prevention's National Center for Health Statistics, American men now weigh, on average, 196 pounds (89 kg) on average, 15 pounds (7 kg) more than 20 years ago, and women weigh 168 pounds (76 kg) on average, which is 16 pounds (7 kg) more than 20 years ago.

144.   There's a flower called the corpse flower, which is called that because it smells like putrefying and decaying flesh, which only blooms every seven to 10 years.

145.   According to a study done in 2012 by Japanese researcher Hiroshi Nittono, looking at images of cute animals like puppies and pandas at work not only improve your mood but also boosts your attention to detail and overall performance.

146.   An Iowa artist named Patrick Acton built a complete model of Hogwarts out of six hundred and two thousand matchsticks held together by almost 60 liters of wood glue.

147.   Sugar gliders are such social creatures that if they're deprived of social interaction they can actually become depressed and die.

148.   In the Middle Ages, doctors believed that farting into jars and sniffing them, would prevent death or more specifically the black death plague which they called therapeutic stink.

149.   The richest woman in Germany Susanne Klatten met her husband while she was working in an internship for BMW under a fake name. In the 1980s he had no idea who she actually was until she was sure about the relationship when she revealed herself.

150.   There are approximately 10 quintillion insects on the planet. That's 10 with 18 zeros behind it or roughly 200 million insects per human.

151.   In 1992, thousands of plastic yellow ducks broke free from a cargo ship in the middle of the Pacific Ocean, and for the past 23 years, these ducks have since turned up in locations all over the world, and have even been used to track ocean currents.

152.   Research conducted at the University of Stanford concluded that a racially diverse group has the ability to solve problems more effectively than a group with only one race in it.

153.	If you watch any classic Clint Eastwood film, you will often see his character smoking like Dirty Harry, despite the fact that Clint never smoked habitually in real life, and actually practiced healthy dieting and meditation since his youth.

154.	In South Korea, children under 17 are blocked from playing online games past midnight, which is monitored by their KSSN, the Korean Social Security Number.

155.	On April Fool's Day in 1989, billionaire Richard Branson designed a hot air balloon to look like a UFO, and hired a dwarf in an ET costume to come out and scare whoever was near it when it landed.

156.	The band Blink-182 incorporated under the name Pennywise Poo Poo Butt Inc so that their accountants, managers and attorneys would have to say that when doing business.

157.	When James Bond actor, Daniel Craig first ran off with his current wife Rachel Weisz in 2010, he actually had a fiancée at the time. And when she found out, she spent a million dollars on his credit line in revenge.

158.	Robert Hubbard was executed in 1666 for starting the great fire of London by claiming he threw a firebomb through a bakery window. However, this was despite the fact that he was heavily crippled, the bakery had no windows, and it was proved at his trial that he wasn't even in the country at the time.

159.	Jennifer Lopez's common nickname in parts of Hong Kong and China is Lord of Butt.

160.	Pharrell Williams was fired from three separate McDonald's restaurants when he was 17 for being lazy and stealing McNuggets.

161.	Every December 25th, the inhabitants of the Chumbivilcas Province in Peru celebrate Takanakuy. This is where men settle grudges from the past year by calling each other out and having a fist fight. Then everybody goes drinking to numb the pain and move on to a new year.

162.	There exists a set of 19 questions among doctors such as "do we have the right patient" and "what operation are we performing" known as the "safe surgery checklist" which has been proven to reduce surgical deaths by more than 40 percent.

163.	65% of smartphone users download zero apps per month.

164.	The great pyramids in Egypt were actually shiny like glass at one point 4,000 years ago. Craftsmen were tasked to polish the stone surfaces to perfection.

165.	In 2010, Mattel made and sold Wonder Woman's invisible jet as a collectible. The package was an empty plastic shell with nothing inside and the packaging had weights to give the illusion that there was actually something inside, and people bought this.

166.   Actor Don Johnson once asked famed journalist Hunter S. Thompson what is the sound of one hand clapping. Hunter S. Thompson answered by reaching up and slapping Johnson upside the head.

167.   Blind people forget many memories since they don't have visual imagery and can't look at pictures to reminisce. A 3D printing company known as Touchable Memories prints 3D objects from old photos so that the blind can touch them, feel, and relive their cherished moments like never before.

168.   Jamaica, Colombia, and Saint Lucia are the only countries in the world where a boss is more likely to be a woman than a man.

169.   Believe it or not, you can determine the temperature outside by counting the chirps made by crickets. According to the Farmer's Almanac, to convert cricket chirps to degrees celsius, you count the number of chirps in 25 seconds, divide by three, then add four to get the temperature.

170.   There's something called a moonbow or lunar rainbow that's a rainbow that can be seen at night and happens very rarely. In order for this to happen, a full moon is needed, it must be raining opposite to the moon, the sky must be dark, and the moon must be less than 42 degrees high.

171.   The longest solar eclipse in the 21st century lasted six minutes and 39 seconds, and it won't be surpassed in duration until the eclipse of June 13, 2132.

172.   Venus and Uranus are the only planets that rotate clockwise. The other six planets in the solar system rotate counterclockwise.

173.   Pope Francis broke a record when he hit one million Instagram followers within 12 hours of starting the account. The previous record was set by David Beckham at one million within 24 hours. He christened the account on a Saturday with a photo of him kneeling in prayer with an accompanying message that said, "Pray for me," in nine languages.

174.   Before Samuel L. Jackson became a movie star, he was Bill Cosby's camera stand-in 'On The Cosby Show'.

175.   Leonardo da Vinci was dyslexic. Also strangely, not because of his dyslexia, he chose to write all of his notes to himself backwards in mirror writing, meaning that you can only read them in the reflection of a mirror. However notes that he wrote to other people, he wrote in a normal direction.

176.   A college student in 1979 only had to work about 182 hours per year in order to pay for tuition. The average student in 2013 had to work over 991.

177.   Penguin One, an organic chemical compound, got its name from the fact that its molecular structure resembles a penguin.

178.   The heaviest human ever recorded was Jon Minnoch and weighed 1,400 pounds (635 kg). He later lost approximately 924 pounds (419 kg), the largest human weight loss ever documented.

179.   The idea for the film 'The Human Centipede' came from a joke made by the writer/director Tom Six on how child molesters should be punished.

180.   During the late 1800's, a baboon named Jack was employed by the railroad in Cape Town South Africa as a signalman. He never once made a mistake and worked for the railroad until his death.

181.   Scientists have begun arguing that we may actually have more than five basic senses including magnetoception, the ability to detect magnetic fields and Chronoception, the sense of time passing.

182.   In 1898 Bayer introduced diacetylmorphine, marketed as a cure for morphine addiction and cough suppressant. Today that drug is better known by the name heroin.

183.   In the 1930s an Argentinean engineer named Juan Vilar created a rain-making machine and successfully made it rain in several places at once. He then disappeared without a trace.

184.   Marvel's The Avengers movie caused shawarma sales to skyrocket nationwide in America in 2012, purely because of an extra scene in which Thor, Captain America, Bruce Banner, and the rest of the heroic clan are quietly enjoying shawarma after casually saving the world.

185.   The most densely populated island on the planet is Santa Cruz del Islote, off the coast of Colombia. It measures only about 0.012 kilometers, but is home to over 12,000 people.

186.   A biotech startup has managed to print 3D rhino horns that are genetically similar to a real horn. The best thing about it is the company plans to flood Chinese and Vietnamese markets, where the demand is high, and bring down the price, and thus, demands.

187.   The movie Straight Outta Compton didn't play in Compton because there are no theaters there.

188.   A man in the United Kingdom was so fed up that his city wasn't repairing potholes he went and spray painted penises on them earning him the nickname "Wanksy."

189.   There is a natural rock formation off of the coast of Iceland that looks like a giant elephant.

190.   Donald Trump was actually the inspiration for the character Biff Tanned in the Back to the Future trilogy.

191.   There is a bookstore in Australia where books are wrapped in paper with short descriptions so that no one can judge a book by its cover.

192.   In Albania, nodding your head means no, and shaking your head means yes.

193.   A human taste bud has an average lifespan of seven to 10 days. Taste bud cells undergo continual turnover, even into adulthood, but taste buds in rats last from two days to over three weeks.

194.   There were over 13 couples celebrating their honeymoon on the Titanic, however none of them survived upon impact and the subsequent sinking of the boat.

195.   Dogs love the herb anise the same way that cats love catnip. In fact, anise is the scent on the artificial rabbit that is used in greyhound races to get the dogs to run.

196.   The hardest bone in the human body is the jawbone. Also known as the mandible, it's also the largest and strongest bone in the human face.

197.   Believe it or not, you consume 1/10th of a calorie by licking a U.S. stamp, but if you were to lick a stamp in Britain, it's 5.9 calories per lick and the adhesive on a larger commemorative or special British stamp contains a whopping 14.5 calories.

198.   Camels actually have three eyelids to protect their eyes from blowing sand. The upper and lower eyelids have eyelashes, however there's a third one that's a thin membrane that they can see through even in a sandstorm.

199.   Your sense of smell and taste begin to improve dramatically within 48 hours of quitting smoking.

200.   Potatoes have almost all the nutrients that humans need to survive. To prove this, the executive director from the Washington State Potato Commission, ate nothing but potatoes for 60 days and was just fine.

Part 2

201.   Caromont Farms, in Esmont, Virginia, posted a message on its Facebook page earlier this year, looking for volunteers to snuggle with its baby goats. Not surprisingly, the sign up list filled up immediately.

202.   After its tourism sector boomed, Kazakhstan's foreign minister thanked Sacha Baron Cohen back in 2012 for the release of Borat after the country saw a 10 times increase in issued visas.

203.   In 2014, a woman named Nancy Cohen was moved into a nursing home. Her relocated cat, Cleo, showed up two weeks later, even though she had never been there before. She started hanging out on benches until somebody noticed her, and now they live together at the facility.

204.   The Taxi Fabric Project in Mumbai, India lets upcoming designers reupholster and completely transform taxi cab interiors.

205.   There is a unique tree near Piemonte, Italy called The Double Tree of Casorzo. It's actually two trees in one, a cherry tree growing on top of a mulberry tree.

206.   According to Daniel J. Buysse, a psychiatrist at the University of Pittsburgh Medical Center, about two percent of the population are considered the sleepless elite. This means that they are night owls and early birds simultaneously.

207.   When Neuroscientist James Fallon was studying the brains of psychopathic killers, he scanned his own brain as a control, only to discover that he himself was a psychopath. When he told his friends and family, the universal response was "That explains a lot."

208.   Argentine ants have a worldwide mega-colony. In fact, if they got on an airplane and traveled to a different continent, they would actually be welcomed by a foreign branch of the colony.

209.   A study once found that, while sober, rats prefer silence, but on cocaine, they prefer jazz.

210.   In the 1930s, two psychologists adopted a baby chimp and tried to raise her as their own child alongside their real infant son, Donald, to see if it caused the chimp to learn human behavior. They stopped the experiment after nine months because their son actually started behaving more like the chimp.

211.   Gun laws in Japan are so strict that even when a police officer killed himself with one once, he was posthumously charged with breaking the law.

212.   Ravens are one of the smartest animals on earth. They actually try to hide their food from each other but are only sometimes successful because they're all so smart.

213.   Various studies have shown that coffee prevents cancer, reduces risk of diabetes, and can improve overall health.

214.   John F. Kennedy's grandmother, Mary Josephine Fitzgerald, not only outlived her grandson, but she was never told about his assassination.

215.   In the early 1930s, Warner Brothers began producing animated shorts specifically for the purpose of promoting music owned by the company. They were called Looney Tunes.

216.   When Google first announced Gmail on April 1st with an unbelievable one gig of free storage, back in 2004, which at the time seemed impossible with Hotmail only offering 2 megabytes, people thought that it was an April Fool's Day joke.

217.   Believe it or not, outer space is only an hour away if you could drive a car straight into the sky at 96 kilometers an hour or 60 miles an hour.

218.   In the early 1800s, Napoleon demanded a method of communication that would not require light or sound. It was called night writing and was developed as a tactile military code. Night writing became the basis for braille.

219.   Niccolo Paganini, regarded by many people to be the greatest violin virtuoso of all time, was so good that in the early 1800s, people began to question if he had sold his soul to the devil for his talent. He was actually forced to publish his mother's letters to him in order to prove that he had human parents.

220.   At one point during the 1985 Geneva Summit, Reagan and Gorbachev agreed to pause the Cold War in case of an alien invasion.

221.   A poisonous lagoon at the quarry in Buxton, England was dyed black for safety. The previous beautiful, azure blue water color was so inviting that the signs did not keep swimmers out.

222.   The world's deepest, darkest, oldest, and quietest motel room is 70 meters underground, at Grand Canyon Caverns in a 65,000,000 year old cave.

223.   Knowledge of silk production was thought to be very valuable and the Chinese kept it a secret for over 3,000 years. In fact it was so secret that anyone who revealed it was sentenced to death by imperial decrees.

224.   A Japanese gymnast named Shun Fujimoto once broke his knee at the Olympics in 1976 but didn't tell anybody and performed miraculously despite his injury, even winning his team a gold medal.

225.   There's a town in Australia where the entire town, 200-plus people, live underground in abandoned opal mines. Residents here have electricity and plumbing, and have been known to find vast amounts of opal when renovating.

226.   Artist Susan Beatrice recycles old watch parts and turns them into intricate steampunk sculptures.

227.   George Hotz, then 17 years old, was the first to unlock a first-generation iPhone and sold the iPhone for a Nissan 350Z and three locked phones.

228.   There's a pepper, grown in Japan, known as the "Shishito pepper". Only one out of every 10 is spicy, and there's no way to know which one beforehand.

229.   There's a mental disorder called maladaptive daydreaming, which causes people to excessively daydream to escape reality as a defense mechanism due to trauma, usually from abuse.

230.   More people have died from selfies than shark attacks.

231.   Treadmills were actually created to punish English prisoners in 1818.

232.   Dr. Duncan MacDougall, Haverhill, once attempted to prove that the human soul had weight by placing dying patients on a giant scale at the exact moment of death. Believe it or not, at the exact moment of death, there was a slight decrease in weight.

233.   Experiences that you have throughout your life leave chemical markers on your DNA, essentially ingraining superficial experiences into your descendants.

234.   Photographer Chompoo Baritone created a photo series that aims at exposing the truth by mocking Instagram users who prop and filter their lives to make them seem more amazing than they really are.

235.   There is a phenomenon that exists called, cellular memory. It occurs when organ transplant recipients experience the same thoughts and cravings as their organ donors.

236.   There is a fish that exists called the Blue Lingcod that has blue flesh. When it's cooked the blue color vanishes completely.

237.   On July 5, 1996, the first mammal ever was successfully cloned. Dolly the sheep was cloned from an adult cell at the Roslin Institute in Scotland. She was named after Dolly Parton because she was cloned from a mammary cell.

238.   Mosquitoes can detect carbon dioxide from 75 feet away. In fact that's how they find their victims.

239.   A galactic year, also known as a cosmic year is the duration of a complete rotation of the Milky Way, which is approximately 200 million terrestrial years.

240.   The human aorta is the largest artery in the human body, and is about the size of a garden hose.

241.   There is a dog breed called Basenji that doesn't have the ability to bark. It can produce a yodeling howl sound though. It's a small to medium

sized, square-shaped animal that is believed to be bred intentionally without the ability to bark.

242.   In 2008, the Japanese created a silicon toy called Mugen Puti Puti designed to mimic the sensation of popping bubble wrap for an infinite number of times.

243.   Mexican shamans began to use Coca-Cola in their religious rituals to heal worshipers. When Pepsi discovered this, they offered commissions to Shamans for using Pepsi instead.

244.   Keiko, the orca who starred in Free Willy, was released into the wild in July of 2002 in Iceland after being in captivity for 23 years. A few weeks after his release he showed up at a Norwegian inlet from the sea, looking to make human contact and gave children rides on his back.

245.   If you're looking for a job, the application and resume are not nearly as important as a reference. In fact, knowing someone who works at the company increases your chances of getting an interview and makes you 40% more likely to get the job over someone with a fancier resume.

246.   Jim Wenqi, a blind man, and Jia Haixia a double amputee, together planted 10,000 trees in Yeli Village located in Northern China and plan on planting another 10,000.

247.   According to the world drug report of 2014, Scotland had the highest rate of cocaine use in the world.

248.   While on his deathbed in 1778, French philosopher Voltaire was asked to renounce Satan to which he replied "Now is not the time to be making new enemies" which are thought to be his last words.

249.   Some of the crew working on 'American Horror Story Freak Show' would have to actually leave set at times because 'Twisty the Clown' was so scary while others would complain of nightmares after filming.

250.   Famed writer H.G. Wells' last words on his deathbed in 1946 were "Go away, I'm all right."

251.   Studies in the UK for automotive accidents concluded that short female drivers who sit close to the steering wheel are the most likely to be killed by an airbag.

252.   McDonald's in Hong Kong will soon host cheap "McWeddings" for couples at a cost of around $1,200 and will actually provide food, drink, and an apple pie for 50 people.

253.   A study conducted in 2013 by the BBC found that 56% of pilots fell asleep while flying and 29% had woken up to find that the copilot was also asleep.

254.   A German engineering company has created the world's first rope free elevator system that uses a magnetic technology which allows elevators to travel sideways as well as up and down.

255.   Economics professors at Emory University found that those who spend below average on their weddings and on their wedding rings have lower divorce rates.

256.   There is only one species of warm-blooded fish on Earth, the Opah.

257.   Pixar spent three years studying the physics of curly hair in order to correctly render Merida's hair in Brave.

258.   If you come across a stranded dolphin, do not help it help it back into the water. More often than not, they beach themselves purposely because they are sick or injured, and are trying to avoid drowning.

259.   In 1888 a pigeon keeper and a beekeeper challenged each other's creatures to a 3.5 mile (5.6 kilometer) organized race in Germany. The bee won by 25 seconds.

260.   When the Confederate Army was low on gun powder, bat caves were raided for poop. Bat poop contains high nitrate content which is a key ingredient for the production of gunpowder.

261.   In 1991, drug lord Pablo Escobar got to build his own prison known as La Cathedral. It featured a soccer field, a giant dollhouse, a bar, a Jacuzzi, and a waterfall. It's where he stayed for only one year and one month after he was caught torturing his guests.

262.   Wild chimpanzees look both ways before crossing the road. The National Museum of Natural History in Paris began studying their vigilance and found that 57% of the time, they would run across the road to be extra safe.

263.   Astronomers have discovered the largest known diamond in the universe is a star named Lucy that is ten trillion, billion karats. This white dwarf has a carbon interior that crystallized as it cooled which formed a giant diamond in the sky. Scientists couldn't resist naming it after The Beatles' song 'Lucy in the Sky with Diamonds'.

264.   In 2013, a dog named Killian saved a baby boy from an abusive babysitter when he alerted his owners by growling and standing between the baby and the sitter whenever she was present. The parents later recorded the abuse and the sitter was convicted.

265.   Panama is the only place in the world where one can see the sun rise on the Pacific Ocean, and set on the Atlantic.

266.   In 1905, 11-year-old Frank Epperson from the San Francisco Bay area invented the popsicle by accident. He left his sugary soda powder that he mixed with water outside overnight and the next morning, it was frozen. He

originally named it the eppsicle, but the name was eventually changed to popsicle.

267.   There's a phobia called allodoxaphobia that's actually the fear of people's opinions. People with this live in constant fear and anxiety of hearing other people's opinions of them.

268.   A group of flamingos is called a flamboyance of flamingos.

269.   In 1922, Charles Osborne got a case of the hiccups that lasted until 1990. He was hiccuping 40 times a minute for 68 years and possibly the weirdest thing is that when it stopped, it stopped for unknown reasons.

270.   The New York Presbyterian Morgan Stanley Children's Hospital has a CT scan room that has been turned into a pirate themed island. Children enter the room by walking on a plank and then lay on a boat-shaped table.

271.   Steven Jay Russell escaped four times from prison. The first time, he simply walked out. Upon recapture, Russell lowered and paid his bail by pretending to be a judge, escaped his next capture by impersonating a doctor, and did so again by then faking his death. Eventually he received a 144-year sentence that he is still currently serving.

272.   In 2010, musician Dave Grohl was admitted into a hospital due to a drug overdose. The drug was that he had actually consumed too much caffeine from coffee while recording a new album.

273.   Studies conducted by the University of Toronto concluded that the more that one trusts people, the better they are at spotting liars.

274.   A Japanese soldier was stranded on an island for 30 years after the Second World War had ended. He continued to stand his post in uniform until his commander came to the island to personally dismiss him in 1974.

275.   In 1978, Soviet geologists found a family of six that survived in the middle of Serbia who hadn't seen another human since 1936.

276.   Pumbaa was the first ever character to fart in a Disney movie.

277.   Purple is known as a royal color because back when they relied on only natural dyes purple came from sea snails and it was the hardest dye to extract and produce, so only royals could afford it. In fact, it would take 12,000 snails to produce 1.4 grams of purple dye.

278.   Ants cannot be injured from impact with the ground after being dropped from any height, mostly because they just don't have enough mass.

279.   The Concorde jet, that had its last flight in 2003, had a maximum speed of 1,350 miles (2170 km) per hour. It could fly from London, England to New York City in about three hours, about half the time of other passenger planes.

280.   On the set of the movie, 'Apocalypse Now', the production cast design decided to actually use real bodies instead of fake ones. It was only

discovered when a pungent odor became too strong for the rest of the cast to ignore.

281.	There's an annual conference called "The Boring Conference" on boring things. In the past, people have given talks on barcodes, sneezing, and the sounds of vending machines.

282.	Astoundingly the human brain, the universe, and the internet all have similar network patterns and the same growth dynamics.

283.	Norway offers amazing incentives for people who own electric cars such as, free parking, free charging, and the use of bus lanes. Now so many people in Norway have bought electric cars that the incentives actually have to be rolled back.

284.	Sylvan Goldman the inventor of shopping carts, had to hire models to push the carts around in his store to make them more appealing to customers when they first launched.

285.	The first ever 3d feature film was called the Power of Love and premiered in 1922 in Los Angeles. Unfortunately, the 3d version of the film is presumed lost and the 2d version was later shown under the name Forbidden Lover.

286.	Christopher Robin Milne, the son of Winnie the Pooh author, A.A Milne, and the person who the character Christopher Robin was based off of, actually hated the books his father wrote and thought it was his father's way of exploiting childhood.

287.	The stethoscope was invented in France in 1816 by Rene Laennec because he felt uncomfortable placing his ear on a woman's bare chest in order to listen to her heart.

288.	Owen, a baby hippo from Kenya, was swept away from his mother during a tsunami. He then mistook a 130 year old tortoise for another hippo and the two actually became best friends.

289.	The graffiti artist David Choe, who painted Facebook's first office in 2005, was paid in shares and is now worth over $200,000,000.

290.	The Sword-billed hummingbird is the only bird with a bill longer than its body.

291.	High school student Hayden Godfrey started working several jobs, saved his money for a year and a half, and eventually bought a flower for each of the 834 girls at this school, simply because he wanted them to feel joy.

292.	Watching your favorite movie over and over is good for you. The repetition calms you because knowing the outcome of a story helps you to feel safe in an unpredictable world. It also helps comfort you by recapturing lost feelings, according to a study in 2012 by Cristel Antonia Russell and Sidney J. Levy.

293.   Ironically 'Finding Nemo', a movie about the anguish of a captured clown fish, caused home aquarium demand to triple. Then that demand was met by large-scale harvesting of tropical fish from the wild, which devastated clown fish populations.

294.   In a real world transaction involving Bitcoin a man named Laslow, a computer programmer, paid 10,000 Bitcoin for two large Papa John's pizzas. Only four years later those same Bitcoin were worth 5.12 million dollars.

295.   Even Al Qaeda has gone on record as denouncing the actions of ISIS as anti-Islamic.

296.   A guy named Seth Putnam wrote a song about how being in a coma was stupid, and soon after went into a coma himself. After he awoke, when asked how it felt to be in a coma, he said, "Being in a coma was just as stupid as I wrote it was."

297.   Leonardo da Vinci's The Mona Lisa wasn't famous until it was stolen from the Louvre in 1911.

298.   A hyena's laugh, which is called giggles by zoologists, can be heard up to 42 feet (13 kilometers) away.

299.   Human bone is ridiculously strong. A cubic inch of it can bear the weight of five standard pickup trucks making it four times as strong as concrete.

300.   Barbie's full name is Barbara Millicent Roberts. Her creator, Ruth Handler, invented her back in 1959 and named her after her daughter, Barbara. Ken also has a full name too which is Ken Carson.

301.   There are giant pink slugs found only in the sub-Alpine reaches of Mount Kaputar, Australia. They can reach up to eight inches long and on a good day, you can see hundreds of them.

302.   On D-Day, at least 500 canvased dummies were dropped away from the Normandy Beaches to distract from actual drop zones. The dummies, called ruperts were just under three feet tall, came with battle sounds and were made to self destruct upon landing so that the Germans couldn't find them.

303.   Prostitution exists among some penguins and chimpanzees. It was first reported in 1998 by Fiona Hunter, a researcher at the University of Cambridge, and Lloyd Davis of the University of Otago. They were studying the mating patterns of the Adelie Penguins, when they noticed that they prostitute themselves for things like stones or food.

304.   Xiao Yun, from China, was missing for 10 years, and was presumed dead, but was then found living in an internet cafe. A runaway at the age of 14, she was good at the game Crossfire, so other gamers paid to watch her

play it and she slept at internet cafes for the rest of her life and public bath houses until she was found at the age of 24.

305.   When Don Karkos fought in World War II, he was hit with shrapnel that blinded his right eye. 64 years later, while working in a barn, a horse head-butted him in the exact same spot, threw him against a wall and restored his vision suddenly.

306.   The FBI now tracks animal abuse like it tracks homicides and assaults. They're logic is that they classify animal cruelty as a group A felony, because if you abuse animals, there's a good chance that you'd do the same to a person.

307.   According to a study of surgical residents participating in the Rosser Top Gun Laparoscopic Skills and Suturing Program, surgeons who play video games make 37% fewer errors and complete 27% faster. Video game skills are a strong indicator of surgical skills.

308.   The CIA once created a gun that could shoot darts that caused heart attacks. Upon penetration of the skin, the dart only left a tiny red dot. The poison itself worked rapidly and then denatured quickly afterwards. This was all revealed in 1975, in a congressional testimony.

309.   Wu Hsia, from China, had an ex-girlfriend and current girlfriend jump off a bridge into a river to see who he would rescue. He rescued his current girlfriend.

310.   Oysters make pearls so that they can feel better. When a grain of sand or debris gets stuck in their bodies, they ease the pain and irritation by coating it with multiple layers of nacre. It's a mineral that lines the inside of their shells, and thus, a pearl begins to form.

311.   In the 19th century, Americans purposefully filled their parks with squirrels for entertainment purposes. Before that, they were rarely found outside of forests.

312.   Hippopotamus milk is pink.

313.   Caesar salad has nothing to do with any of the Caesars. It was first concocted in a bar in Tijuana, Mexico, in the 1920's.

314.   Your fingernails grow faster when you are cold.

315.   Snails take the longest naps, some lasting as long as three years.

316.   Crocodiles and alligators are surprisingly fast on land. Although they are rapid, they are not agile. So, if being chased by one, run in a zigzag line to lose him or her.

317.   Octopuses have three hearts.

318.   Since 1978, 37 people have died by Vending Machine's falling on them. 13 people are killed annually. All this while trying to shake merchandise out of them. 113 people have been injured.

319.   Wild dolphins call each other by name.

320.   A grenade blast underwater is more deadly than on land.

321.   To escape the grip of a crocodile's jaws, push your thumbs into its eyeballs - it will let you go instantly.

322.   Mel Blanc (the voice of Bugs Bunny) was allergic to carrots.

323.   Because of the rotation of the earth, an object can be thrown farther if it is thrown west.

324.   Half the foods eaten throughout the world today were developed by farmers in the Andes Mountains (including potatoes, maize, sweet potatoes, squash, all varieties of beans, peanuts, manioc, papayas, strawberries, mulberries and many others).

325.   Right-handed people live, on average; nine years longer than left handed people.

326.   If one spells out numbers, they would have to count to One Thousand before coming across the letter "A".

327.   Ten percent of the Russian government's income comes from the sale of vodka.

328.   The expression 'to get fired' comes from long ago Clans that wanted to get rid of unwanted people, so they would burn their houses instead of killing them, creating the term 'Got fired'.

329.   It has been estimated that humans use only 10% of their brain.

330.   In the United States, a pound of potato chips costs two hundred times more than a pound of potatoes.

331.   If you go blind in one eye you only lose about one fifth of your vision but all your sense of depth.

332.   Celery has negative calories! It takes more calories to eat a piece of celery than the celery has in it.

333.   Studies have shown that children laugh an average of 300 times/day and adults 17 times/day, making the average child more optimistic, curious, and creative than the adult.

334.   The average woman consumes 6 lbs of lipstick in her lifetime.

335.   The phrase "rule of thumb" is derived from an old English law, which stated that you couldn't beat your wife with anything wider than your thumb.

336.   Each king in a deck of playing cards represents a great king from history. Spades - King David, Clubs - Alexander the Great, Hearts - Charlemagne, and Diamonds - Julius Caesar.

337.   Jupiter is bigger than all the other planets in our solar system combined.

338.   Emus and kangaroos cannot walk backwards, and are on the Australian coat of arms for that reason.

339.   There are 1 million ants for every human in the world.

340.   The three most recognized Western names in China are Jesus Christ, Richard Nixon, & Elvis Presley.

341.   The Pentagon in Arlington, Virginia, has twice as many bathrooms as is necessary, because when it was built in the 1940s, the state of Virginia still had segregation laws requiring separate toilet facilities for blacks and whites.

342.   Conception occurs most in the month of December.

343.   One third of all cancers are sun related.

344.   The average lead pencil will draw a line 35 miles long or write approximately 50,000 English words. More than 2 billion pencils are manufactured each year in the United States. If these were laid end to end they would circle the world nine times.

345.   Nearly 80% of all animals on earth have six legs.

346.   Larry Lewis ran the 100-yard dash in 17.8 seconds in 1969, thereby setting a new world's record for runners in the 100-years-or-older class. He was 101.

347.   Ninety percent of all species that have become extinct have been birds.

348.   The only nation whose name begins with an "A", but doesn't end in an "A" is Afghanistan.

349.   The Earth experiences 50,000 Earthquakes per year and is hit by Lightning 100 times a second.

350.   Hershey's Kisses are called that because the machine that makes them looks like it's kissing the conveyor belt.

351.   Statues in parks: If the horse has both front legs in the air, the person died in battle; if the horse has one front leg in the air, the person died as a result of wounds received in battle; if the horse has all four legs on the ground, the person died of natural causes.

352.   It has NEVER rained in Calama, a town in the Atacama Desert of Chile.

353.   The Main Library at Indiana University sinks over an inch every year because when it was built, engineers failed to take into account the weight of all the books that would occupy the building.

354.   400-quarter pounders can be made from 1 cow.

355.   If we had the same mortality rate now as in 1900, more than half the people in the world today would not be alive.

356.   The plastic things on the end of shoelaces are called aglets.

357.   Ants closely resemble human manners: When they wake, they stretch & appear to yawn in a human manner before taking up the tasks of the day.

358.   A raisin dropped in a glass of fresh champagne will bounce up and down continually from the bottom of the glass to the top.

359.   More Monopoly money is printed in a year, than real money throughout the world.

360.   The longest one-syllable word in the English language is "screeched.""Dreamt" is the only English word that ends in the letters "mt."

361.   All of the clocks in the movie "Pulp Fiction" are stuck on 4:20, a national pot-smokers hour.

362.   A dragonfly has a lifespan of 24 hours.

363.   The microwave was invented after a researcher walked by a radar tube and a chocolate bar melted in his pocket.

364.   All polar bears are left-handed.

365.   If you yelled for 8 years, 7 months and 6 days, you will have produced enough sound energy to heat one cup of coffee.

366.   February 1865 is the only month in recorded history not to have a full moon.

367.   The top 3 health-related searches on the Internet are (in this order): Depression, Allergies, & Cancer.

368.   Dentists have recommended that a toothbrush be kept at least 6 feet away from a toilet to avoid airborne particles resulting from the flush.

369.   A family of 26 could go to the movies in Mexico City for the price of one in Tokyo.

370.   The muzzle of a lion is like a fingerprint - no two lions have the same pattern of whiskers.

371.   The average person spends 12 weeks a year 'looking for things'.

372.   The number "four" is considered unlucky in Japan because it is pronounced the same as "death".

373.   Venus is the only planet that rotates clockwise.

374.   One in eight million people has progeria, a disease that causes people to grow faster than they age.

375.   It's estimated that at any one time around 0.7% of the world's population is drunk.

376.   During his entire life, Vincent Van Gogh sold exactly one painting, "Red Vineyard at Arles".

377.   The word "set" has more definitions than any other word in the English language.

378.   In 10 minutes, a hurricane releases more energy than all of the world's nuclear weapons combined.

379.   Switzerland is the only country with a square flag.

380.   Chocolate can kill dogs; it directly affects their heart and nervous system.

381.   There are more beetles than any other animal. In fact, one out of every four animals is a beetle.

382.   If you keep a goldfish in the dark room, it will eventually turn white.

383.   In bowling, three strikes in a row was called a turkey. The term originated in the 1800s when at holiday time, the first member of a team to score three strikes in a row won a free turkey.

384.   Giraffes have no vocal cords.

385.   The idea of Pokémon evolving is actually based on the caterpillar becoming a butterfly. Pokémon creator Satoshi Tajiri loved collecting and studying the creatures as a child and based his worldwide hit on the process.

386.   Banana trees are not actually trees – they are giant herbs.

387.   To 'hang ten' in surfing, means to have all 10 toes over the edge of the board when riding a wave.

388.   The term Quarantine is one that is as old as time, segregating the ill or the dangerous to protect the rest of the tribe but where does the phrase come from? The Italian phrase quaranta giorni is said to be the origin of the word quarantine, it means simply 40 days and refers to a time when during the plague ships arriving in Venice were required to stay out at sea for the entire 40 days before docking.

389.   1,800 cigarettes are smoked per person each year in China.

390.   Have you ever yawned and a bit of saliva shoots out of your mouth into the air? So have many apparently, you're not alone. This process is known as Gleeking and is caused by your salivary glands being randomly stimulated.

391.   In 2015 the Korean Herald revealed a study that found out that the number of fried chicken outlets in Korea stood a whopping 36,000. This figure means the country has almost the same number of these outlets as there are McDonald's branches across the world.

392.   The only country in the world to begin with a Q is Qatar, the nearest English pronunciation to the local way would be Cutter and the name comes from Qatara referring to Zubara, a town in the country. The only country ending in Q is Iraq.

393.   Fort Knox has an escape tunnel installed in the lower part of the vault. This tunnel is there in case anyone accidentally becomes trapped inside the vault.

394.   In ancient Rome, gladiators were held in the highest respect, but one of the rarer sights were female gladiators or gladiatrix, a much less common

fighter who had the same purpose as their male counterparts but have all but disappeared from history.

395.   A 16-year-old may legally vote in Serbia but only if they are an employed citizen. The voting age for those not employed stands at 18, a similar figure to most of the world.

396.   In 2015, it was discovered that the number 1 cause of death for policemen is suicide, mainly due to the stress caused by the job itself.

397.   A 120 pound woman annihilated a 72 ounce steak challenge in Portland, U.S.A. after clearing the plate in a staggering 2 minutes 44 seconds, a whole 4 minutes faster than the previous holder. That's an average of almost 0.5 ounce per second.The creator of The Sims; Will Wright, created the game after experiencing a tragic house fire in 1991 left him with a vision of a game surrounding a "virtual dollhouse" and the franchise was born.

398.   Bananas are curved because they grow towards the sun.

399.   The internet speed at NASA is capable of downloading the average film in milliseconds, as its speed is a staggering 91 GB a second.

400.   A single snowflake is known as one of the most delicate and miniscule items in the world. However, the largest measured snowflake was a whopping 15 inches wide.

Part 3

401.   Pteronophobia is the fear of being tickled by feathers.

402.   In Elizabethan England, the spoon was so novel and prized that people carried their own folding spoons to banquets.

403.   71% of office workers stopped on the street for a survey agreed to give up their computer passwords in exchange for a chocolate bar.

404.   So far, two diseases have successfully been eradicated: smallpox and rinderpest.

405.   The Olympic flag's colors are always red, black, blue, green, and yellow rings on a field of white. This is because at least one of those colors appears on the flag of every nation on the planet.

406.   There are only three types of snakes on the island of Tasmania and all three are deadly poisonous.

407.   All major league baseball umpires must wear black underwear while on the job in case their pants split.

408.   Ninety percent of New York City cabbies are recently arrived immigrants.

409.   In the 16th and 17th centuries in the country of Turkey, anyone caught drinking coffee was put to death.

410.   The city with the most Rolls Royces per capita is Hong Kong.

411.   In 18th century England, gambling dens employed someone whose job was to swallow the dice if there was a police raid.

412.   A Boeing 767 airliner is made of 3,100,000 separate parts.

413.   There is a bar in London that sells vaporized vodka, which is inhaled instead of sipped.

414.   The longest bout of hiccups lasted nearly 69 years.

415.   The largest ocean liners pay a $250,000 toll for each trip through the Panama Canal. The canal generates fully one-third of Panama's entire economy.

416.   According to Genesis 1:20-22, the chicken came before the egg.

417.   The moon is moving away from the Earth at a tiny, although measurable, rate every year. 85 million years ago it was orbiting the Earth about 35 feet from the planet's surface.

418.   Sonic the Hedgehog's full name is actually Ogilvie Maurice Hedgehog.

419.   In Egypt around 1500 B.C., a shaved head was considered the ultimate in feminine beauty. Egyptian women removed every hair from their heads with special gold tweezers and polished their scalps to a high sheen with buffing cloths.

420.   The stage before frostbite is called "frostnip".

421. There is enough fuel in full jumbo jet tank to drive an average car four times around the world.

422. A kiss stimulates 29 muscles and chemicals that cause relaxation.

423. There is a company that will (for $14,000) take your ashes and compress them into a synthetic diamond to be set in jewelry for a loved one.

424. Your heart beats over 100,000 times a day.

425. Snakes are true carnivores as they eat nothing but other animals. They do not eat any type of plant material.

426. The chicken is one of the few things that man eats before it's born and after it's dead.

427. A duel between three people is actually called a truel.

428. The Himalayan Honey Bee – the largest of the honey bees – makes a hallucinogenic honey that tribes collect.

429. The brain is our fattiest organ, being composed of nearly 60% fat.

430. The collars on men's dress shirts used to be detachable. This was to save on laundry costs as the collar was the part that needed cleaning the most frequently.

431. Sunsets on Mars are blue.

432. The Vatican City is the country that drinks the most wine per capita at 74 liters per citizen per year.

433. Eight of the ten largest statues in the world are of Buddhas.

434. A small population of Mammoths survived on the Wrangel Island until 1650 BC, about 900 years after the construction of The Great Pyramid of Giza were completed.

435. The Flintstones was the most profitable network cartoon franchise for 30 years, that's before The Simpsons came along.

436. Homosexuality was still classified as an illness in Sweden in 1979. Swedes responded by calling into work "sick," saying they "felt gay."

437. If a female ferret does not have sex for a year, she will die.

438. People don't sneeze in their sleep due to their brain shutting down the reflex.

439. If you made $1 every second, it would take you 2,921 years to have more money than Bill Gates (over $92.1 billion dollars).

440. Iguanas have three eyes. Two normal eyes and a third eye on top of their head that only perceives brightness.

441. 'Digging a hole to China' is theoretically possible if you start in Argentina.

442. Some areas in Scotland and Japan switched to blue street lights at night, and saw a decrease in crime & suicide rates.

443.   The oldest condoms ever found date back to the 1640s (they were found in a cesspit at Dudley Castle), and were made from animal and fish intestines.

444.   Female kangaroos have three vaginas.

445.   The northern leopard frog swallows its prey using its eyes — it uses them to help push food down its throat by retracting them into its head.

446.   Experiments show that male rhesus macaque monkeys will pay to look at pictures of female rhesus macaques' bottoms.

447.   There's an opera house on the U.S.–Canada border where the stage is in one country and half the audience is in another.

448.   Humans are the Only Animals That Enjoy Spicy Foods.

449.   Dogs can smell cancer. Researchers have found that dogs are able to pick up on a specific scent that cancer produces in a person—which is undetectable to humans.

450.   The average four year-old child asks over four hundred questions a day.

451.   More than 2,500 left-handed people are killed every year from using equipment meant for right-handed people.

452.   Potato Chips Cause More Weight Gain Than Any Other Food.

453.   If "The Simpsons" aged normally, Bart would now be older than Marge was in the first season.

454.   The population of Ireland is still 2 million less than it was before the potato famine, 160 years ago.

455.   The average hummingbird's heart rate is more than 1,200 beats per minute.

456.   If the human brain were a computer, it could perform 38 thousand-trillion operations per second. The world's most powerful supercomputer, BlueGene , can manage only .002% of that.

457.   You have a 1 in 200 chance of being related to Genghis Khan.

458.   Along with the five traditional senses of sound, sight, touch, smell and taste, humans have 15 "other senses." These include balance, temperature, pain and time as well as internal senses for suffocation, thirst, and fullness.

459.   There is a single mega-colony of ants that spans three continents, covering much of Europe, the west coast of the U.S., and the west coast of Japan.

460.   Airplane food isn't very tasty because our sense of smell and taste decrease by 20 to 50 percent during flights.

461.   Some of the first examples of graffiti come from 1st century Pompeii, where messages like "I don't want to sell my husband" and "Successus was here" were written on walls.

462.   Sloths will mistakenly grab their arms instead of the branches of a tree, which can lead to fatal falls.

463.   The world's longest musical piece lasts 639 years.

464.   France didn't stop executing people by guillotine until 1977.

465.   Craving ice is a symptom of iron deficiency.

466.   Though closely identified as a female fashion staple today, high heels were first designed for men.

467.   Your sense of touch fades as you age.

468.   Tuskless elephants are evolving in response to poaching.

469.   Male pufferfish create "crop circles" to attract mates.

470.   There's a city in Turkey called Batman, located in the province of Batman near the Batman River.

471.   A Shiba Inu dog named 'Body' makes $180,000 a year modeling menswear on Instagram.

472.   According to textbooks used to teach children in North Korea, Kim Jong-un learned to drive at the age of three.

473.   There are so many different types of apples, if you were to eat a new one every day it would take you almost 20 years to try them all.

474.   In India it's not uncommon to enjoy marijuana in milkshake form. In fact, there's evidence of its consumption in this manner dating all the way back to sometime between 500 and 1500 BC.

475.   The CEO of Netflix, Reed Hastings, offered a form of partnership to Blockbuster in the late '90s, and the CEO of Blockbuster, John Antioco, laughed in his face.

476.   The Toyota Supra, which Paul Walker's character Brian drives off at the end of Furious 7, actually belonged to the late actor.

477.   Apple got the idea of a desktop interface from Xerox.

478.   Scientists have found a way to unboil egg whites in a matter of minutes. The major ingredient to pull off this reversal was urea, one of the main components in urine.

479.   Dr. Seuss was confronted by a feminist named Alison Lurie, who stated that there are no strong female roles in his books. Near the end of his life, Dr. Seuss replied, stating that his characters are animals, and, "If she can identify their sex "I will remember her in my will."

480.   Central American stingless bees have been cultivated by Mayans for thousands of years, and have been regarded as pets with their hives hung in and around the home. Some hives have been recorded to last over 80 years, being passed down through the generations.

481.   Recent polling indicated that 35% of U.S. workers would willingly forego a substantial raise in exchange for seeing their direct supervisor fired.

482.	Jonathan the tortoise is a giant tortoise who lives on the island of St. Helena in the South Pacific Ocean that's believed to have been born in 1832 and is still alive to this day.

483.	If you multiply 111,111,111 by 111,111,111, it gives the magical, mathematical result of 12,345,678,987,654,321.

484.	The original release date of Halo 2 for the PC was delayed because Microsoft discovered that one of the developers hid a picture of his ass in it.

485.	The lowest class of meat is called canner and comes from very old cows with little fat in their tough meat and is used in both dog food and school lunches

486.	In 2013 Volkswagen succeeded in building a car that gets 235 miles per gallon called the XL1. Almost the entire car is made out of carbon fiber and only weighs 81 kilograms.

487.	Most of the time, the ice-cream that you see in TV commercials and other ads, is actually mashed potatoes. This is because regular ice-cream wouldn't be able to stand up to the heat of the onset lights while filming.

488.	If you are an Indian American, and you own a motel, there is a 70% chance that your last name is Patel.

489.	The reason men have nipples is because all embryos start off as females in the womb.

490.	According to researchers night owls, or people who stay up late and sleep in, tend to be more extravagant, impulsive, and novelty seeking. They also tend to be more likely to develop addictive behaviors, mental disorders, and antisocial tendencies.

491.	In Stockholm Sweden there was a temporary campaign implemented called the Speed Camera Lottery where good drivers could win money from the fines of other speeding drivers.

492.	The Salar De Uyuni in Bolivia is the world's largest salt flat at ten thousand five hundred and eighty-two square kilometers, and turns into the world's largest mirror when it rains. It's so beautiful that it's been called the border between heaven and earth.

493.	In Japan, Nestle has introduced over 200 different flavors of Kitkat since 2000, including ginger ale, soy sauce, crème brulee, green tea, and banana.

494.	Bob Marley was seen as a white man in his native Jamaica due to having a British father, and he suffered racism and discrimination while growing up.

495.	As of 2016 Madeline Scotto was a 101-year-old woman that is still teaching math at the same elementary school in Brooklyn that she graduated from back in 1928.

496.   The country of Liechtenstein has an incarceration rate of 19 per 100,000. With a population of only 37,000, this means that there are approximately seven people in prison within the nation.

497.   20-year-old Julien Barreaux from France spent six months looking for the person who killed his online character in a virtual knife fight during a game of Counter Strike. He finally found the culprit living only a few miles away, and then stabbed him in the chest.

498.   Flipping a coin isn't actually 50/50, but rather 51/49 biased for the side that was facing up when flipped.

499.   The Russians partied so hard once that the entire city of Moscow ran out of vodka.

500.   Bob Ross did the 'Joy of Painting' completely free of charge, and only made money through his art supply store.

501.   In 2015 a goat was placed in a Siberian Tiger enclosure in the Far Eastern Safari Park in Russia, and it was supposed to become the tiger's food, except that the tiger and the goat became friends.

502.   According to research done in 2014, people who are perfectionists are at an increased risk of experiencing suicidal thoughts because of the strong social pressure that they feel.

503.   Cerro Rico in Bolivia, is known as the mountain that eats men, because of the large number of men who have died there while working in the mines. In fact, historians have estimated that about 8 million men have died in the mines since the sixteenth century.

504.   The Muppet Show received a letter from a man informing them that the Swedish chef doesn't actually speak Swedish. The head writer wrote back, "Thank you for bringing this to our attention. We were going to fire the chef on the spot but he has a wife and family and promised to take "Swedish lessons."

505.   The day after Robin Williams' suicide, the National Suicide Prevention Lifeline fielded the greatest number of calls in its history.

506.   The Lego movie incorporated actual fan-made short Lego films into its plot. You can see them on the monitors in the scene where the citizens discover their creativity.

507.   Platypuses don't have stomachs.

508.   The police in west Germany located a man who had a warrant for unpaid fines. They confronted him just as a slot machine that he was at struck a jackpot and he avoided jail time by paying the fine on the spot.

509.   A school in Pune, India encourages students to conserve water by pouring leftover drinking water from the bottles in a large tank before they go

home every day. They use this to water for plants and trees or for other non-drinking purposes.

510.   Tasmania has an extra day of Easter, known as Easter Tuesday. It is not celebrated anywhere else on Earth.

511.   In 2013, Google established a company called Calico that focuses on health, well-being, and longevity. However what's weird about it isn't that its goal is to extend human life but that it's to cure death.

512.   Scotland has the most concentrated pattern of private ownership in the entire world. Only 432 people owned half of the private land there.

513.   After visiting Cambodia in 2002, Angelina Jolie bought a sprawling area of land in the northern province of Battambang which was infamous for being poached and turned it into a nature reserve. She was awarded citizenship in response to her actions in 2005.

514.   Viganella, Italy is cut off from direct sunlight for 83 days in the winter due to the surrounding mountains so they set up a giant, computer controlled mirror on the top of the mountainside to reflect the sun's rays onto the town.

515.   Slovakia and Slovenia are so often confused that the staff of Slovak and Slovenian embassies have to meet once a month to exchange wrongly addressed mail.

516.   The mortar used in the construction of the great pyramids of Giza is of unknown origin. It's been analyzed and while the chemical composition is known, it cannot be reproduced and is stronger than stone. This is why it's still holding up today and was built sometime between 2540 and 2560 BC.

517.   According to a study done in 2013 by Doctor Peter Jonassen from the University of Western Sydney School of Sciences and Psychology, people who wake up late at night are more likely to display antisocial personality traits, such as machiavellianism, narcissism and have psychopathic tendencies.

518.   The extinct Dodo bird got its name from the Dutch. They called the bird Dodoor Ursine which loosely translates to fat-asses.

519.   One of the top vasectomy doctors in Austin is named Dick Chop.

520.   Drug lord Pablo Escobar offered to pay off Columbia's $20 billion foreign debt in order to avoid extradition to the United States.

521.   When given the choice between normal water and morphine water, secluded rats always choose the drugged water, and would always die. However rats provided with space, friends, and games rarely took the drug water and never became addicted or overdosed despite many attempts made by humans to trick them.

522.   During the 18th century you could pay your admission to the zoo in the tower of London by bringing a cat or a dog to feed the lions.

523. Members of the band Good Charlotte used to heavily protest against KFC's treatment of chickens. Then in 2012 and 2013 they appeared in a number of KFC commercials in Australia, and even tried to set a new world record for eating KFC on Australia's Got Talent.

524. Abraham Lincoln once said, "Women are the only things that cannot hurt me that I am afraid of."

525. Africanized bees, known as "killer bees"are breed hybrids that accidentally escaped quarantine and since have spread throughout the Americas.

526. A stray junkyard dog named Lillico walked up to 13 kilometers every night through the streets of San Carlos, Brazil, to collect a food parcel. Upon returning home she shares the food with her family, a dog, a cat, some chickens, and a mule.

527. Your body paralyzes itself when you sleep to keep you from acting out your dreams. However, it is in fact possible to wake up still paralyzed, known as "sleep paralysis".

528. In 2013 a cat named Cookie went missing while on holiday with her owner in Grasse, Southern France. Eighteen months later, Cookie returned dirty and emaciated, having traveled a journey of 1127 kilometers all the way home.

529. At the age of only five Ayan Qureshi took and passed Microsoft's IT technician exam, making him the youngest computer specialist in the world.

530. If you earn more than $27,665 Canadian a year, you are part of the richest 4% of the planet.

531. A tomato plant was found on an isolated 40-year-old volcanic island known as Surtsey, found off the coast of Iceland. It was from a previous scientist who took a dump and subsequently a plant grew from there.

532. There's a restaurant called "Tacsiyapo Isdaan Floating Restaurant" in Tarlac City, Philippines, where you are actually allowed to smash plates on the wall to help release pent-up anger.

533. If we were able to capture just 0.1% of the ocean's kinetic energy caused by its tides, we would be able to satisfy the current global demand for energy five times over.

534. Sniper bullets travel so fast that the rotation of the Earth will actually move the target, so shooters have to adjust their aim accordingly.

535. The tires for the Bugatti Veyron cost $42,000 a set and they only last 15 minutes at top speed.

536. According to some experts it costs only $14 to produce a pair of Beats by Dre headphones. That's a huge profit for Dr. Dre considering the cheapest pair sells for $200 while the most expensive pair retails for 700.

537.   A study in 2013 shows that bottlenose dolphins have the longest memories in the animal kingdom. In fact they can remember the whistles of other dolphins that they've lived with even after 20 years of separation.

538.   A man named Paz crashed Paris Hilton's 30th birthday party and stole her $3,200 birthday cake when he realized that no one there was actually going to eat it. He ended up splitting the cake into 125 pieces and served it all to the homeless.

539.   The metallic smell of money is actually your body oils breaking down in the presence of iron or copper. You can see this by using a paper towel to pick up a penny and smelling it, no odor.

540.   Sarcasm is believed to boost creativity in all parties involved in the conversation.

541.   When cats look at you in the eye and blink slowly, they're actually trying to tell you that they're in love with you.

542.   The 'Rekonect Notebook' is a magnetic journal that allows you to remove, reattach, and rearrange the pages whenever you want.

543.   There is an island called Hans Island, which is disputed territory between Canada and Denmark. The militaries of both countries periodically visit to remove the other guy's flag and leave a bottle of Danish schnapps or Canadian whiskey.

544.   Adele isn't allowed to send out her own tweets because when Twitter first came out, she was notorious for tweeting while drunk.

545.   Inspired by the viral photo of Donald Trump sporting a man bun, DesignCrowd held a Photoshop contest to see what past and present politicians would look like if they had one.

546.   Have you ever noticed that old books have a distinct smell? Well that's because organic compounds in paper break down over time and release chemicals that smell like vanilla, almonds, and grass.

547.   The pangolin is a mammal that looks like a reptile because of its scales. Its scales are made of keratin which is the same material as human fingernails.

548.   Hans Zimmer, the music composer for over 150 movies has never had any formal music education.

549.   A teenager in Taiwan died after playing the video game Diablo 3 for 40 hours straight without eating.

550.   The phrase happy wife, happy life is actually pretty accurate. A study conducted in 2014 shows that men who are unhappily married may still be happy with their lives in general if their wives are satisfied with their marriages.

551.   Former Venezuelan President Hugo Chavez, stated that Muammar Gaddafi was welcomed in Venezuela, but stated that Charlie Sheen was not. With a quote saying: "there are limits..."

552.   There's a Detroit company called 'Extreme Kidnapping' where people pay up to $1500 to get tied up and kidnapped for fun.

553.   Back in 1993, it was discovered that Heidelberg University in Germany was using human corpses in crash tests.

554.   Hydrogen peroxide is not recommended for cuts and wounds and actually slows healing by killing the healthy skin cells.

555.   In 2010, after the BP oil spill, Stephen Colbert declared that every time he said the word "Bing", the Microsoft search engine would donate $2500 to oil spill cleanup efforts. He managed to say "bing" 40 times, thereby raising $100,000 for his charity, the Colbert Nation Gulf of America fund.

556.   Singles Day in China is the world's biggest online shopping day since unattached individuals celebrate by buying themselves gifts.

557.   When Paris fell to the Nazis in 1940, French soldiers cut the elevator cables to the Eiffel Tower. They did this so that if Hitler wanted to hoist a swastika flag, they would have to climb hundreds of stairs to get to the top.

558.   The original floats in the Macy's Thanksgiving Parade were released into the air, after the parade, because Macy's didn't know what to do with them. However, they included a ticket that would fall to the ground after they popped. If you found a ticket, you could redeem them for a prize at Macy's.

559.   California uses inmates to fight forest fires, and prisoners gladly take the jobs, because it reduces their sentence, gets them outside, and pays better than the typical job.

560.   The whiptail lizard is an all-female species. The males have gone completely extinct. Interestingly, they are not hermaphroditic. The females actually lay and hatch from unfertilized eggs.

561.   The Harry Potter series has been translated into more than 70 languages.

562.   President Barack Obama has won two Grammy Awards before he was elected. They were for best spoken word album, one for an audio recording of his 1995 memoir Dreams from My Father, and the second was for The Audacity of Hope.

563.   The Golden Gate Bridge uses the largest bridge cables ever made. They were so long that they could actually encircle the world more than three times at the equator.

564.   The world's largest coin was issued by the Royal Canadian Mint back in 2007. It was 20 inches in diameter and one inch thick. It was made of

99.999% gold bullion, weighs 220 pounds and is worth an estimated $1 million.

565.   In 1967, St. Paul, Alberta, Canada, built the world's first UFO landing pad. The 130-ton structure consists of a raised platform with a map of Canada embossed on the backstop consisting of stones provided by each province in Canada. The pad also has a time capsule to be opened on the 100 year anniversary of the pad's opening in 2067.

566.   There are wildlife overpasses, green bridges and ecoducts that exist that were built over roads to allow wildlife to cross safely to the other side. They are up to 197 feet wide. The larger ones are to accommodate large mammals such as bears, wolves and moose and deer. They're covered in soil and vegetation to provide a suitable habitat for a wide range of groups of animals.

567.   In Japan, if you're in someone's home and you need to use the bathroom, you need to change out of your house slippers and into toilet slippers. Not only that but then you need to remove the toilet slippers before exiting the washroom.

568.   There's a nightclub in Devon, U.K., who gave out free lollipops to reduce late-night rowdiness in hopes that drunken clubbers wouldn't be able to shout or cause disturbance while sucking on them, and it worked.

569.   Einstein actually had an illegitimate daughter that was born in 1902.

570.   In the 1990s, Saddam Hussein had the Quran transcribed by an Islamic calligrapher in his own blood. He had over seven gallons of blood drawn over a two-year period.

571.   The voice of Chewbacca from Star Wars was created by using bear vocalizations, as well as the sound of walruses, badgers, and the howls of sick animals.

572.   The opossum is the only marsupial in North America.

573.   Walmart employs 2.3 million people around the world.

574.   Boston has poems on their sidewalks that can only be seen when it rains. They are painted with special waterproof paint that only appears when wet.

575.   At the 2008 Olympics in Beijing, white mice were fed 24 hours before the athletes were fed to protect the athletes from food poisoning. If there was a problem, the food could be traced and destroyed before being fed to the athletes.

576.   A 19-foot-long (1.5 meter) Australian alligator has a bite force of 3,700 pounds (1700 kg). That's the highest bite force ever recorded.

577.   On January 12th, 2011, 49 out of the 50 states of America had snow on the ground. That's almost 71% of the country. The only state without snow was Florida.

578.   Theodore Roosevelt's mother and first wife both died on Valentine's Day of 1884. His mother died of typhoid fever, and 12 hours later his wife died from Bright's disease and complications from giving birth to the couple's first child two days before.

579.   Actor Steven Seagull received a PETA humanitarian award in 1999 for preventing the export of baby elephants from South Africa to Japan.

580.   The Island of Discussion in Scotland is where, historically, those with arguments were put on the island with cheese and whiskey to sort out their problems and couldn't leave until they came to a mutual agreement.

581.   Breakups are actually more painful for men. In a study of around 5,705 participants from 96 countries, it was found that while women experience intense pain immediately after a breakup, they get over it pretty quickly, men on the other hand, move on quickly but remain damaged for longer.

582.   There is a limestone wall in Bolivia that is home to over 5,000 dinosaur footprints, some of them dating back nearly 68 million years.

583.   Crows have actually been shown to be as smart as great apes. They are able to show imagination, anticipation of possible future events, and are able to solve problems which require abstract reasoning.

584.   There is a Chinese Segway rip-off company called NineBot, which used the money that it got from selling rip-off Segways to buy the original Segway Company.

585.   There exists a giant American wasp with a sting so painful one peer-reviewed journal advises anyone who gets stung to lie down and scream to avoid further injury.

586.   In the 1970s, people in Cambodia were killed for being academics or for merely wearing sunglasses.

587.   April 11th, 1954 is known as the most boring day in history. Literally not a single memorable thing happened that day on the entire earth. No one significant died, no major events occurred, and the only interesting thing that actually happened on that day is that nothing happened on that day.

588.   In the Meiji era in japan there was a custom called Autoguru where people dyed their teeth black. It prevented tooth decay and during the time was actually seen as beautiful.

589.   Napoleon Bonaparte wore his black, felted, beaver fur hat sideways instead of with the points at the front and back so that he could be easily spotted on the battlefield.

590.   In China, there's a delicacy called Virgin Boy Eggs. These eggs are actually soaked in the urine of boys under the age of 10 and they collect the urine from school washrooms. It's believed that eating this can have health benefits. You can buy one for about 24 cents.

591.   In South Korea, you could have a plastic surgery called smile lipped, where they raise both corners of your mouth and give you a permanent smile.

592.   In China, you can buy baby Buddha shaped pears. The farmers clamp a mold onto a growing fruit to get the shape. In addition to baby pears, a company called Fruit Mold manufacturers heart-shaped cucumbers, square watermelons and other more deliciously odd shapes.

593.   At the Austrian Brewer's Starkenberger's castle, you can actually swim in beer. They have seven 13-foot pools filled with 42,000 pints of warm beer and some water where you can sit and relax completely immersed. The beer's rich in vitamins and calcium and it's thought that sitting in it is good for the skin and can help cure open wounds and psoriasis.

594.   It can actually be considered rude to tip in Japan. If you do decide to tip something, the proper etiquette is to place the money in a tasteful, decorative envelope, seal it, and then hand it to the recipient with a slight bow.

595.   The Philippines is the only country in the world that denies divorce to the majority of its citizens. They can file for legal separation, which will allow them to separate their possessions and live apart, but does not legally end the marital union and thus, does not permit remarriage.

596.   German sneaker company Nat-2 has created the first vegan wooden sneaker. They're made of up to 90% real sustainable wood, which is applied to an organic cotton and vector engraved in a way that the material bends and becomes soft and flexible like fine leather.

597.   Tigers are nicer than lions. Lions fight to the death over a kill, but tigers that come across other tigers while hunting often share their meals. Male tigers even wait for females and their cubs to eat first.

598.   According to psychologist Adrian Furnham, perfectionism can be a curse that often leads to depression. The reason for this is because perfectionists often have an unrealistic view about failure and are overly critical of themselves, which results in having a very negative impact on their daily lives.

599.   Research conducted at the University of Warsaw concluded that the average person is able to accurately track three to four moving objects at any one time. However, an avid action gamer can track six to seven.

600.   Scientology isn't legally considered a religion at all in many countries. In fact, Switzerland identifies it as a commercial enterprise, France and Chile as a cult, and Norway as a nonprofit.

Part 4

601.   During the Iranian embassy siege in London, England back in 1980, when given the choice of who from the group of hostages would be released, they chose Ali Guil Ghanzafar, whose loud snoring was keeping them awake.

602.   The Megamouth shark, first discovered back in 1976, is a species of shark that is so rare that only 60 of them have ever been captured or identified on record.

603.   For eight consecutive years, a Greyhound dog named Jasmine, who survived in a shelter, was the surrogate mother to over 50 rescued animals, including puppies, foxes, four badger cubs, 15 chicks, eight guinea pigs, 15 rabbits, a deer, and a goose!

604.   In a study conducted by data scientist Matt Daniels, all members of the Wu-Tang Clan are all in the top 20 of artists with the largest vocabulary in the world.

605.   Eiffel Tower designer, Gustave Eiffel included a secret apartment for himself near the top, where he would entertain elite members of the science community.

606.   Research from the University College of London concluded that teenagers are scientifically less empathetic than adults. Due to the continual development in their brains, teenagers are less likely to use the neural area that is associated with guilt and empathy when they make decisions.

607.   Leonidas of Sparta was not a young man at the Battle of Thermopylae, like depicted in the film 300. In reality, he was actually more like 60-years-old.

608.   Al Capone was known for sending flowers to rival gang members' funerals. In fact, at one time, he actually spent over $5,000 on a single funeral.

609.   The average fast food customer eats about 12 pubic hairs a year.

610.   The word "best" in best man historically refers to his skill with a sword. This is because he may have been needed it if the bride tried to run away, or if her family tried to stop the wedding.

611.   Jellyfish are 98% water, so when they wash up on the shore, they will eventually simply evaporate into the sun.

612.   In 2015, Oscar Santillan, an artist from Ecuador, removed one inch off the peak of England's highest mountain, Scafell Pike. In response, the British demanded that that inch be returned to them, and accused him of vandalism.

613.   After an 8.0 magnitude earthquake that hit Mexico City in 1985, a hospital collapsed, yet four newborn babies survived for seven days trapped under the rubble. They have become known as the miracle babies for surviving without nourishment, water, or human contact for so long.

614.   The CEO of Japan Airlines, Todu Yamanaka makes less than the pilots, takes a bus to work, and eats in the cafeteria. When interviewed about his, he said that businesses who pursue money first, fail.

615.   Chuck Palahniuk, author of the Fight Club, preferred the film adaptation so much that it actually made him embarrassed of his own book.

616.   The mathematical proof that one plus one equals two actually takes 162 pages to explain. It was documented in a three-volume work called "Principia Mathematica", which details the foundations of mathematics.

617.   In an attempt to get fit and lose weight, 54-year-old Cong Yan from Jilin, China walked daily with an 88-pound rock balanced on his head.

618.   Seven Cent Brewery located in Australia has created a beer using the yeast isolated from the belly button lint of it's brewers.

619.   London England has a clothing optional restaurant called Bunyadi. It costs up to $95 a person for food and drinks and you can choose between clothed and naked and pure seating areas where you will be served by semi-nude staff.

620.   The Dutch apparel company, Cover, has created jackets and bags that feature technology that blocks every in and outgoing signal making the wearer completely untraceable by modern tracking devices, such as computer chips embedded in credit cards and can even take you off the cell phone grid.

621.   Product and graphic designer, Ricky Ma, constructed a life-sized robot that looks exactly like Scarlett Johansson. It took him a year and a half and cost him $50,000.

622.   Mount Everest actually shrank one inch in 2015, due to the earthquake in Nepal.

623.   Ring announcer Michael Buffer has made over 400 million dollars by licensing the use of the trademark catchphrase, "Let's get ready to..."

624.   FANUC, a Japanese robotics company, has a factory that can run unsupervised for 30 days at a time. Robots build other robots at a rate of 50 per 24 hour shift. These factories are called lights-out factories, because no human presence is needed.

625.   The Van Cats of Eastern Turkey, which are a naturally occurring breed, all have white fur, mismatched eyes, and love to swim.

626.   In 2009, a man named Alexei Roskov from Russia, drank three bottles of vodka, and then jumped out of a five story window, walked back up, and jumped out again, because of his nagging wife, and he survived.

627.   Drew Manning is a personal trainer, who in 2011, wanted to prove that it was possible to get back in shape, even if you become extremely overweight. He gained 32 kilograms, or 70 pounds of fat, over a six month period, before he started the tough journey back to regaining his prior form.

628.   You can see underwater sea life and coral reefs using Google Maps.

629.   Adnan and Sana Klaric, a married couple from Zenica, Bosnia, started cheating on each other in online chat rooms. When they finally decided to meet up with the person that they were each cheating with, they quickly realized that they had been cheating on each other, and soon after, filed for divorce.

630.   The Pronghorn Antelope has 10-times the vision of humans, which has left scientists to believe that on a clear night, they can actually see the rings of Saturn.

631.   Russian Special Forces use a knife that fires a bullet out of the bottom of the hilt. The safe way to fire it involves holding the blade to absorb the recoil.

632.   A terminally ill six-year-old boy named Levi Mayhew was offered a gift from the Make-A-Wish Foundation. Instead of using it for himself, he wished for a trip to Disneyland for the little girl writing him letters out of encouragement, and she went to Florida, carrying a cutout photo of him on all the rides that she could.

633.   Serial killer Rodney Alcala acted as his own attorney in his trial in 2010. For five hours, he interrogated himself on the witness stand, asking questions addressed to Mr. Alcala in a deep voice and answering them in his normal voice.

634.   There is an entire industry to help students cheat to get their degrees, by having their papers written by unemployed graduates and professors and it's actually kind of brilliant, because students can't get caught for plagiarism, because the papers are brand new.

635.   Scorpion venom is the most expensive liquid on Earth, at 39-million dollars per gallon.

636.   Usain Bolt ate nothing but chicken nuggets while he was in Beijing for the 2008 Summer Olympics, because he found Chinese food to be odd.

637.   When Teddy Roosevelt was a child he had debilitating asthma, except that doctors didn't understand the disease at the time and told him to smoke cigars, drink coffee, and whisky.

638.   Domestic animals are a lot smarter than you might realize. In fact some pets will actually pretend to be sick just to get special attention from their owners.

639.   In Finland there's an annual contest called Eukonkanto where men race to carry their wives through an obstacle course. The winner receives his wife's weight in beer.

640.   Sloths can swim three times faster than they can move on land and can hold their breath underwater for up to 40 minutes.

641.   1.5 million people were evicted from their homes in Beijing in preparation for the 2008 Olympics.

642.   At El Diablo restaurant in the Canary Islands, food is served with the geothermal heat from an actual volcano.

643.   A photo of nine-year-old Daniel Cabrera from the Philippines doing his homework in the street, assisted by the light of a local McDonald's resulted in the world donating money, school supplies and a college scholarship to both him and his family.

644.   When Benjamin Franklin died in 1790, he willed the cities of Boston and Philadelphia $4,400 each but with the stipulation that the money could not be spent for 200 years. By 1990, Boston's trust was worth over $5 million.

645.   In ancient Egypt, men could take time off work to care for menstruating daughters and wives.

646.   New Zealand will deny people residency visas if they have too high of a BMI, and there have been cases of people rejected simply because of their weight.

647.   Stephen Hawking has said outside of our own universe, lies another, different universe, and in this universe, Zayn is still in One Direction.

648.   On July 23, 1983, Air Canada Flight 143 with 69 people on board ran out of fuel at an altitude of 12.5 kilometers. Miraculously, the pilot managed to glide the plane down safely, as he was a very experienced glider pilot. Additionally, 2,300 pounds of jet fuel had been put in instead of 2,300 kilograms.

649.   The city of Lexington, Kentucky is letting residents pay parking tickets with canned food donations during the holiday season.

650.   Hong Kong billionaire Cecil Chao is offering 120 million dollars to turn his lesbian daughter straight.

651.   Don't ever place a cucumber behind your cat. It's stressful for the cat to find a new object in its territory and could leave it anxious for days.

652.   Sir Ian McKellen actually broke down and cried while filming the Hobbit, because he had to film with just a green screen instead of with the other actors. In fact, he was quoted as saying, "This is not why I became an actor."

653.   In 2015, Daniella Perez, a woman in a wheelchair who had no feet, won a treadmill and a walk-in sauna on the Price is Right.

654.   In 1955, cigarettes were sold in vending machines that only accepted quarters, but a pack of cigarettes only used to cost 23 cents. Instead of raising the price, cigarette manufacturers actually included two pennies within each package.

655.   In the town of Laguna, Brazil, a pod of Bottlenose Dolphins have been cooperatively fishing with fishermen since 1846. The dolphin herd mullet fish towards the shore and signal the fishermen to cast their nets.

656.   In 2014, a man spent over $40,000 buying out two IMAX theaters in Beijing because his ex-girlfriend seven years prior had dumped him for not being able to afford movie tickets.

657.   During World War I, Allied soldiers would fire thousands of rounds at random over the German trenches to boil the coolant water in their machine guns so that they could make tea.

658.   There's a hotel atop the Foronon del Buinz mountain in the Julian Alps that accommodates only nine people. Guests can stay there for free as long as they're willing to make the 8030 feet (2530 meter) hike to get there.

659.   In 1965, a 16-year-old high school student Randy Gardner stayed awake for 11 days and 24 minutes. That's 265 hours straight. He holds the record for a human intentionally staying awake without the use of stimulants.

660.   To honor Jamaican sprinter Usain Bolt, Berlin gave him his own 12-foot-high (3.66 meters) piece of the Berlin Wall. It weighed nearly three tons.

661.   The richest man in Hong Kong, billionaire Li Ka-shing, dropped out of school before he turned 16. He has an estimated net worth of $20.1 billion.

662.   LSD or acid was legal in California up until 1966.

663.   In 1980, Detroit gave Saddam Hussein the key to the city.

664.   The olm salamander has a maximum lifespan of over 100 years.

665.   South Africa's Witwatersrand Basin which is only 2.7 square miles (3 square kilometers), has produced more gold than any other continent; about 50,000 tons over 120 years, which is nearly half the gold ever mined.

666.   There's a pub in Athlone, Ireland, called Sean's Bar that has been open since 900 AD.

667.   The seawater in Boston Harbor in Massachusetts Bay has been found to contain caffeine. Although tiny, the traces are there. 140 to 1,600 nanograms in the Boston Harbor and 5.2 to 71 nanograms in Massachusetts Bay.

668.   Samuel J. Seymour was the last surviving witness of Abraham Lincoln's assassination. He lived long enough that he was able to talk about his experience on a TV show in 1956.

669.   Potatoes absorb and reflect radio wave signals the same way that human bodies do. So in the past engineers have actually used them to test and improve Wifi signals on planes.

670.   An ornithologist named George Archibald managed to save the whooping crane species from becoming extinct, by spending 37 years acting

as a mate to a female whooping crane who thought she was human. He finally got her to mate with a real bird and the rest is history.

671.　William Shakespeare has added over 2200 words to the English language. Some of those words are, newfangled, bedazzled, and swagger.

672.　The Dead Sea has an unusually high salt concentration with about eight to nine times more salt than natural seawater. This means that people can easily float in the Dead Sea because of its natural buoyancy.

673.　There's an artist named Mariusz Kedzierski, who was born without arms, but never gave up on his dreams and has won global awards for his photo realistic portrait drawings.

674.　Stress literally kills your brain. Studies have found that months of exposure to stress can permanently destroy neurons in your brain, which affects learning, impulse control, reasoning, and memory.

675.　A hungry sea lion pup once walked into a fancy San Diego restaurant, and sat down at a prime table with an ocean view.

676.　During World War I, Woodrow Wilson kept a flock of 48 sheep on the White House lawn to save money on groundskeepers. The sheep also earned 52,823 dollars for the Red Cross through the auction of their wool.

677.　In 1928, the founder of the Kodak Company was so frustrated by the different numbers of days in each month that he insisted that the company operate on a 13 month year. Each month had exactly four weeks, and they did this all the way up to 1989.

678.　10 squats will get you a free subway ticket in Mexico City. The government offers this to residents in hopes of fighting obesity in the country where 70% of adults are actually overweight.

679.　There's a village in Kerala, India called Kodinhi, with just 2,000 families and has around 200 pairs of twins and no one knows why this high occurrence of multiple births happens.

680.　According to a survey, 51% of people believe that sharing a Netflix password with a significant other means the relationship is serious.

681.　Thanks to 3D printing, it is now possible for blind expectant mothers to have a three-dimensional ultrasound printed for them to sense the image of their unborn child.

682.　Banks have therapists known as wealth psychologists who help super-rich clients who are mentally unable to cope with their immense wealth.

683.　Blair McMillan from Guelph, Ontario, Canada, was concerned that his family was becoming too attached to technology, so they spent the entirety of the year 2013 living like it was 1986, with a rotary phone, boom box and tube television.

684.   Research conducted by NASA in 1995 concluded that the perfect nap lasts for about 26 minutes.

685.   Tesla Motors doesn't spend any money on advertising. Instead, they put all of their money into making their cars as good as possible.

686.   Sleeping throughout the night only became common within the last 200 years. Before then, people had a first and second sleep, often working, reading or even making love for an hour or so between sleeps.

687.   A wealthy man named Howard Lutnick donated more than $65 million to Haverford College because, when he was going there years ago, he lost both of his parents to cancer; however, the college let him go tuition-free for all four years, and that was his way of paying them back.

688.   Alexander the First, the king of Yugoslavia, refused to attend public events on Tuesdays after three of his family members died on that day of the week. However, after finally being forced to make an appearance on a Tuesday in October of 1934, he was assassinated.

689.   Theophilus Van Kannel invented the revolving doors in 1881. He did so because he hated chivalry, especially the idea of opening doors for women.

690.   The petals of a sunflower are actually each single-petalled flowers. The sunflower itself is actually a cluster of hundreds of flowers.

691.   Colonel Sanders got fired from dozens of jobs including being a lawyer, and found himself broke at the age of 65. That's when he decided to start KFC.

692.   Liam Neeson actually used to be a schoolteacher and did it for two years but got fired for punching a 15-year-old boy in the face when the student pulled a knife out in class.

693.   Research gathered at Vienna University concluded that the older a father is when he has a child, the less attractive the child will be.

694.   The quickest red card ever given out in soccer history was just three seconds into the match, when player Lee Todd, who played for Chippenham in the U.K., exclaimed, "Eff me, that was loud," after the starting whistle was blown.

695.   Back in 2005, there were 71 potential witnesses to a murder in a Belfast bar who all claimed to be in the toilet during the attack. The four-by-three toilets became nicknamed, "The TARDIS."

696.   A nine-year-old orphaned child from Rwanda named Justus Uwayesu lived in a garbage dump until American Red Cross workers helped him. Today, he's 23 and is attending Harvard on a full scholarship.

697.   A 10-year psychology study undertaken in Germany since the 1980s found that men who kiss their wives before leaving for work lived, on average, five years longer, earned 20-30% more and got into fewer car accidents.

698.   There's a Romanian woman who knitted a vest made out of her own hair. She gathered all of the hair that fell out when she combed it from the age of 40 to 60 and eventually had enough hair to produce the article, totalling 2.2 pounds (one kilogram).

699.   You can buy toothpaste infused with caffeine that gives you a boost in the morning. Unlike coffee, Power Energy Toothpaste takes effect almost immediately, making you more alert before you're even finished brushing.

700.   The oldest inhabited house in Scotland is Traquair Castle. Located less than 30 miles from Edinburgh, it has been lived in for over 900 years and was originally a hunting lodge for the kings and queens of Scotland.

701.   There's a mobile game that was released in 2014 titled "Run Forrest Run" that was inspired by the Paramount Pictures 1994 classic, "Forrest Gump," where you literally run through his entire life story.

702.   Carrie Fisher wore no underwear in Star Wars because George Lucas convinced her that there were no underwear in outer space.

703.   Hopscotch, written by Julio Cortazar, published in 1966, is a 154-chapter-long book that makes sense no matter what chapter you choose to read first or last.

704.   In 2015, President Barack Obama personally thanked Japan for karate, karaoke, manga, anime and, of course, emojis.

705.   Coffee beans aren't actually beans, they're fruit pits.

706.   In 2012, the entire village of Sodeto in Spain won the lottery, except for one man who was never offered a ticket, as those that were selling them forgot to ask him.

707.   In 1914, British World War I soldier Thomas Hughes tossed a beer bottle with a letter to his wife into the English Channel, which was discovered in 1999 by a fisherman, who then delivered it to Hughes' 86-year-old daughter.

708.   In 2013, a 10-year-old boy named Griffin Sanders from Colorado saved his great-grandmother's life in a speeding vehicle after she fell unconscious. He did this by driving it himself, which he learned by playing Mario Kart.

709.   Since the beginning of recorded history, the world has only been at peace for a total of 268 years. That's only 8% of the time.

710.   Giraffes only sleep for 30 minutes a day and need the least sleep out of all mammals.

711.   Soviet Union leader Joseph Stalin's son, Yakov, was captured while fighting the Nazis in 1941, but Yakov died in captivity because Stalin refused to trade a marshal for a lieutenant.

712.   The Mexican drug cartels made a combined estimate of $29 billion in 2010. That's about the same earnings as Google.

713.	After the release of Rocky IV, a joke was making its way around Hollywood that, since Rocky had run out of opponents, that he would have to fight an alien in the fifth installment. However, shockingly, screenwriters Jim and John Thomas took the joke seriously and wrote a screenplay based on that joke, which ultimately became the plot for the movie Predator.

714.	There are actually some women in the world with four color receptor cells in their eyes, which can allow them to see 100 million colors. To put that into perspective for you, a typical human only has three color receptors and can only see about one million colors.

715.	Elephants are one of the only animals who can suffer from post-traumatic stress disorder.

716.	Between the 1940s and 1970s, Harvard, Yale, and other Ivy League schools actually took nude photos of each freshman student in an attempt to link physical attributes to intelligence. Notable names include George Bush, Diane Sawyer, Meryl Streep and Hillary Clinton.

717.	Researchers have found that for a century female students have consistently earned higher grades than male students. And although fewer women choose to pursue science, technology, engineering and math careers, they excel in these subjects.

718.	One penny doubled every day becomes over five million dollars in just thirty days.

719.	It takes seventeen muscles to smile and forty-three to frown.

720.	In some species of turtles, the temperature determines if the egg will develop into a male or female. Lower temperatures lead to a male, while high temperatures lead to a female.

721.	The eyes of a horse can actually move independently. So, it has panoramic vision.

722.	Icelanders consume more Coca-Cola per capita than any other nation.

723.	The Atlas moth defends itself by imitating a snake's appearance and behavior. Along with convincing wing patterns, the moth will fall to the ground when threatened, and flop around to look like a writhing snake.

724.	Andrew Jackson's political opponents referred to him as a 'jackass'. So, he adopted the name and used it as his campaign symbol. It would eventually become the symbol of the entire democratic party in America.

725.	Japan now has retirement homes for senior dogs so they can get the adequate love and care that they need for their final years.

726.	The term, 'swansong', comes from an ancient belief that a swan is silent for its entire life until it sings one beautiful song just before dying.

727.	You can actually fix your vision while you sleep. Orthokeratology lenses reshape your corneas overnight so you don't need to wear corrective lenses while you're awake. When you remove them in the morning, you can see just as clearly as you would with prescription lenses.

728. Watermelon contains high levels of vitamin B6, so eating it can actually help relieve stress and anxiety.

729. It is dangerous to feed moose. Moose that are fed by humans become aggressive If the next human doesn't feed them, and may actually end up attacking them.

730. North Korea doesn't have a law against marijuana. In fact people can smoke pot openly in the country and not be criminalized.

731. There's an animal called the Kashmir musk deer or vampire deer that were spotted for the first time in over 60 years in Afghanistan. These creatures are extremely rare because poachers sell their scent glands for more money than gold.

732. People have actually begun putting QR codes on their loved ones gravestones. Scanning them will lead you to online tributes to the dead where you can read their obituaries.

733. The time machine in "Back to the Future" was originally going to be a refrigerator, but was changed when the creators thought kids would trap themselves in fridges while trying to replicate the scene.

734. China is currently constructing the world's longest and highest glass-bottom bridge and it will be over 1400 feet (430 meters) long.

735. Most dalmatian puppies are born with solid white coats. The spots are invisible until the puppies are about 10 days old.

736. Bulls are actually colorblind. The matador's cape could be any color. It's the motion that attracts the bull's attention to charge, not the color red.

737. Catfish have approximately 100,000 taste buds all over their bodies, most of them on their whiskers.

738. Cranberries are called bounce berries by some people because they actually bounce when they're ripe.

739. Europe is the only continent without at least one desert region. In order to qualify as a desert, an area must get less than 10 inches of rain per year.

740. If you have an irrational fear of Friday the 13th, you have what's called Friggatriskaidekaphobia.

741. According to National Geographic, an elephant's trunk has 150,000 muscle units.

742. Gloucestershire Airport in England used to blast Tina Turner music to scare off birds and it worked better than blasting bird distress calls.

743. The modern Ouija Board got its name in 1890 by asking the board what it should be called. It's spelled out Ouija, and when asked what it meant, the board said, "Good luck."

744. In 2010, an Ikea located in Wembley, England unleashed 100 cats into a store just to see what would happen.

745. Renowned film actress from the 1930's and 50's Hedy Lamarr, was also a mathematician. She was also the inventor of the frequency hopping spread spectrum, a technology still used today for Bluetooth and WiFi.

746. In 2012, a stray cat became a seeing eye-guide for a blind dog named Terfel who uses its paws to gently lead him around the house.

747. Sandy Island located between Australia and New Caledonia was chartered on maps for over a century until a crew of scientists sailed to the location in 2012 and found that it didn't actually exist.

748. If all the world's population, approximately 7.4 billion people, piled into the Grand Canyon, they wouldn't even come close to filling it up.

749. A man once faked a mental illness to get out of prison because he thought living in an asylum would be better. However, once he got to the asylum he tried to get out but the doctors actually diagnosed him as a sociopath because faking a mental illness to get out of prison is exactly the type of manipulative behavior you'd expect from a sociopath.

750. The Sapra Salpa is a fish that can cause hallucinations if its head is eaten. It used to be consumed as a recreational drug during the Roman empire.

751. A man in New York named Robert Samuels is a professional line sitter who makes up to $1,000 a week just by standing in line for people.

752. Action gamers are better learners. They excel at predicting the sequence of upcoming events and become better learners by playing fast-paced games.

753. A single share of Coca-Cola stock that was purchased in 1919 for $40, would be worth $9.8 million today.

754. Robert Emmet Odlum, the first person to jump off of the Brooklyn Bridge, was a professional high-diver who wanted to demonstrate that people did not die by simply falling through the air and he proved himself correct by falling 41 meters safely through the air only to die when he hit the water.

755. South Carolina high school student Alex Stone was arrested, suspended, and had his locker searched because of a creative writing assignment where he mentioned buying a gun to shoot his neighbor's pet dinosaur.

756.   There's a genetic disease called Laron Syndrome that results in short stature, long life expectancy and near immunity to cancer and diabetes, among other things.

757.   In 1942, a British forest guard in India made an alarming discovery when he found at 16,000 feet (4,877 meters) above sea level, at the bottom of a small valley in a frozen lake, hundreds of unknown skeletons.

758.   During Roman times, salt was worth its weight in gold, and soldiers were sometimes paid in salt, hence the word salary.

759.   It is impossible for quick sand to suck you under because you simply aren't dense enough to sink in it. However, it liquefies the more you disturb it, as long as you don't panic, you'll only sink about half your body length.

760.   There is a Korean eatery in Zhengzhou City, China, known as Zhengzhou Island, where people are allowed to dine at no charge if they happen to be among the five most beautiful patrons of the day.

761.   A study from 1978 followed up on 515 people who were prevented from attempting suicide using the Golden Gate Bridge between 1937 and 1971. Ninety percent were either alive, or died of natural causes, with the study concluding that suicidal behaviors are crises oriented, rather than inexorable.

762.   In 2008, it took Apple a year to sell 10 million iPhones. In its first week of sales in 2015, the iPhone 6 sold 13 million units.

763.   By law, no U.S. officer's ever allowed to out-rank George Washington, and he was posthumously promoted to history's only six star general in 1976.

764.   'Panda nanny' is a real job position, where you get to spend 365 days a year with panda babies for an annual salary of 32 thousand dollars.

765.   The platypus has no nipples and milk simply oozes from their skin.

766.   When a coal mine catches fire it can burn for decades or even centuries. There are thousands of these fires across the world.

767.   Believe it or not, socks are among the most needed items at homeless shelters, yet among the least often donated.

768.   A dog named Greyfriars Bobby in Scotland sat by his owner's grave for 14 years until he eventually passed away.

769.   An anonymous sent thousands of all black faxes to the Church of Scientology to deplete all of their ink cartridges.

770.   All new employees and recently promoted executives at the Japanese company, Dentsu, have to climb Mount Fuji. This has happened every July since 1925.

771.   The horse head used in The Godfather was a real horse head, not a prop. John Marley was not informed beforehand, so his scream was authentic, not scripted.

772.   Momentary Ink, prints your tattoo designs as customary, temporary tattoos, that last 3-10 days so that you can try out your ideas before you commit to one.

773.   Glass is 100% recyclable and it can be recycled endlessly without loss in quality or purity.

774.   You can have brain surgery and not feel any pain because the brain itself does not have any pain receptors.

775.   Silbury Hill near Avebury in Wiltshire, England, is the largest prehistoric man-made mound in Europe. It stands 130 feet (40 metres) high, and its purpose is still unknown.

776.   The diameter of the planet Uranus is 31,763 miles (9400 metres) across. That's four times bigger than earth.

777.   The Vatican has its own soccer team. Vatican City is the smallest independent state in the world, and therefore has its own national soccer team or, as they call it in Europe, football team.

778.   From 2012 to 2015 how to kiss was the most popular how to search on YouTube. That was followed by how to tie a tie, how to draw and how to get a six pack in three minutes.

779.   There are parts of the Atacama Desert in Chile that have not seen a drop of water since record keeping began.

780.   The Milky Way has between 100 and 400 billion stars, but we can only see about 2,500 of them at any one point from the globe since our solar system resides roughly 27,000 light years away from the galactic center.

781.   Historians believe that William Shakespeare was born and died on the same date. He was born on April 23, 1564 and he died on April 23, 1616.

782.   In 2001 and 2002, Argentina had five presidents in two weeks. the string of presidents started when Fernando de la Rua resigned in December of 2001. The last of the five was appointed in January of 2002 amid major protesting.

783.   Googling 'do a barrel roll' makes your whole browser flip over.

784.   Amish men are actually clean shaven prior to getting married but are required to grow their beards after marriage. This and all aspects of Amish life are dictated by a list of written and oral rules known as Ordnung, which outlines the basics of the Amish faith and helps to define what it means to be Amish.

785.   In 2015, a man who skipped out on his bill at a Houston area restaurant was seen running into a vacant building across the street. The police officers who arrived jokingly called out "Marco" to which the suspect accidentally replied, "Polo." He was immediately arrested.

786.   Believe it or not it's possible to donate your voice. There's an organization called vocal ID that encourages people to donate their voices so that they can recreate synthetic voices that are just as unique as fingerprints to suit individuals who have speech impairments.

787.   Only three humans have ever died outside of the Earth's atmosphere. They were all on the Soyuz 11 the only manned mission to board the world's first space station which ended in disaster when the crew capsule depressurized.

788.   Edward Jones or Boy Jones was known in the Victorian era for getting caught breaking into Buckingham Palace when he was 14 years old and stealing Queen Victoria's underwear.

789.   Billboards have been banned in Vermont since 1968 in order to preserve the natural beauty of the state.

790.   The Goliath tigerfish is the largest of the tigerfish clan and can be found in the Congo River Basin. In fact it's so big it's been known to eat small crocodiles and has even attacked humans on several instances.

791.   A recent study found that a 45 to 60 minute nap during the day could improve learning and memory by as much as five fold. Researchers say that a short nap at the office or in school is enough to improve learning success.

792.   The Chinese government takes its officials and members of their families on prison tours to give them an introduction to what awaits them if they should engage in corruption.

793.   In 1972, the king of Morocco, Hassan the Second, grabbed the radio during an assassination attempt and told the rebel pilots who were firing at him inside his Boeing 727 to stop firing the tyrant is dead, which made the assassins break off from their attempt.

794.   When you kiss someone for the first time, you get a spike in the neurotransmitter Dopamine making you crave more. Endorphins are also released bringing on waves of euphoria.

795.   Sadie Renee Johnson from Oregon started a wildfire in 2013 in order to give her bored firefighter friends some work, except that it spread to 206 square kilometers and cost nearly eight million dollars and two months to bring under control.

796.   In 2015, a stray cat in Russia known as Masha kept a two-month-old abandoned baby boy warm in freezing temperatures overnight.

797.   Jerusalem is one of the oldest cities in the world. It has been destroyed twice, besieged 23 times, captured, and then re-captured 44 times, and attacked a total of 52 times.

798.   In 1915, a millionaire named, Cecil Chubb bought his wife the Stonehenge for approximately 10,000 dollars. Except that, she didn't like it, so in 1918 he gave it to Britain and today it's valued at around 51 million dollars.

799.   In the traditional aboriginal Canadian version of lacrosse, teams consisted of 100 to 1,000 men and fields were 500 meters to three kilometers long. Games could last up to three days straight.

800.   Research conducted by the University of Exeter concluded that every individual shark has its own distinct character and personality. Some sharks are shy, while others are more social.

801.   Billionaire Elon Musk didn't like the school that his kids were attending, so he conceptualized and built his own named Ad Astra, which means 'to the stars'.

802.   The SR 71 Blackbird was the world's fastest air breeding man-made aircraft and out ran nearly 4,000 missiles fired at it during its service.

803.   When syphilis first surfaced, most countries named it after one another. The English called it the French disease. The French called it the Spanish disease, and the Japanese called it the Chinese Pox.

804.   In the late 1800's, archaeologists found a ring inside a ninth-century Viking grave in Sweden inscribed with the phrase, "For Allah". This linked trade between Swedish Vikings and the Islamic world all the way back to 1,000 years ago.

805.   According to the Centers For Disease Control And Prevention, on average people who smoke die 10 years earlier than non-smokers. And every person who dies because of smoking, at least 30% of people live with a serious smoking related illness.

806.   Jell-O is made from gelatin that is produced by boiling the bones, skin, and hides of animals such as cows and pigs. People have been eating it since 1897, and it accounts for about 80% of the gelatin market.

807.   Abraham Lincoln was in the National Wrestling Hall of Fame. He had an awesome physical size at six foot four, was widely known for his wrestling skills, and had only one reported defeat in a dozen years.

808.   Echidnas have a four-headed penis. Also known as spiny anteaters; they don't even use their penis to urinate and it only leaves the body during an erection.

809.   The Golden Silk Orb Weave spider's web is so strong that it can capture a bird, of which the spider then eats.

810.   Marigolds and other plants that contain the pigment Xanthophyll are added to chicken feed to make their egg yolks appear more orange.

811.   In Peru, fried or roasted guinea pig is considered a delicacy. Known as cuy, it's been a staple in Peru's diet for around 5,000 years.

812.   The Aztec people often used cocoa beans as currency.

813.   Argyria is a condition which turns a person's skin a bright blue color. It's caused by chronic exposure to silver.

814.   In 1998, construction worker Travis Bogumill was accidentally shot with a nail gun that drove a 3.25-inch nail into his skull. The nail lodged in the area of the brain that typically involves processing math. He was completely

fine after the nail was removed, except his math skills weren't what they used to be.

815.   In the year 1900, inventor Ludwig Ederer invented an alarm mechanism that was built into your bed. When you set the alarm to a specific time, the bed rose to a 45-degree angle and tipped you out of bed.

816.   Murder rates were so high during the 1970's and 1980's in Miami, Florida, that the Dade County Medical Examiner's office actually had to rent a refrigerated trailer from Burger King to handle the overflow of corpses.

817.   After the Fukushima nuclear disaster in 2011, more than 200 Japanese pensioners all over volunteered to tackle the nuclear crisis.

818.   Research conducted by psychologists at Bernell University determined that those who use Facebook to brag about diets and exercise, and accomplishments, are typically narcissists.

819.   There exists a special shaped knife for cleaning out Nutella jars entirely.

820.   Sir Richard Branson once lost a bet with AirAsia's CEO, Tony Fernandes, on the winner of the 2010 Grand Prix in Abu Dhabi. He had to work as a female flight attendant on Tony's airline.

821.   When your eyes move, your brain purposely blocks your vision, which is why you can't see the motion of your own eyes in a mirror. This is called 'saccadic masking' and without it, your life would be like watching a constant movie that's filled with a shaky hand-held camera.

822.   When Steven Spielberg first applied to USC Cinematic Art School, he was rejected three times by the admissions officer. When Steven was awarded his honorary doctorate from that school, he agreed to accept it, only if it was personally signed by that same admissions officer, and it was.

823.   A man named Chito, rescued a dying crocodile, who named it Pocho, but it recovered and refused to leave the man's side, and they are inseparable to this day.

824.   In ancient Egypt, little people were seen as people with celestial gifts, and they were treated like Gods and given the highest social positions.

825.   Michael Nicholson, a man from Michigan, has one bachelor's degree, two associates' degrees, and 22 master's degrees, 3 specialist's degrees, and one doctoral degree, making him the most credentialed person in history.

826.   Cheetah cubs have long, tall hairs that run from their neck, all the way down to the base of their tail, called mantle. It makes a cheetah cub look like a honey badger and makes them blend into the tall grass keeping them from threats, like lions and hyenas.

827.   Native American people intentionally bent trees to mark trails, and many remain today as hidden monuments.

828.   A millionaire Chinese businessman named Xiong Shuihua, decided to bulldoze entire rundown huts in his village where he grew up and decided to build luxury flats, then gave the keys to the residents instead, for free.

829.   Happier cows really do produce more milk, and simply calling cows by individual names ups production by 3.5 percent.

830.   The skull that Russians kept as evidence of Hitler's death is actually the skull of a woman.

831.   Caterpillars completely turn to liquid in a cocoon, but as a moth/butterfly can still remember their life as a caterpillar.

832.   The steamboat Arabia, which sank in 1856, was excavated in 1988 under almost 14 meters of dirt in a field at a farm. Interestingly many artifacts were recovered and preserved so well that some of the food was actually still edible.

833.   Diana Kim, a photographer from Hawaii, who after 10 years documenting the homeless, found her own father among them.

834.   Wildlife photographer Alan McFadyen spent 42 hundred hours and took 720 thousand photos, over a six-year period before he finally got the perfect shot of a Kingfisher diving into water without making a splash.

835.   Owning a hamster, gerbil, or ferret is illegal in Hawaii. You're also not allowed to own an alligator, a piranha, or a toucan either.

836.   In 2013, Ben and Jerry's received the Compassion in World Farming's Good Dairy award for their high quality treatment of their cows, which includes making sure that they get regular massages. They also pay their employees double minimum wage.

837.   There's an area in France covering 39 square miles known as Zone Rouge. It's so polluted with unexploded chemical munitions, human and animal remains from both World Wars, humans are prohibited by law from entering that area.

838.   There's a ghost town in Tianducheng, China that was built in 2007 that looks just like Paris. It includes a 354 foot replica of the Eiffel Tower. They also have replica Italian, German, and English towns, but they too are ghost towns.

839.   In 2006, a group of researchers in Iceland found a really old clam. In order to find out its age, instead of counting the rings on the outside of the clam, they opened it and counted the rings on the inside, ultimately killing the clam. The clam itself ended up being 507 years old, one of the world's oldest animals.

840.   In 2014 Japanese designer Akiro Mizuchi created edible chocolate Legos that were actually functional.

841.   The pound key on your keyboard, or 'hashtag' as you know it, is called an octotroph.

842.	Budokan or Otakon was known as the Mayan god of wind and storms. His name means one-legged in the Mayan language, and the word hurricane was derived from his name.

843.	There is a twitter account called big _ben_clock and it tweets bong bong bong-bong-bong every hour. It's been doing this since 2009.

844.	Sandwiches taste better when someone else makes them. A psychologist named Daniel Kahneman explains that this is because when we make our own sandwiches, we anticipate their taste and therefore pre consume them and therefore are less hungry afterwards.

845.	Interestingly blood has similar properties to eggs in cooking and can actually be used as a viable substitute in baking.

846.	In 2015, a passenger on British Airways took a poop that smelled so bad that pilots actually decided to turn the plane around.

847.	The reflex that causes people to sneeze when looking at the sun is called the "photic sneeze reflex". It's also known as Autosomal Dominant Compelling Helio-ophthalmic Outburst Syndrome, which abbreviates to ADCHOO.

848.	A pine tree planted in 2004 in Los Angeles Park in memory of former Beatle, George Harrison, died after being infested by beetles.

849.	Studies have shown that when a woman frequently texts her partner in a relationship, they are both happier with each other. However, when a man sends the majority of texts, both partners feel less happy and a woman often considers ending the relationship.

850.	A German officer once asked Picasso, "Did you do this?" when he saw a photo of the painting Guernica, a painting about the effect of German bombardment on the Spanish town of Guernica, to which, Picasso simply responded, "No, you did."

851.	There is an Asian elephant named Koshik that can imitate human speech by sticking it's trunk in its mouth. He can actually say, 'Hello', 'good', 'no', 'sit down', and 'lie down' in Korean.

852.	We actually have the ability to eat an entire bag of chips without really noticing, because chips have a vanishing caloric density. What that means is that it tricks our tongue and brain into thinking that we haven't actually eaten anything.

853.	Famed artist Bob Ross painted a grayscale landscape in 1984 after meeting a colorblind man who believed that he would never be able to paint to show him that he can.

854.	The eye color of owls typically indicates what time of day the owls prefer to be active and hunt. Their eyes can be yellow, orange, dark brown, or even black.

855.   Ancient Babylonians took beer brewing extremely seriously. Anyone found brewing bad beer was punished in one of two ways; death by drowning in that barrel of beer or by drinking their crappy beer until they died.

856.   Tokyo has its own superhero. His name is Mangetsu Man, a self-made hero who's taken up the responsibility of keeping the city clean. He wears a full moon head, purple bodysuit, oversized Ugg boots, with matching gloves, and uses a voice dictation app to hide his voice.

857.   Researchers from the University of Michigan have found a way to allow people to have vision at night. In 2014, they developed a graphene contact lens that allows users to change the kind of light that they see.

858.   A company in Singapore made a pair of soft drinks called Anything and Whatever. The two lines of drinks had six flavors each but both had generic packaging designs so there was no way to tell what flavor was in each can.

859.   Kamala Devi, a 56 year old Indian woman, was ambushed by a leopard and actually managed to kill it with the only thing that she had on her, an iron sickle.

860.   For the film, 'Gone Girl', David Fincher wanted Ben Affleck to wear a Yankees cap for a scene. Affleck, a diehard Red Sox fan, adamantly refused, and this led to a four-day production halt until the two came to an agreement that he would wear a Mets cap.

861.   In the 1800s, researchers found one of the first ever iron maidens in a castle in Nuremberg, Germany. An iron maiden is a device of torture where the person is put inside a sarcophagus with spikes on the inner surface. When the doors were closed, the spikes would puncture several organs, including their eyes, but not deep enough to kill them, just deep enough that they would bleed to death over several hours.

862.   Yahoo was originally called Jerry's Guide to the World Wide Web after one of its creators, Jerry Yang.

863.   In 1881, dentist Alfred Southwick got the idea for the electric chair after witnessing a freak accident when an intoxicated man died after he accidentally touched a live generator terminal.

864.   The barreleye fish has a completely transparent head. It inhabits depths of around 2,000 feet (600 meters) to 2,600 feet (800 meters) where the darkness approaches absolute black.

865.   Some insects smell with their genitalia. There's a genetic disease called fish odor syndrome where a person excretes an excess of chemicals called TMA in the urine, sweat, and breath that causes them to smell like rotting fish.

866.   The average person has two million sweat glands.

867.   The parliament of Iceland is the oldest still-acting parliament in the world. It was founded back in 930 A.D. Political gatherings typically lasted for two weeks in June, which was a period of uninterrupted daylight and nice weather.

868.   The Maya found slightly crossed eyes beautiful. Parents of babies would actually hang objects like stones right between their baby's eyes to try to get them to go cross-eyed.

869.   Lyme disease got its name because it was first recognized back in 1975 when researchers found that a large number of children in Lyme, Connecticut were being diagnosed with juvenile rheumatoid arthritis.

870.   A group of porcupines is called a prickle.

871.   D-day was originally set for June fifth, but had to be postponed for 24 hours due to bad weather.

872.   The green ink used in American money was actually invented at McGill University in Montreal, Canada in 1857 by Thomas Dairy Hunt.

873.   A team of archaeologists found what they believe to be the world's oldest board game in a 5,000-year-old bronze age burial site in Turkey. They believe that board games originated in Egypt in the Fertile Crescent.

874.   The Tumbler for the Dark Knight trilogy is actually a working vehicle, not a CGI model.

875.   The most expensive guitar pick costs, $4,674 and is made out of a meteor. It's made by the company, Star Picks.

876.   There's a UK based company named 'Gumdrop' that recycles gum into bins that are made out of entirely recycled gum.

877.   There is a territory in Costa Rica called Territorio De Zaguates, which means land of the strays, which is basically a huge no-kill dog shelter where you can hike for free with dogs.

878.   On November 7th, 1907, a Mexican railroad worker called Jesus Garcia single-handedly saved the population of a nearby town called Nacozari Sonora by driving a train loaded with dynamite away. The train exploded six kilometers away from the town and killed the brave man in the process.

879.   To burn off 200 calories, you could chew gum for 18 hours, apply lip balm 1500 times, or sing a song 23 times.

880.   Planes used to be a lot more comfortable. In the 1940s, the Boeing 377 Stratocruiser had reclined club chairs throughout the cabin. On intercontinental flights, every seat could adjust into a bed so that each passenger could sleep.

881.   Raccoons are actually very smart. They can open complex locks in under 10 tries and can still repeat the process if the locks are rearranged or

turned upside down. They'll also remember solutions to problems for up to three years.

882.   Former two time heavyweight champion, George Foreman, is now the pastor of North Houston's Church of the Lord Jesus Christ. The 68 year old reverend was inspired to join the church as he himself grew up in poverty and wanted to help others after a successful career.

883.   In January of 1966, the U.S. accidentally bombed Spain. An Air Force bomber carrying four nuclear weapons collided with its refueling tanker over the Spanish town of Palomares, sending the bombs screaming towards earth.

884.   ESPN, the sports television channel is actually owned by Disney with a majority ownership of 80% but that's not all. Disney also owns Pixar, Lucasfilm, Marvel, ABC Broadcasting Company and A&E, as well as the History Channel.

885.   In 2015, Japan lifted its 67 year old ban on dancing that it put in place after World War II. They forbade dancing in venues without a special dance license. The law was originally put into place after the second World War in an effort to crack down on dance halls that were often a hot spot for prostitution.

886.   If you feel strongly that someone is watching you, that's because they probably are. Your brain has a primal gaze detection system that determines whether someone is staring directly at you or not.

887.   Clinical studies done at Stanford University show that people who have auditory hallucinations, such as schizophrenia, have voices that are shaped by cultural influences. In Africa and India, most describe them as voices of family members or spirits, but most Americans say that they hear violent, torturous, and hateful yelling from strangers.

888.   There are actually 3D printers that can print your dinner. The Foodini Food Printer makes everything from pizza to burgers to chocolate using fresh ingredients.

889.   A free kitchen, operated by volunteers in India at the Golden Temple in the Western Indian City of Amritsar serves 100,000 hot meals a day and has been doing so for over 300 years.

890.   The average claw machine is only programmed to give the claw full strength every 20 tries.

891.   Basma Hameed, a Canadian woman originally from Iraq, learned how to tattoo so that she could cover her burn scars that she received on her face as a child. The results were remarkable and she now has a business helping other burn victims by tattooing discolored scars to match their own skin tone.

892.   There exists an American company known as "Creative Home Engineering" that specializes in making hidden rooms for your home. There's

even one that requires a chess board played in a certain combination in order to unlock the room.

893.   The United Kingdom and Portugal hold the longest standing alliance in the world which started 1386 years ago.

894.   Born in the 1930s, identical twins Oskar Stohr and Jack Yufe were separated shortly after birth. Oskar was raised in Germany and attended Hitler Youth Academy while Jack practiced Judaism in Trinidad. They finally met at the age of 21 and they didn't get along at first, but eventually became close brothers later in their 50s.

895.   When a cat brings back a dead animal, it's actually acting out its natural role as a mother and teaching, showing its owners how to catch and eat prey, just like they would teach their young in the wild.

896.   Your blood actually appears green underwater at about nine meters or so because there is no red light under water, therefore, there is no red light that can bounce off of your blood into our eyes.

897.   In 2012, following the death of 'Meow', a cat who weighed 18 kilograms, the Guinness Book of World Records stopped recording the heaviest pets in the world to discourage deliberate overeating.

898.   You can differentiate between East from West Berlin from space because the different types of street lamps used to give off different shades of light.

899.   Jerome Rodale, a longevity expert and father of organic farming announced at the age of 71, during an interview that he's decided to live to be 100. He also declared, "I've never felt better in my life." and minutes later, while filming, he died of a heart attack.

900.   There is a boiling lake located in Dominica that is so hot, the centers temperature has never been determined.

901.   The Grasshopper mouse is carnivorous, immune to venom, eats scorpions, and howls like a wolf to claim its territory.

902.   The Spanish Paralympic basketball team was forced to return the gold medals that they won in the 2000 Australian Paralympics after almost all players were found to be not disabled.

903.   Some non-venomous snakes, like the Tiger Keelback, will actually protect their babies by eating poisonous frogs while being pregnant. They then pass the poison onto their eggs which makes their newborns poisonous when they're born.

904.   On December 31st, 1946, a man named Alphonse Rocco claimed to be a detective and gave a pedestrian a camera and asked her to take a picture of a suspect. The detective turned out to be a gangster and the

suspect turned out to be his ex-wife and the camera turned out to be a concealed shotgun, firing via the shutter button.

905.   In Bridgeport, in the UK, there is a cat named the Artful Dodger who regularly catches the bus by himself to travel 10 miles to the neighboring town. He waits at the bus stop so often that the driver brings tins of cat food and knows what stop to let the cat off at.

906.   Dr. Seuss' first book was rejected 27 times. He was almost ready to give up but bumped into a friend on the street in New York City back in 1937 who had just begun working in publishing. Seuss said that if he had been walking on the other side of the street, he probably would have never been a children's author.

907.   Scaphism was a form of ancient punishment where the victim was tied and force fed a rich diet of honey and milk and then left in the sun. He accumulated diarrhea while his excretion attracted flies and insects who would then eventually eat the man inside out.

908.   In September of 1940, two planes collided over Brocklesby, Australia, and interlocked the engines of the plane on top which stopped working. The ones on the plane underneath continued to work however and the pilot of that plane landed both planes safely and all four crewmen survived.

909.   Kim jong-nam is Kim Jong un's older brother and was supposed to be Kim Jong Il's successor. However he fell out of the line of succession when he tried to fake a passport so that he could get into Disneyland in Japan.

910.   Japanese engineer Kuniako Saito invented a new, tiny, personal transportation system, the "WalkCar", similar to an electric skateboard, but small enough to fit right in your backpack.

911.   The world record for the largest number ever counted belongs to Jeremy Harper. He streamlined the entire process online and raised money for charity. He reached one million. It took him three months.

912.   The first guest to enter Disneyland was college student Dave MacPherson. He didn't ride a single attraction because he had to get back to school. He was awarded a lifelong ticket to Disneyland, with up to three guests, and the ticket has since been extended to include Disney parks around the world.

913.   Norwegian student Kristoffer Koch spent 27 dollars on bitcoins, forgot about them, and then years later realized they were worth 886 thousand dollars.

914.   Inmates at a Bolivia prison live as a society. They have jobs, buy or rent their accommodation and often live with their families.

915.   There's a fish called the black dragon fish that looks like the creature from the Alien movies.

916.   In 1994, a 34-kilogram bag of cocaine fell out of a plane and landed in the middle of a Florida crime watch meeting.

917.   A Chinese millionaire began selling cans of fresh air for 80 cents a can in response to China's worsening air pollution and made over $6 million.

918.   It is in fact possible to find DNA traces from cigarette butts. An artist named Heather Dewey Hagboard used cigarette butts and old chewing gum that she found thrown away on the streets to create 3d portraits of people whose DNA was found on those objects.

919.   Naturally purple eyes exist and this is due to a disorder called Alexandria's Genesis which causes pale skin and purple eyes.

920.   Despite being much smaller in size, the Wolverine can successfully attack much larger animals including caribous and elk.

921.   Residents of the village of Shitterton in England, grew so tired of people stealing a sign with the village name on it, that they replaced it with a 1.5-ton block of stone with the village name inscribed upon it.

922.   There are pink bananas that exist called Musa velutina, and they peel themselves when ripe. They're often grown as an ornamental, but have soft sweet flesh and can be eaten. The seeds however are quite hard and can chip a tooth.

923.   According to research our voices change when we find people attractive. These vocal modulations tend to be subtle and the speaker usually isn't conscious of the change.

924.   The world record for the most passengers carried on a commercial aircraft was set on May 24th, 1991 when over 1000 Ethiopian Jews were evacuated to Israel. The flight started with 1086 people in the plane but ended with 1088 people because two of them had babies on route to Israel.

925.   The African grey parrot, N'kisi, has a whopping 950 word vocabulary that even impressed the famous primatologist, Jane Goodall. N'kisi has seen photos of her, and when they met asked "got a chimp?"

926.   In 2002, an unnamed Croatian diver got lost in an underwater cave, and stabbed himself in the chest to avoid the agony of drowning. It was the first documented case of someone committing suicide while diving.

927.   In medieval Germany, married couples could legally settle their disputes by fighting a marital duel. To even the field, the men had to fight from inside a hole with one arm tied behind his back. The woman was free to move and armed with a sack full of rocks.

928.   The Soviet tenor, Victor Ivanovich Nikitin, was so good that when he sang to Soviet troops at the east from World War II, German troops on the other side stopped shooting just to listen.

929.	In 2001, a lion cub, bear cub, and tiger cub were found neglected in a drug dealer's basement, but they have lived together ever since they were adopted by a sanctuary, and are considered inseparable because of the strong friendship that they have.

930.	There's a guitar shaped forest in Argentina. The 7,000 trees were planted by a farmer named Pedro Martin Ureta. He planted them in 1979 as a tribute to his late wife. He's never been able to see it himself from above, because he's terrified of flying.

931.	A third grade girl was expelled for a year because her grandmother sent her a birthday cake to school along with a knife to cut it. The teacher used the knife to cut the cake, and then reported the girl to the authorities for having a dangerous weapon.

932.	A man in Saudi Arabia installed a community fridge outside of his home and his neighbor's to donate any extra food that they have, so that those in need could get something to eat without having to beg for it.

933.	Self-discipline better predicts success than IQ.

934.	According to research done by scientists, in order to lose 63 pounds for his role in The Machinist, Christian Bale's daily diet consisted of one can of tuna fish and/or one apple per day, black coffee, and water.

935.	The scientific name for brain freeze is actually sphenopalatine ganglioneuralgia. Brain freezes happen because the cold dilates arteries which causes a sudden rush of blood to the brain, which causes pressure and causes pain.

936.	Rabbits actually have the ability to sleep with their eyes open. They go into a trance-like state, which is half sleep. The benefit of this is in the wild, it allows them to get away from predators in a hurry.

937.	According to Lita Proctor, the Program Coordinator of the National Institute of Health's Human Microbiome Project, we have enough bacteria in our bodies to fill a large soup can. That's up to five pounds of bacteria.

938.	The colossal squid has the largest eyes ever studied in the animal kingdom, measuring almost 11 inches, which is roughly the same size as a volleyball. In fact, researchers believe that they may be the largest eyes that ever existed.

939.	Some sharks can live up to 100 years old. Although most of them live 20 to 30 years in the wild, while some species such as the spiny dogfish live well beyond 100 years.

940.	Cats actually sweat through their paws. Cats do have sweat glands, but their skin is covered in fur, so the amount of cooling that the sweat can provide them is minimal. The paw pads have the most sweat glands, so they sweat there mostly.

941.   Researchers in the UK have created a robotic rectum for proctologists to practice their physical rectal exams. It allows medical professions to learn without the use of real life volunteers.

942.   The tree that owns itself is a white oak tree in Athens, Georgia, that is widely assumed to be legally owned by itself, and eight feet of land surrounding it. According to newspapers, a deed written by Colonel William Jackson, was written to the tree, giving ownership of the land to itself in the 1800's.

943.   A man named Nigel Richards from Malaysia, memorized the French dictionary to win the French Scrabble championship, and he doesn't even speak French.

944.   One of the top-five things that people regret when they're dying is working too hard and missing out on family time.

945.   A 20-year-old anonymous British man from Birmingham dresses up as Spiderman in the night to help homeless people by buying them food from the supermarket.

946.   Potoos are a type of bird that uses body posture to camouflage themselves to look like the part of a tree stump.

947.   Baby elephants will suck on their trunks for comfort just like human babies suck on their thumbs.

948.   Designer Alexander McQueen's former apprentice, Emma Sandham-King, made the world's first Harris tweed suit designed for a horse to celebrate the 2016 Cheltenham Festival. It took four weeks and more than 18 meters of tweed to complete the three-piece suit, which was worn by a racehorse named Morestead.

949.   There was a newborn baby that was abandoned in a forest in Kenya for two days back in 2005, that was rescued by a stray dog who carried the baby all the way back to her own litter of puppies.

950.   There is a subspecies of butterfly known as the "8998 butterfly". It's named this way for its markings, which uncannily resemble the number 89 on one wing, and the number 98 on the other.

951.   In 1896, the world's first speeding ticket was given to a Britain man that was going four times the speeding limit. Walter Arnold, who was going eight miles per hour in a two mile per hour zone was caught by a policeman on a bicycle, and was fined one shilling, which was about eight U.S. cents.

952.   Shark teeth are coated with fluoride which acts like toothpaste and keeps the shark's mouth healthy and clean.

953.   To punish tree thieves who cut down trees illegally, some cities spray trees with fox urine around Christmas time. It freezes on them and is odorless

outdoors, but would stink up your whole house if you brought it indoors. The smell is apparently eye-watering.

954.   Some restaurants in China actually lace their food with opiates to keep customers coming back.

955.   The Hanover Country School Board in Virginia tried to ban 'To Kill A Mockingbird' in 1966. When she heard about this, author Harper Lee sent a letter to the school board asking if they were literate and offered some money to enroll them in first grade.

956.   In 2012 a man named Robert Biggs was attacked by a mountain lion while he was out hiking. Unbelievably a bear saved his life by attacking the lion and driving it away.

957.   In 2014 Margaret Loughry won the northern Ireland lottery jackpot which consisted of 46 million dollars. She donated 44 million of it to her own hometown to help transform it into a tourist destination.

958.   Video games can be good for children with autism because it helps them practice skills like self-awareness flexibility and self-control.

959.   Honey bees have five eyes, two compound eyes that help them see around themselves, simultaneously, and three simple eyes that are positioned on the top of their heads that help with its orientation.

960.   After winning the 2014 FIFA World Cup, German footballer Midget Ozel, donated his 300,000 euro victory bonus to help support 23 Brazilian kids' surgery operations.

961.   At the center of every single raindrop is a mineral dust particle, as it is physically impossible for raindrops to form from pure water alone.

962.   There is a small village in Holland known as "Dementia Village", inhabited by those people with dementia. It's designed to be a normal environment with a secured perimeter so that patients can safely roam to the grocery store, restaurants, cafes, and gardens.

963.   A Stanford study concluded that there is a high correlation between walking and creative thought output. Compared to sitting, those who walked demonstrated a 60% increase in creative thought output.

964.   Snapchat founder Evan Spiegel's net worth was $1.5 billion at the age of only 24 making him one of the world's youngest billionaires.

965.   Kowloon Walled City in China existed from 1810 to 1993. In its later years, it was controlled by triads with thousands of residents who were involved in drugs, gambling, and prostitution before the city was demolished.

966.   Rajendra Singh, known as the water man of India, revived five rivers and brought water back to 1000 villages in India using native water preservation techniques.

967.   The pyramids of Giza were more ancient to the ancient Romans than Rome is ancient to us.

968.   Gobekli Tepe, located in Turkey, is thought to be the world's oldest temple. Constructed 6000 years before Stonehenge, it's estimated to have been built before the invention of the wheel, even the idea of farming, or the tools that could have constructed its own existence. Basically, it shouldn't have existed itself.

969.   When Apple began designating employee numbers, Steve Jobs was offended that Steve Wozniak received number one while he only got number two. He believed that he should be second to no one, so he took number zero instead.

970.   In 2015, Apple recovered 2, 200 pounds (1 tonne) of gold from recycled iPhones, iPads, and Macs. That's worth over $40 million. Gold is frequently used in consumer electronics because it's highly averse to corrosion and an excellent conductor of electricity. While silver is actually the best conductor, it corrodes more easily.

971.   In ancient Olympics, women were not allowed to compete, and married women weren't even allowed to be in the stands to watch. Only young women and virgins were permitted. Fathers brought their daughters in hopes that they would marry one of the champions.

972.   Brazilian police on Marajo Island ride water buffalo when they patrol instead of horses.

973.   All Starbucks coffee shops in Saudi Arabia have a gender wall. It separates single men from women and families.

974.   Most Bolivian families have a dried llama fetus under the foundation of their houses for luck. They're most commonly found at Bolivia's witches' market where you can also find toad talismans, owl feathers, and stone amulets.

975.   Austrian inventor Valentin Vodev has invented a scooter slash stroller hybrid. With the click of a button, the stroller transforms into a scooter and can travel as fast as 10 miles (16 km) per hour.

976.   The coconut crab grows over three feet long and is not only the largest land crab but is also the largest arthropod, the group that includes insects, spiders, and crustaceans.

977.   Most meteors are actually the size of a grain of sand and disintegrate in the air. The larger ones that actually reach the Earth are called meteorites and are very rare.

978.   Believe it or not, green bell peppers are just less mature, less ripe versions of red, orange, and yellow peppers.

979.	Back in 2007, a priest was arrested for stalking late night talk show host Conan O'Brien. He was writing threatening notes on parish letterhead, contacting his parents, and showing up at his studio.

980.	The stop sign originated in Detroit, Michigan, back in 1915 and was originally black lettering on a white background. Then it was black lettering on a yellow background before it was finally red and white.

981.	Hippopotomonstrosesquippedaliophobia means the morbid fear of long words.

982.	Jupiter is the fourth-brightest object in our solar system. Only the sun, moon, and Venus are brighter. It is one of the five planets that you can see from Earth with the naked eye.

983.	Most predators have eyes facing forward, while most prey have eyes on their sides of their head.

984.	Every single restaurant that has appeared on season two of Kitchen Nightmares has closed.

985.	In 2013, a man threatening to jump from the South Carolina Ravenel Bridge was convinced not to jump after being offered a pizza.

986.	Studies conducted at Indiana University Media School discovered that watching cat videos actually boosts viewer's energy and positive emotions and decreases negative feelings.

987.	Smart people underestimate themselves while ignorant people think they're brilliant. It's a cognitive bias called the Dunning-Kruger Effect. It's where the highly-skilled assume that things that they find easy are also easy for others and that the unskilled are so incompetent that they can't recognize their own stupidity.

988.	In 2000, cigarette giant Phillip Morris introduced fire-safe cigarettes which actually posed a greater risk of starting fires when left unattended.

989.	Prairie dogs have a complex means of communication. It's so advanced that not only do they have different calls depending on the type of predator, but they also make sentences that describe the predator.

990.	The concept of rap-battle has existed since the 5th century, where poets would engage in "flighting", which was a spoken word event where poets would actually insult one another in verse.

991.	There are red bananas that taste sweet, creamy, and a little bit like raspberries.

992.	Singapore is the only country in the history of the modern world to gain independence against its own will.

993.	Cold showers are actually healthier than hot ones. Among other benefits they improve immunity and circulation, ease stress and relieve depression.

994.   Tashiro Jima is an island in Japan that's also known as Cat Island. The stray cat population there is larger than the human population.

995.   Scientists at Junagadh University in India have extracted gold from the urine of rare indigenous breeds of cattle. They analyzed 400 Gir cows and found traces of ionized gold salts that they were able to isolate, precipitate, extract, solidify and melt between three to 10 milligrams of gold per liter of urine.

996.   Skunks are actually immune to snake venom.

997.   The first occurrence of identical bird twins ever was discovered in the emu.

998.   Bears are the only mammals that don't pee or poo during the winter hibernation months, and doctors have actually studied how the bears recycle their urine to help human patients with kidney failure.

999.   Both Demi Lovato and Selena Gomez were on the TV show Barney and Friends when they were kids. In fact, the long-time friends were constantly shown together dancing and singing on screen.

1000.   There is a knife and fork hybrid that exists called a nork.

Part 6

1001.   The air quality in Beijing got so bad in December of 2015 that schools were closed, car travel was restricted, and barbecuing was banned.

1002.   Japanese death row inmates aren't told the date of their execution, therefore they wake up every single day wondering if today may be their last.

1003.   The Sacramento Public Library started a Library of Things earlier in 2016 which allowed patrons to check out, among other things, sewing machines and other items that patrons may find useful but may not need to own long term.

1004.   When the world's top soccer player Cristiano Ronaldo was asked to donate his cleats for a charity auction benefiting 10 month old Erik Ortiz Cruz who had a brain disorder that could cause 30 seizures a day he instead paid the whole $83,000 for his surgery himself.

1005.   Bicultural people may change their personality when they switch languages. According to a study conducted by university professors across America, language unconsciously affects people's interpretation of events. Women speaking Spanish were seen as more independent and assertive than women speaking English in similar situations.

1006.   Black Panthers are not a real species. What they are, are jaguars and leopards who have 'Melanism', which causes them to have black skin. It's actually the opposite effect of having albinism.

1007.   Conservationists in South Africa are infusing a special red dye into the horns of live rhinos. The mixture renders the horn completely useless to poachers that are trying to sell it commercially and also has a toxin for human consumption.

1008.   President Andrew Jackson's pet parrot was kicked out of Jackson's funeral in 1945 for cursing.

1009.   In 30 seconds, you will on average, produce 72 million red blood cells, shed 174,000 skin cells and have 25 thoughts.

1010.   In 2014, a stray dog named Arthur followed a Swedish racing team through the Amazonian jungle and rivers to complete a 688-kilometer race just because one of them had given it a meatball during one of the earlier halts.

1011.   Although natural gas only became commonly used in the 1800s, the Han Dynasty of China drilled for natural gas, transported it in pipelines and gas containers and burned it on stoves as far back as 200 BC.

1012.   There are so many castles in France that some are up for sale cheaper than two-bedroom apartments in big cities like New York City and Sydney.

1013.   Bearded vultures wear makeup. They like to alter their appearance by rubbing their necks and heads in iron-rich soil to change their white feathers to a bright reddish-orange. The older and more socially dominant birds wear the most makeup to show off and appear more intimidating.

1014.   A lot of old movie theaters used to have something called cry rooms where you could literally take your children if they were becoming disruptive. This way you could still enjoy the movie while not disturbing the other movie goers.

1015.   There's a spray that makes everything smell like a cat's head. Cat owners have been known to compare their cat's head to the smell of sunshine or freshly baked bread. A company in Japan spent four months sniffing cats to bottle the scent.

1016.   It would take you 10 years to view all of the photos that were shared on Snapchat in the last hour alone.

1017.   A group called the Manike Club in Japan created zoo jeans to raise money for the World Wildlife Fund and the local Kamine zoo in Hitoshi city. Lions, tigers, and bears designed the genes by tearing into them and creating distressed jeans. The jeans are then auctioned off for charity.

1018.   There's a competition called the World's Biggest Liar held annually in England. Competitors from around the world are given five minutes to tell the biggest and most convincing lie they can think of. Believe it or not politicians and lawyers are banned from entering the competition because they're thought to be too good at lying.

1019.   The Burj Al Arab in Dubai is the only seven star hotel in the entire world. However the hotel's management never uses this term to describe itself. The notion was brought about by a British journalist who described the Burj Al Arab as "above and beyond anything she had ever seen" and called it a seven star hotel.

1020.   Roger Frisch, a concert violinist was awake when he had brain surgery to get rid of his tremors. His surgeons got a private concert during the surgery as Frisch played the violin while the doctors worked on his brain.

1021.   A 17 year old refugee named Aslan Al Hakim refused to leave his puppy Rose in Syria during the refugee crisis, and carried her more than 300 miles to safety.

1022.   A grandmother in Vicenza, Italy accidentally sent two adults and three children to the hospital when she made them cocoa with packets that expired back in 1990.

1023.   In Japan eating Christmas dinner at KFC is so popular that two hour lines form at some locations waiting for people to get in.

1024.   In the Philippines there's banana ketchup. During World War II there was actually a shortage of tomatoes, so they had to use bananas as a replacement to replace ketchup. It's made from mashed bananas, sugar, vinegar, and spices.

1025.   In rich countries, obesity is more common among the less educated, but in poor countries obesity is common among the highly educated.

1026.   Confidential data from the maritime industry that leaked revealed that one giant container ship can emit the same amount of cancer and asthma-causing chemicals as 50 million cars. That is while the top 15 largest container ships together in the world may be emitting as much pollution as all 760 million cars on earth.

1027.   The human heart has three types of blood vessels; arteries, veins and capillaries. Arteries carry oxygenated blood away from the heart. Capillaries connect them to the veins, and veins return the used blood back to the heart.

1028.   7% of the population triggers a sneeze reflex when they stare at a bright light such as the sun or a strong light bulb and of that 7%, 94% of those people are Caucasian.

1029.   Simo Hayha, the deadliest sniper in World War II, with over 505 confirmed kills, never once used a telescopic sight.

1030.   Sturre Bergwall was known in the 90s as a notorious killer in Sweden. He confessed to over 30 murders and other crimes. But, as it turns out, he was actually just a compulsive and manipulative liar and he never once killed a person or committed a crime.

1031.   La petite Syrah, a wine bar and bistro in Nice, France, charges extra for rude customers. People who just ask for coffee have to pay €7.50 while adding a please drops the price to €4.25. And if you say "hello, a coffee please." Then you only have to pay €1.40.

1032.   In the 1960's and 70's, professional bowlers were international celebrities who made twice as much money as NFL stars at the time.

1033.   It's believed that the term sandwich was named after John Montagu, fourth Earl of Sandwich, a town in the county of Kent in southeast England. He would ask his servants to bring him slices of meat between two slices of bread while he was gambling at a table so that he wouldn't have to leave the game.

1034.   President Reagan saved Harley Davidson Motorcycles by raising tariffs 45% on Japanese bikes that entered the country.

1035.   According to a study published in the proceedings of the National Academy of Sciences, female named storms have historically killed more people because people neither consider them as risky, nor take the same precautions as the male named storms.

1036.   In 2008, a Jamaican beach called "Coral Spring Beach" was actually stolen and the thieves were never caught. They achieved this by stealing massive amounts of sand until it basically wasn't a beach any more.

1037.   We not only have fingerprints, but also toe prints that have been used in criminal cases.

1038.   The headphone jack on your smartphone has remained relatively unchanged other than size since 1878.

1039.   Rats are a delicacy in Thailand.

1040.   The Taj Mahal in India took over 22 years to build. Construction began in 1632 and finished in 1653. It was built when Emperor Shah Jahan was filled with grief over his passing wife and wanted to create a testament to their love.

1041.   Our mouths secrete approximately one liter of saliva per day.

1042.   Reykjavik in Iceland actually heat their sidewalks and streets to keep them free of ice and snow. Since they began installing these heated roads over a decade ago, they've enjoyed significant savings from not having to spend taxpayer money on snow removal services.

1043.   Bald eagles build nests that are typically around five feet (1.5 metres) in diameter. They often use the same nests year after year and they could become even bigger, as big as nine feet and weighing as much as two tons.

1044.   The Chinese soft shell turtle is the first animal known to be able to pee out of its mouth. This was first discovered by researchers at the National University of Singapore, who noticed that turtles would stick their heads into puddles of water and wiggle their tongues, but they weren't drinking.

1045.   A group of hippos is called a crash.

1046.   In Venezuela, a liter of water costs more than a liter of fuel. Even with the sudden price hikes in 2016 of 1,329% for 91 octane-related gasoline and over 6,000% for 95 octane, gasoline still remains cheaper than clean drinking water.

1047.   At one point after its launch, Kim Kardashian's emoji app was making $1,000,000 a minute.

1048.   An American teenager named Ethan Couch, who killed four pedestrians while drunk driving, was given no prison time after claiming Affluenza, a mental illness for being too wealthy.

1049.   In 2015, Russia opened a military Disneyland called Patriot Park where visitors, including children, can ride in tanks, shoot guns and buy and sell military gear.

1050.   Luna moth doesn't have a mouth so it doesn't eat. It only lives for about one week and its sole purpose is to mate.

1051.   Alexander Solonick was a Russian hitman known as super killer, famous for killing around 30 mob bosses before becoming one himself.

Ironically he was strangled to death just two years later after he started his own criminal organization.

1052.   The Kids Wish Network was named the worst charity in the United States in 2013. According to a report only 3 cents out of every dollar raised actually went to granting the wishes of children while the rest of the money went directly into the pockets of the charity organizations operators.

1053.   In 2001, the uncle of a boy named Jessie Arbogast, wrestled a 7-foot bull shark to retrieve the severed arm of his nephew. After saving Jesse, the uncle dived back in, seized the shark, and wrestled it to shore, where a ranger shot it. The arm was pried from its gullet, put on ice, rushed to the hospital, and unbelievably successfully sewed back on.

1054.   Neil Harbisson is the world's first cyborg artist. He has an antenna implanted in his skull that allows him to hear color and see sound, and he can also connect to nearby devices such as bluetooth and the internet.

1055.   The reason that buildings in Hong Kong have gaping holes in them is to allow dragons free passage from their mountain homes to the sea.

1056.   In the Godfather film, McCluskey's shooting was done by building a fake forehead on top of actor Sterling Hayden. A gap was cut in the middle, filled with fake blood, and bunged up with prosthetic flesh. The plug was then yanked out with a fishing line to make a hole suddenly appear.

1057.   According to the patent for toilet paper, the creator, Seth Wheeler, made a drawing that officially shows that toilet paper should go over, not under.

1058.   A woman once took part in a search for a missing tourist in Iceland only to realize hours later that she was indeed, the missing person.

1059.   A Russian suicide bomber with the intent of killing hundreds in Moscow on New Year's Eve of 2015 had her plan foiled when her wireless carrier sent her a text message wishing her a Happy New Year which triggered her belt bomb killing her, and her alone.

1060.   If somebody reports their company for tax evasion in the United States, he or she will receive 15 to 30% of the amount collected. One person named Bradley C. Birkenfeld was a whistleblower on the USB AG Swiss Bank tax evasion scheme and received $104 million as a reward.

1061.   In 2013, a man in Michigan whose house was set to be demolished, switched his house numbers with his neighbor, and the crew ended up demolishing the wrong house.

1062.   It's possible to die from drowning up to 24 hours after leaving water. It's known as dry drowning where victims can be walking and talking while their lungs are actually filled with water.

1063.   Chinchilla fur is so thick and soft that fleas will suffocate if they try to live in it.

1064.   The Pigg-O-Stat is a device that has been around since the 1960s where radiologists can safely immobilize babies and young children who can't sit still during an x-ray.

1065.   Researchers from the University of Queensland and the University of New South Wales have found that people with dark eyes are more agreeable, while people with blue eyes tend to be more competitive.

1066.   There is an unnamed species of octopus that currently exist that scientists think are so cute that they're actually pushing to have it named "Opisthoteuthis Adorabilis."

1067.   Antarctica contains 90% of all the ice on the planet in an area that's just under one and a half times the size of the United States. The amount of ice there is staggering. In some parts, such as east Antarctica, ice averages 1.2 miles (1.9 kilometres) thick, but despite its thick ice, Antarctica is classified as a desert because so little moisture falls from the sky every year.

1068.   According to scientists at Los Alamos National Laboratory's Lujan Neutron Scattering Center, the world's largest gold crystal was found years ago in Venezuela. It's the size of a golf ball and weighs half a pound and is estimated to be worth $1.5 million.

1069.   There's a new dining craze known as 'Dinner in the Sky' available in 15 countries around the world where you actually eat your food in a racing chair suspended 60 meters above ground.

1070.   McDonald's opened their first ski-through fast food restaurant in 1996 located in Sweden. You can actually ski up to the counter, order your food, and ski off. They call it 'McSki'.

1071.   Peter Mayhew, the actor who played Chewbacca in Star Wars actually had to be accompanied by crew members dressed in brightly colored vests while filming in the forests of the Pacific Northwest. This was to ensure that he wasn't shot by hunters who would mistake him for Bigfoot.

1072.   The Center for Retail Research in Britain found that the most stolen food item in the world is cheese. In fact, 4% of all cheese sold was actually stolen.

1073.   There are actually miniature guide horses that the blind can use as an alternative to seeing-eye-dogs. They have several perceived advantages to that of a dog, including the average lifespan of 30 years and having 350-degree vision.

1074.   In 1967, during the Nigerian Civil War, both sides agreed to a 48-hour ceasefire because Pele was in town to play an exhibition soccer game and everyone wanted to be free to watch it without having to worry about the war.

1075.   London has a cereal cafe known as 'The Cereal Killer Café' where you can eat hundreds of different kinds of cereal from around the world.

1076.   The Lion King was originally called "The King of the Jungle." That is until the Disney team learned that lions don't live in a jungle.

1077.   There are special bins in Mexico City where you can put your dog poo in it and in exchange you get free wifi, and in fact the more poo the longer the free wifi.

1078.   Coca-Cola has made over 3,500 different kinds of beverages. That means that if you drink one per day it would take over nine years for you to try them all.

1079.   Fennec foxes mate for life. The male fox has become especially aggressive towards each other when mating season approaches in order to protect their mates.

1080.   Russian billionaire Vasily Klyukin wanted hospitals to be more welcoming, so he designed one to resemble a luxury yacht called White Sails Hospital, that a Tunisian businessman plans to build over the next 15 years.

1081.   There is a normal barbie called The Lammily Doll where the doll has brunette hair, cellulite, stretch marks, freckles, acne and more. She was also given the proportions of a typical 19 year old.

1082.   When Gary Knell the president and CEO of the Sesame Street workshop was asked whether Bert and Ernie were gay he responded that they're not gay, they're not straight, they're puppets, they don't exist below the waist.

1083.   Elvis Presley only failed one class at school. That was music class.

1084.   Towards the later years in his life Voltaire developed a habit of living near country borders so that he could escape by crossing the border if his writing angered the authorities.

1085.   After hurricane Katrina, the Amir of Gatar donated 100 million dollars to help rebuild housing, hospitals, and schools. He visited the area a few years later after the disaster to check on its progress.

1086.   There is a 70 meter long organ on the coast of Zadar, Croatia. The organ, designed by architect Nikola Basic has 35 tubes that make music whenever waves crash into them.

1087.   The last individual of a single species is called an endling. When it dies the species is then extinct.

1088.   Tiny pseudoscorpions which are usually about 2 to 8 millimeters long are often found in rooms with dusty books. They actually protect the books by feeding on booklice and dust mites.

1089.   In 2014 a homeowner in England accidentally left a spare bedroom window open for three months. This allowed about 5000 wasps to sneak through and build a massive nest on the bed. Disturbingly, the wasps chewed through about 20 centimeters worth of mattress and pillows but pest control managed to at least salvage the crochet blanket in the house.

1090.   Despite their size difference, praying mantises can easily catch and eat hummingbirds.

1091.   White coke is a clear colored coca-cola commissioned by Soviet marshal Gregory Zhukov in the 1940s. He requested it because he was a fan of coke, but didn't want to be seen drinking it in public, so we asked for a color to resemble vodka instead.

1092.   In 1992, the CEO's of Southwest Airlines and Steven's Aviation settled the dispute over who would get to use the slogan "Plane Smart" by arm-wrestling instead of dealing with a long drawn-out legal battle.

1093.   Babies are actually capable of giving a thumbs up in the womb.

1094.   The Khum Bak river resort in Sri Lanka is a hotel that's shaped like a giant elephant.

1095.   When he was only 13 years old, Ashton Kutcher thought about committing suicide, so that he could donate his heart to his brother, who desperately needed a heart transplant for his cardiomyopathy.

1096.   The pink fairy armadillo is the smallest species of armadillo. It is a mere four inches long and weighs about a hundred grams.

1097.   In Las Vegas, an average of five to seven adults is reported missing every day and more than 200 a month.

1098.   40 to 50 million years ago, Antarctica's climate was very similar to modern day California's.

1099.   If you leave towels, chairs, or sun umbrellas overnight to save a spot on busy Italian beaches, officials will take what you left behind and fine you about $220 to get your property back.

1100.   The very last McDonald's hamburger and fries in Iceland is on display at a bus hostel in Reykjavik right now. You can even watch real-time footage of it over a live stream. A man purchased it back in October 30th of 2009, and it's still on display.

1101.   In South Korea, if you win gold at the Asian Games or any medal at the Olympics, you are exempt from the country's military service, which is mandatory for able-bodied males.

1102.   The walnut-sized male blanket octopus tears off the tentacles of passing Portuguese man o' war jellyfish as a defense mechanism.

1103.   Tigers have a retinal adaptation that reflects light back to the retina, which makes their night vision six times better than humans'.

1104.   According to the Death Penalty Information Center, since 1973, 156 people have been exonerated and freed from death row.

1105.   There is a Switzerland-based company that for the cost of $29,000 will name your baby for you.

1106.   Kamikaze or exploding ants from Southeast Asia kill themselves when under threat. They have a toxic substance in their heads and in two large glands on the sides of their bodies that are filled with poison. Under threat they literally explode their heads or rupture their bodies to spray the poison to cover the predator.

1107.   In medieval times, bras were called breast bags.

1108.   The 2016 Olympics in Rio was the first time in Olympic history that South American country had hosted the games.

1109.   The phrase always a bridesmaid, never a bride was popularized by Listerine in ads featuring a lovelorn woman unable to find a husband due to her halitosis. The same ad coined the term halitosis.

1110.   According to an analysis done by Swift Key, Canada uses the poop emoji more than any other country. Hearts are number one in France, even beating the standard smiley and Australia leads the world in alcohol and drug related emojis.

1111.   The original creator for the Barbie Doll, Jack Ryan, had previously designed military grade missiles.

1112.   In January of 2016, McDonald's Japan introduced for a limited time French-fries drizzled with two kinds of chocolate sauce.

1113.   United States once attempted to buy Greenland in 1946 for 100 million dollars.

1114.   A person who sleeps too much, sits too much, and isn't active enough, is more than four times as likely to die early.

1115.   In 2012, a woman named Rebekah Speight, of Dakota City, successfully sold a Chicken McNugget on ebay for, 8100 dollars because it simply looked like George Washington.

1116.   Ukrainian engineer, Vladimir Tatarenko, has designed an airplane with a detachable cabin. In the event of an emergency, the cabin breaks off, deploys parachutes, and floats passengers safely to sea or ground.

1117.   Tim Hawking added swear words to his dad, Stephen Hawking's, voice synthesizer as a prank.

1118.   Following Marilyn Monroe's death, Joe DiMaggio was so devastated that he held a private funeral barring all of Hollywood's elite, delivering roses to her grave three times a week for over 20 years. He never remarried, and his final words were I'll finally get to see Marilyn.

1119.   In order to protect the city's water, the Los Angeles department of water and power purchased 80 million hollow black balls to cover its reservoirs to stop the sunlight from triggering dangerous chemical reactions.

1120.   After losing a battle in world war two because of taking a tea break, the British army perfected the art of brewing tea inside of a tank by creating the British army boiling vessel. A built-in kettle for armored vehicles.

1121.   It is illegal to die in London's houses of parliament.

1122.   Pteridophobia is the fear of ferns.

1123.   Dog blood type is different than the types found in people. In fact, there are six major blood types, but amazingly, 42% of dogs have the same type, which is universal.

1124.   According to National Geographic explorer Zeb Hogan, the wels catfish is the largest freshwater fish in Europe. It can grow up to 15 feet long, weigh as much as 660 pounds, and live for decades, possibly as long as 80 years.

1125.   Sweat is actually odorless. It's only when bacteria on the skin and hair metabolize the proteins and fatty acids in sweat that it produces an unpleasant scent.

1126.   Baby blue whales can consume up to 150 gallons of its mother's milk a day.

1127.   The word dude was first used in the 1800s as an insult towards young men who were too concerned with keeping up with the latest fashions.

1128.   John Cena, WWE superstar, has granted more than 400 Make-A-Wish requests, more than anyone else in the charity's history.

1129.   Mathematician Paul Erdos could calculate in his head, given a person's age, how many seconds that they had lived, when he was four.

1130.   According to his brother, Vincent Van Gogh's last words were, "The sadness will last forever."

1131.   Believe it or not, coloring books for grownups are a huge trend, and publishers actually struggle to keep up with demand. The books are used successfully to reduce stress, relieve anxiety and as rehabilitation aids for patients that are recovering from strokes.

1132.   Sam Griner from the 'Successful Kid' memes used his success to start a GoFundMe page, which raised nearly $100,000 for his dad's kidney transplant.

1133.   There is a town in Arizona called nothing and it's a ghost town. So quite literally nothing is there.

1134.   Bob Marley's song No Woman, No Cry is actually No woman, Nuh cry in Jamaica. This actually translates to no woman, don't cry and the song is about growing up in the ghetto and persuading a woman that things will get better so don't cry.

1135.   Istanbul has an estimated 150,000 stray dogs. A company called huge din has created a vending machine where food and water for the dogs can be dispensed when people recycle the plastic bottles.

1136.   Guide dogs are able to go against their owners instructions when they think their order is unsafe. This is called intelligent disobedience.

1137.   Underwater hockey is a sport where two teams compete to push a puck across the bottom of a swimming pool into the opposing team's goal. It originated in England in 1954 and is also called Octopush.

1138.   There's a tradition in Glasgow of placing a traffic cone on the head of the Duke of Wellington Statue. The cost of removing the traffic cone costs an estimated 10,000 pounds a year.

1139.   It's illegal not to flush the toilet in Singapore. For failing to flush, you will be fined $150 and police officers have been known to check.

1140.   Buzz Aldrin's maiden name was, coincidentally, Moon.

1141.   Just one percent of friendships formed in the 7th grade are still intact by the 12th grade, according to a study by Psychological Science.

1142.   Architects in Iceland wanted to push the appearance of utility towers beyond their basic functional structures. So, they created a design proposal called "The Land of Giants." Essentially, it turns electrical pylons into human-shaped sculptures.

1143.   Portuguese artist David Oliveira uses wire to draw in the air by creating sculptures that look like pencil sketches.

1144.   There is a prison in Finland where the only thing keeping inmates in is a yellow picket fence.

1145.   'Anhedonia' is the word for a feeling when you cannot find joy in things that usually bring you joy.

1146.   In 2001, Pizza Hut paid the Russian space agency to send a pizza to the International Space Station at a cost of one million dollars.

1147.   20-year-old Kiran Cable from South Wales was with his girlfriend so much that his friends say that he actually disappeared from their lives so much so that after 18 months of unreturned calls and emails. Fifty of Cable's friends decided to surprise him with a mock funeral that included a coffin, a hearse, and even a eulogy.

1148.   In the 1970s Senator Larry Pressler refused to take a bribe that was offered from the FBI. He was called a Hero for doing so but he didn't think turning down a bribe should be considered heroic.

1149.   You are most likely to come up with a great idea when doing monotonous tasks such as exercising driving or showering. This is because we are the most relaxed and least distracted so dopamine is flowing through our bodies and triggering our thoughts.

1150.   The Great Gatsby originally sold very poorly with only 20,000 copies sold in the first year it was published. F.Scott Fitzgerald died believing that his work was a failure.

1151.   It isn't entirely true that no two snowflakes are alike. Snowflakes actually fall in only one of 35 different shapes.

1152.   By the end of your life, odds are you will have spent over 20,000 minutes kissing. That's literally two weeks of your life with your lips locked with someone else's.

1153.   Dolphins are the only other species that are documented to have sex just for pleasure and not just for procreation.

1154.   There are only four words in the English language that end with -dous. They are tremendous, horrendous, stupendous, and hazardous.

1155.   A tiger's stripes are on their skin, not just their fur. More collect phone calls are made on Father's Day than any other day of the year. AT&T; reported, on average, 83 million calls were made on Father's Day, compared to 106 million on Mother's Day, but 27% more Father's Day calls were collected.

1156.   Pearls will actually dissolve when immersed in vinegar. A pearl is mostly calcium carbonate, which is susceptible to even the weakest acid solution.

1157.   On March 3rd, 1934, gangster John Dillinger escaped from a jail in Indiana with the help of a wooden gun that was smuggled in to him by one of his attorneys.

1158.   The first technical casualty of the Civil War was killed during a 100-gun salute. A cannon prematurely discharged and killed Private Daniel Hough of the First U.S. Artillery.

1159.   McDonald's in the Netherlands has a place mat called a McTrax where you can make music while you eat. To make it work, you place your phone on the mat, get an app, and then compose your music including your voice.

1160.   According to the Guinness World Records, the United States holds the record for the most medals won at a single summer Olympic games. At the 1904 Olympics, held in St. Louis, Missouri, they won 78 gold medals, 82 silver, and 79 bronze for a total of 239.

1161.   Edgar Allen Poe once published a novel where a ship crew becomes stranded with no food and one member named Richard Parker is sacrificed for food. Disturbingly 45 years later in 1884 a yacht sank on route from England to Australia. The four men crew didn't have enough food to survive and one boy was killed by the other three for food. His name was Richard Parker.

1162.   Despite having DNA evidence of the suspect, German police could not prosecute a 6.8 million dollar jewel heist because the DNA belonged to identical twins and there was no evidence to prove which one of them was actually the culprit.

1163.   Bruises turn colors because your body is breaking down and reabsorbing the hemoglobin that leaked from the broken blood vessels in your body.

1164.   At full sprint a cheetah spends more time flying than in contact with the ground.

1165.   Hundreds of prisoners were left to die in their cells during Hurricane Katrina as officials abandoned Orleans Parish Prison.

1166.   Elephants are more intelligent than you think. One elephant in India was trained to place logs in pre dug holes for a ceremony. On one occasion it refused to place a log in a hole where a dog was sleeping and waited until the dog was chased away to lower the post into the hole.

1167.   In 2007, a Doberman Pinscher (a dog breed) named Khan actually saved a baby girl from a deadly king brown snake attack by grabbing the girl by the diaper and flinging her to safety and taking a venomous bite to the paw in her place.

1168.   In 1809, the Spanish town of Huescar declared war on Denmark then forgot about it for 172 years. Not a single shot was fired, and no one was killed, and a peace treaty was finally signed in 1981 when a historian found the official declaration and realized that they were actually supposed to be fighting.

1169.   There's a popular variation of 'Yo Momma' type jokes in Kenya that goes a little something like this. "Your family is so stupid you gave your chickens hot water so they can lay boiled eggs."

1170.   Google Chrome's dinosaur Wifi error message is actually also a game. So, next time you're angry at your internet for breaking, just press the spacebar and you will witness your T-Rex jump. Just don't let him land on the cactus or it'll be game over.

1171.   There are playgrounds in England, Finland, Germany, and the US designed specifically for aging residents. They feature low-impact exercise equipment designed to promote balance and flexibility such as elliptical machines, static bikes, and flexors.

1172.   Starting on July 19th, 2016, T-Mobile gave all of its customers a year of unlimited data to play Pokémon GO. They also offered 50% off mobile accessories such as portable power packs and more because so many people's phones were dying.

1173.   In June of 2016, there was a massive theft of Twitter usernames and passwords involving nearly 33 million customers. According to the security company, LeakedSource, over 120,000 people had used the password one, two, three, four, five, six.

1174.   There's a sport called joggling where you jog and juggle at the same time. It was invented by a man named Bill Giduz who would juggle balls on a running track to increase his coordination when he realized that the pace of the three-ball juggling pattern easily matched a wide range of running cadences.

1175.   When General Motors unveiled the Camaro name in 1966, Automotive Press asked Chevrolet product managers "What is a Camaro?" And they were told it's a small vicious animal that eats mustangs.

1176.   Steve Jobs refused to let his own kids have iPads and limited their use of technology to a minimum.

1177.   LSD was first synthesized in 1938, but it wasn't until five years later that its creator, Albert Hofmann, accidentally consumed it discovering its hallucinogenic properties. It was then packaged nine years later for psychiatric uses.

1178.   The world's first ligers were born in 2013. A white lion and a tiger had four male cubs which are now the rarest big cats on earth.

1179.   After American physicist Richard Feynman was named the world's smartest man by Omni Magazine, his mother was actually quoted as saying, "If that's the world's smartest man, God help us."

1180.   In the entire Lord of the Rings trilogy, no two female characters ever speak to each other.

1181.   In the late 1900s, Howard Hughes bought an entire casino named Silver Slipper just so that he could tear down their neon sign. This is because it was visible from Hughes' bedroom, and apparently it was keeping him up at night.

1182.   Tom Monaghan, the founder of Domino's Pizza met his wife on his first pizza delivery back in 1962.

1183.   Violet Jessop was a ship nurse on the Britannic, the Olympic and the Titanic. While on board the Olympic, it collided with a warship and nearly sank. While on the Titanic, it hit an iceberg and sank, and the Britannic hit an underwater mine and sank, yet Violet survived all three.

1184.   Justo Gallego Martinez, a 90 year old former monk, has been building an unauthorized cathedral in Spain since 1961. He mostly works alone for 10 hours a day, 6 days a week.

1185.   The earth's day-night cycle is growing longer year by year. And 620,000,000 million years ago, an earth day was only 21.9 hours.

1186.   During the cold winters, the Alaskan wood frog becomes a frog shaped block of ice. It literally stops breathing and its heart stops beating. Then, when spring arrives, the frog thaws and returns to normal, and goes along its merry way.

1187.   More salt is used for deicing roads with 8% of global manufactured salt going there compared to 6% for human consumption.

1188.   Every time that you recall an event, your brain distorts it just a little bit. Basically when you remember something that happened in the past, you're actually just remembering the last time that you remembered it, and so on.

1189.   18-year-old, Andrej Ciesielski, was arrested for climbing the Great Pyramid of Giza and taking photos, after which he shared with his thousands of followers, who loved watching him travel the world just to climb stuff.

1190.   There's a class of people in Japan referred to as cyber-homeless, who live at cyber cafes, because they're actually a cheaper alternative to an apartment. The cafes offer free showers and even sell underwear.

1191.   A Chinese man bought and raised two puppies, cared for them despite their frequent killing and eating of chickens and discovered later that they were bears.

1192.   Blowing smoke up your ass actually used to be a common cure for many ailments.

1193.   Japan has a network of roads that actually plays music as you drive over them at the correct speed.

1194.   A South Korean man named Woo Bum-kon committed a mass murder because he was enraged from being woken by his girlfriend trying to swat a fly on his chest.

1195.   Yokohama Japan has an annual festival devoted entirely to Pikachu. The Pikachu outbreak is a week-long festival where masses of dancing Pikachus, along with countless statues, completely take over the city.

1196.   Mike Tyson first snorted cocaine when he was just 11 years old, and was given alcohol when he was just an infant.

1197.   George R.R. Martin was so impressed with Jack Gleeson's portrayal of Joffrey in 'Game of Thrones' that he sent him a personal letter saying congratulations on your marvelous performance, everyone hates you.

1198.   Arch West, the inventor of Doritos was buried with Doritos sprinkled over his body.

1199.   In 2014 a man named Chistian Poincheval invented a range of pills aimed at making people's farts smell like either chocolate or roses.

1200.   One of the biggest reasons why night vision goggles are green is because the human eye is the most sensitive to light wavelengths near 555 nanometers aka green and can differentiate between more shades of this green than any other color.

1201.   In 1923 Bobby the wonder dog tracked 2500 miles (4100 kilometers) across the United States to reunite with his owners after he got lost in Indian during a family road trip.

1202.   Property owners in New York City can actually request to have trees planted on their street for free. They're even allowed to suggest what species to plant.

1203.   In Japan, there's a condition called Hikikomori where around a million people, mostly men, have locked themselves in their bedrooms for years creating social and health problems.

1204.   There's a replica of Noah's Ark in Williamstown, Kentucky. It was built by creationist ministry. It is exactly the dimensions specified in the book of Genesis at 450 feet long, 67 feet high, and 46 feet wide and cost about $100 million to make.

1205.   The Antarctic Polar Desert is the largest desert on Earth. It covers the continent of Antarctica and is the size of about 5.5 million square miles (8.8 million square kilometres).

1206.   The world's most expensive aquarium fish is the Asian Arowana also known as the dragon fish. It's believed by the Chinese to bring good luck and prosperity due to its red color and coin-like scales. This fish has sold for up to $300,000.

1207.   Siberia has a population density of less than eight people per one square mile. This is extra shocking considering that Siberia covers 77% of all of Russia and has an area of more than 50 times that of the U.K., but, yet, has half the population.

1208.   During the American Civil War, if you were drafted, you could actually pay someone $300 to go in your place. This was called commutation and was intended to raise money for the war effort, but was often heavily criticized that it was better at raising money than troops.

1209.   China invented fireworks, but Italy gave them their colors. Colors are created using metallic powders. Calcium makes orange. Sodium makes yellow, and Barium makes green. Also, cylindrical tubes create whistling sounds. Aluminum flakes make hissing noises, and flash powder makes loud boom sounds.

1210.   According to a study done by National Geographic, the same gene that gives humans the urge to travel is also responsible for ADHD and thrill-seeking behavior.

1211.   The reason that paper cuts hurt so much is that the cut often bleeds very little or not at all leaving the skin's pain receptors open to air.

1212.   A man named Chen Si spends every weekend of his life at the Nanjing Yangtze River Bridge which is the world's number one suicide bridge. He does it to save people from jumping, and in fact, he has saved 144 people from killing themselves.

1213.   ISIS has so much money that it's wealthier than several actual countries. The group makes about $1 million to $5 million a day.

1214.   There's an annual photo contest called "The Comedy Wildlife Photography Awards." Entries consist of the funniest animal wildlife pictures that photographers accidentally or intentionally captured throughout their career.

1215.   Boeing has created a new metal called "microlattice" that's 99.99% air. So light in fact that the metal can sit on top of a dandelion without crushing it.

1216.   When he died in 1937, John D. Rockefeller's estate equaled 1.5% of America's total economic output. To put that into perspective for you, today that's the equivalent of four times the amount of Bill Gates net worth when it was at its peak.

1217.   Saltwater Brewery, from Florida, has partnered up with the ad agency, We Believers, to create fully edible six-pack beer can packaging. It's made from byproducts of the brewing process like wheat and barley, and is fully biodegradable and completely digestible. They are just as strong as the plastic ones, but if an animal or bird gets caught in one, they can actually snack on it and quickly decompose it.

1218.   Cobwebs actually have antifungal and antiseptic properties that keep bacteria away, minimizing the chance of infection. In fact, in ancient times, the Greeks and Romans would use cobwebs to treat cuts. Soldiers also used spider webs to heal wounds. They would combine honey and vinegar to clean the wound and then cover it with balled-up spider webs.

1219.   The female Burmese Python is able to incubate her eggs by raising her body temperature by as much as seven degrees warmer than air temperature. They accomplish this by frequently hiccupping or having muscle spasms.

1220.   Ancient Egyptians used to put dead mice into the mouths of people to treat toothaches. They also mashed up dead mouse paste with other ingredients to treat patients with pain.

1221.   In 2015, astronomers located a gigantic cloud of methyl alcohol called methanol surrounding a stellar nursery, measuring over 310 billion miles (500 billion km) across. Over time, it could actually help astronomers understand how some of the most massive stars in the universe are formed.

1222.   Tibetan nuns can actually change their core body temperatures with a form of meditation called gitumo. Using temperature measurements, a team of researchers recorded the internal temperature of the nuns in the freezing cold of the Himalayas. The nuns were able to increase their core body temperature up to almost 101 degrees Fahrenheit (38 degrees celsius).

1223.   Researchers at Murdoch University in Perth have discovered goldfish as long as 12 inches and weighing as much as 4.2 pounds (1.9 kg) in the Bath River in the southwest of Western Australia. They think it's the result of people releasing their goldfish into the water. This is because in the wild, that's how big they can grow.

1224.   According to the National Oceanic and Atmospheric Administration and NASA, July 2016 was the hottest month in 136 years of record keeping.

1225.   Dyslexics see numbers and letters backwards. It's a reading disorder, not a vision or seeing disorder, which means that Braille readers can also be dyslexic.

1226.   According to a study published in the Journal of Behavior Therapy and Experimental Psychiatry, mood can affect how we walk and vice versa. We walk slumped-shouldered if we're sad, bouncing if we're happy. Making people imitate a happy walk actually made them feel happier, and sadder if they were imitating a sad way of walking.

1227.   Queen Elizabeth and her husband, Prince Philip, are third cousins.

1228.   According to Guinness World Records, the oldest tree known to have been planted by humans is 2,300 years old. The sacred fig, or Bow Tree was planted in Sri Lanka in 288 BC.

1229.   In India as well as other parts of the world, standing babas are people who have taken a vow to never sit, lay, or squat for 12 years in order to transport their psyches into a realm of spiritual awareness not experienced by sitters. They stand before a small hammock in which to rest their arms during the day and torso at night. One leg must be on the ground at all times.

1230.   Most mammals don't live long past their reproductive years. Only a few that we know do, such as the killer whales, pilot whales, and possibly some great apes and human beings.

1231.   The national sport of Afghanistan is called Buzkashi where a headless carcass of a calf or goat is kept in the center of a field and two opposing teams, on horseback, try to get hold of the carcass and carry it to the goal area. The game can sometimes last for days.

1232.   In the small town of El Valle de Anton, Panama, there are trees growing that have square trunks. It's believed that this strange anomaly of nature doesn't occur anywhere else in the world. In fact, experts from the University of Florida, took a few tree seedlings to see if they will retain their rectangular shape if planted elsewhere in the world, and they didn't when planted in other locations.

1233.   In 1818, when Abraham Lincoln was nine, his mother, Nancy, died of a mysterious milk sickness that was sweeping across southern Indiana. It turned out the strange disease was due to drinking tainted milk from a cow that had ingested poisonous white snakeroot.

1234.   Mary, Queen of Scots, became queen at only six days old. This is because her father died and she was his successor.

1235.   During its lifetime, an oyster changes its sex from male to female and back several times.

1236.   During his entire life, artist Vincent Van Gogh sold exactly one painting, "Red Vineyard at Arles".

1237.   The spider, Calponia harrisonfordi, was named for the star of "Raiders of the Lost Ark" and "Star Wars", as a thanks to Harrison Ford who narrated a documentary for the London Museum of Natural History in 1994. The spider itself was discovered in 1993 and is very tiny, only around five millimeters in length, and lives in California.

1238.   The only member of the band, Z Z Top, without a beard has the last name, Beard.

1239.   Toto from the "Wizard of Oz" was paid $125 a week. This was more than the Munchkin actors were paid.

1240.   The fastest healing part on the human body is the tongue. This is due to the rich supply of blood that the tongue receives, making it able to heal twice as fast than any other part of the body.

1241.   Montpelier, Vermont is the only state capital without a McDonald's.

1242.   Snakes and lizards flick their tongues in the air to capture scent particles. In other words, they smell with their tongues.

1243.   The aquarium at the Golden Nugget in Las Vegas has a waterslide also called the Shark Chute where you can go through the tank and see the sharks.

1244.   In 2001 Robin Williams met and became friends with Koko the gorilla who communicates in sign language. After hearing about Robin William's death in 2014, Koko signs the word cry and became somber for the rest of the day.

1245.   In 2005, a girl in Ethiopia was kidnapped and was saved by three wild lions. The lions unbelievably chased off her kidnappers and stayed with her until the police found her.

1246.   In 2015 in Colorado, a mysterious teenager was regularly breaking into homes, stealing snacks, specifically Hot Pockets, and watching people's Netflix. He literally steals no cash or valuables, only snacks and Netflix.

1247.   The sun is the most perfect sphere ever observed in nature according to University of Hawaii.

1248.   Polish teenager Iga Jasica unexpectedly woke up in the middle of her brain surgery and calmly asked the doctor, "How's it going?" Amazingly she wasn't in any pain so they talked about cats until the surgery was over.

1249.   In 2003 two men stole a Boeing 727 from an Angolan airport and were never seen again.

1250.   Saudi Arabia is the largest country in the world without a river.

1251.   Disney put 500 stormtroopers on the Great Wall of China to promote Star Wars The Force Awakens.

1252.   The Soviets found that sniper duties actually fit women the best since snipers are patient, careful, deliberate, can avoid hand to hand combat, and need higher levels of aerobic conditioning than other troops.

1253.   The Dai-Ichi Yochien preschool in Japan has a courtyard that collects rainwater into a giant clean puddle that kids can stomp and splash around in.

1254.   There is a rare brain disorder called Foreign Accent Syndrome that causes people to involuntarily speak in foreign accents.

1255.   Adopting children is actually considered taboo in Korea, and because of this South Korea's orphans are almost never adopted unless a foreigner adopts them.

1256.   In 2015 a Russian man got drunk with his friends, dropped dead, came back to life in the morgue freezer, and then headed off to drink some more.

1257.   Despite their bad reputation, great white sharks have only ever attacked people 280 times between 1876 and 2013 globally, and on top of that, only 77 have ever resulted in a fatality. Just for a little comparison, deer kill nearly 200 people a year in the US alone.

1258.   Studies from the University of North Carolina concluded that incredibly beautiful people are actually less likely to be hired for a job if they're being interviewed by someone of the same sex. They're also often very lonely because they're viewed as unapproachable and intimidating, and they're even given less care by doctors when being treated for pain.

1259.   There are only two countries in the world whose flags do not contain either red, white, or blue. Jamaica and Mauritania.

1260.   A newborn Chinese water deer is so adorably small after birth that you could hold it in one hand, but when it grows up, they can weigh as much as 13 kilograms and sprouts fangs, making them look like a vampire deer.

1261.   After mismanagement, the social news site Digg, a company that was once valued at $200 million was sold for a mere $500,000.

1262.   A previously crystal-blue hot spring located in Yellowstone National Park is actually turning green as the result of tourists throwing good luck coins into it since 1950. It has since been dubbed Fading Glory.

1263.   If you went swimming on the moon, you would be able to walk on the water's surface and jump out of the water like a dolphin catching air above water.

1264.   The character of Popeye is actually based on a real-life person named Frank "Rocky" Fiegel. He was a local tough guy in Chester, Illinois, and quite similar to the real Popeye. He had some pretty serious forearms.

1265.   Alfred Binet, the original inventor of the IQ test, created the methodology to identify students who needed help. He actually deplored its use as a ranking for unitary and linear intelligence.

1266.   Lifeguard Thomas Lopez from South Florida was fired after saving someone from drowning because the man he saved wasn't technically in his assigned lifeguard area.

1267.   In 1975, a 17-year-old boy was killed while riding his Moped. He was killed exactly one year after his 17-year-old brother was killed while riding the same Moped in the same intersection by the same taxi with the same driver carrying the same passenger.

1268.   A creature called the Prasinohaema skink lives on the island of New Guinea and has green blood, bones and tissue. No other vertebrate is known to have green blood, and it's extremely toxic to humans.

1269.   The medical term for your butt crack is the intergluteal cleft, also known as the natal cleft and the vertical gluteal crease.

1270.   In 1952, Mr. Potato Head was the first-ever toy advertised on TV. Nearly two million were sold in the first year alone, and Mrs. Potato Head came a year later in 1953.

1271.   The ad agency FDB Brazil created a doll for Nivea that is made of UV-sensitive material and turns a painful-looking bright red if left out in the sun. Applying sunscreen to it turns it white again. The doll was made to teach children the importance of wearing sunscreen.

1272.   If you have an injury to your hand or fingers and there's nerve damage, your fingers won't wrinkle when submerged in water.

1273.   19-year-old Shayla Wiggins from Riverton, Wyoming, found a dead body floating in a river while playing Pokemon Go. She was trying to find a Pokemon from a natural water resource, but she found something else instead.

1274.   Elvis Presley had a twin brother who was a stillborn. His name was Jessie Garon.

1275.   In 1994, Bill Gates bought Leonardo da Vinci's Codex Leicester notebook for $30.8 million. He did it to not only add to his personal collection, but to also help promote Windows Vista's launch by using a program called

Turning the Pages 2.0 that lets people browse through virtual versions of the notebook.

1276.   Robert F. Kennedy failed third grade. Smaller than his siblings, Bobby was often considered the runt of the family and he even attended nearly a dozen schools as well.

1277.   Governments in Iraq and India have imposed an internet blackout during exams to prevent students from cheating.

1278.   You can now hire a self-driving taxi in Singapore. During the testing period, the cars had a driver in the front who could take over the wheel at any time, and a researcher in the back who watches the computers. They're equipped with a detection system that uses lasers to operate like radar and two cameras on the dashboard to scan for obstacles and detect traffic light changes.

1279.   Hurricane names are recycled every six years, with the exception of hurricanes that have been so deadly and costly that the future use of its name for a different storm would be insensitive.

1280.   A Filipino fisherman found a 75-pound natural pearl and kept it hidden under his bed for 10 years. He discovered it in a giant clam and kept it as a good luck charm. It's 170,000 carats.

1281.   According to a new study in the Journal of Hand Therapy, millennials have weaker muscles in their hands from all the texting, snapping, scrolling, and gaming that they do, especially the guys.

1282.   There's a social anxiety called parthenophobia where you have an abnormal and persistent fear of young girls.

1283.   Vampire bats have a protein in their saliva that acts as an anticoagulant, which keeps their victim's blood flowing while they feed. Researchers have actually been studying it to see if it can help dissolve blood clots and help with stroke victims.

1284.   In the 1904 Summer Olympics, gymnast George Eiser won three gold medals, two silver, and a bronze, all while wearing a wooden prosthetic leg.

1285.   There used to be a sport called ferret-legging, where a ferret is strapped in a contestant's pants, without underwear. The contestant who can stand the teeth and claws the longest wins.

1286.   The ALS Association received 101 million dollars in donations compared to 2.8 million the previous year because of the money raised by people doing the ice bucket challenge.

1287.   In the United Kingdom and Ireland, you can purchase cyberbullying insurance. The insurance company, Chub, will pay out as much as $74,600 to help with court costs and relocation fees.

1288.	In Shanghai, you can have your credit score lowered for not sending greetings or visiting your elderly parents.

1289.	There is a hangover clinic in Sydney, Australia. For a whopping $200, you can get one-hour treatments, which includes a half gallon of hydration drip, oxygen therapy, and vitamins to help you recover from a night of too much alcohol.

1290.	The average person yawns about 250,000 times over the course of their life and babies in the womb even do it as early as 12 to 14 weeks.

1291.	One of the deadliest earthquakes in history happened in Shaanxi, China, on January 23, 1556, killing an estimated 830,000 people. It was later revealed that the magnitude of the quake was approximately eight to 8.3, which isn't nearly the strongest tremor on record, but the quake struck in the middle of an unfortunately densely populated area with poorly constructed buildings and homes, resulting in horrific death tolls.

1292.	Scientists from Psychology Today concluded that if a person's body odor smells good to you it means that their immunity genes are opposite to yours. This allows higher chances for people with opposite immunity genes to mate, resulting in offspring with stronger immunity systems.

1293.	Just 2% of the entire world's population is naturally blonde.

1294.	Nissan uses the number 23 in car racing because the number two translates to 'ni' in Japanese, and the number three translates to 'san', hence 23 translates into Nissan.

1295.	Neurologists claim that every time you resist acting on your anger, you're actually rewiring your brain to be a calmer and more loving person.

1296.	In 1987, Steve Rothstein bought a lifetime, unlimited first-class American Airlines ticket for $250,000. He flew over 10,000 flights, costing the company $21 million. They terminated his ticket in 2008.

1297.	A study conducted at Columbia University concluded that people born in the month of May, may have the lowest risk of illness and disease.

1298.	Leonardo da Vinci invented the scissors.

1299.	Lizards can self-amputate their tails for protection. And they grow them back after only a few months.

1300.	Like fingerprints, everyone's tongue print is different.

1301.	Actress Candice Bergen's father left $10,000 to his ventriloquist dummy and zero to her. He said the dummy had been my constant companion from whom I have never been separated, even for a day.

1302.	Microwaves use more electricity to power their clocks than they do to heat up your food.

1303.	There is something called non visible art where works are imagined by the artists and described to the audience. In 2011 a woman named Amie

Davidson bought one of these pieces for $10,000 saying she identified with the ideology of the non visible art project.

1304.   There is a 200 foot (61 meter) long pink stuffed bunny on the top of a hill in the Piedmont region of Italy. It's there for Hikers to enjoy and should decay completely by 2025.

1305.   Cats have adapted to fall from great heights. When they fall they reach terminal velocity and they twist their bodies so that they can position their feet under their bodies to land themselves.

1306.   In 2012 a man named Seth Horvitz ordered a TV from amazon and instead got a military grade assault rifle instead.

1307.   The walled City in St-Malo France is notorious for being a safe haven for pirates.

1308.   A study done in 2010 shows that women find men in red to be more attractive. The color makes men appear more powerful and higher in status which leads to the attraction.

1309.   Martha Stewart once dated Anthony Hopkins, but broke up with him after seeing "Silence of the Lambs". She stated that she was unable to avoid associating Hopkins with the character of Hannibal Lecter.

1310.   Japan was invaded by the strong Mongol army twice, and both times were saved by the harsh storms that crippled the Mongols. They called these storms "kamikaze" or divine winds.

1311.   Zach Braff punched a 12-year-old for spraying fake paint on his Porsche as part of a prank on the show "Punk'd."

1312.   During the Afghanistan War, when his team was ambushed, outnumbered, and under fire, British Corporal Sean Jones ordered his men to affix bayonets to their guns and charge across 80 meters of open ground against the Taliban forces. And unbelievably, it worked. Enemy forces scattered, fleeing the fight, due to the unexpected move.

1313.   Spain cheated in the 2000 Summer Paralympics. 10 out of the 12 players on their roster were encouraged to pretend that they were mentally disabled, and they actually had no mental disability.

1314.   Canada consumes the most donuts and has the most donut shops per capita of any country in the world.

1315.   Jack Nicholson grew up believing that his mother was his sister and his grandparents were his parents. He didn't find out the truth until both his mother and grandmother had died.

1316.   It's possible for stem cells to extend human life. In 2014, researchers in Pittsburgh injected white mice with stem cells. Now normally their usual lifespan is 21 days but after injection they lived for an extra 71 days. This is the equivalent of an 80 year old human being living to be 200.

1317.   One gigabyte of storage cost $300,000 in 1981. Now it says cheap as 10 cents.

1318.   Emotions and Stress can adversely affect your body. Negativity can actually lower your immune systems response against disease.

1319.   In the 1930's, people lacking space in their London apartments used to utilize a baby cage for more space and for fresh air for their babies.

1320.   The word dinosaur comes from the ancient Greek words, deinos, meaning fearfully-great, as in awe inspiring, and sauros, meaning lizard. The name was invented in 1842 by Richard Owen.

1321.   The jaguar is the national animal of Brazil. It's scientific name is Panthera onca and is the largest carnivorous mammal in Central and South America weighing up to 211 pounds.

1322.   In 2013, scientists from the University of Chile spent a year designing a new vaccine that will give anyone who drinks even a small amount of alcohol an immediate, very bad hangover. They developed it to help tackle the problem of alcoholism in the country.

1323.   The sloth only urinates and defecates once a week. Constipation is normal for them, and so, when they do go, it's like giving birth. Their poop comes out looking like a long piece of rotten banana.

1324.   In North Korea, only military and government officials can own motor vehicles.

1325.   Before there was modern refrigeration, people in Russia and Finland put Russian brown frogs in their milk to keep it fresh. According to Moscow State University organic chemist, A. T. Lebedev, the frog's skin secretions are loaded with peptides and anti-microbial compounds.

1326.   The Blue Whale has the highest percentage of body fat of any animal at more than 35%. Whales can weigh up to 180 tonnes which means upto 63 tonnes of fat.

1327.   In the movie 'Saving Private Ryan', directors depicted combat so realistically that veterans actually had to leave the theaters during the opening scene stating that it was the most realistic depiction of combat that they had ever seen.

1328.   A 14-carat gold Lego brick was given out in the early 80s to employees who had worked at the Germany Lego Factory for over 25 years. They are valued at over $15,000.

1329.   Pineapples were considered a status symbol in the 18th century. They were seen as a symbol of wealth and power, and in England, people were able to rent one for a night to show off to partygoers.

1330.   We generally don't think of foods as too sweet until our bones stop growing. This is why kids tend to like sweets a lot more than adults do.

1331.   A wild pig in Australia once stole 18 beers from some campers, got drunk, and then got into a fight with a cow.

1332.   Philip A. Contos was a motorcyclist who died at an anti-helmet rally after he flipped over his handlebars and hit his head on the pavement.

1333.   The Incas measured their units of time by how long it would take to cook a potato.

1334.   MI-5 once had a plan to use gerbils to detect terrorists and spies at airports. This is because their sense of smell can acutely detect increased adrenaline in people, but the project was scrapped when the gerbils proved unable to tell the difference between terrorists and those who were just afraid of flying.

1335.   In 2004, Google anonymously posted math equations on billboards in Harvard Square and Silicon Valley that, if solved, led to a website with another equation, which in turn, allowed you to submit your resume.

1336.   In Sweden, it is illegal to name your baby Metallica, Superman, Veranda, Ikea or Elvis.

1337.   On August 16, 1996, at the Brookfield Zoo, a three-year-old boy fell into a gorilla enclosure and lost consciousness, but Binti Jua, a female gorilla, guarded the young boy from other gorillas, cradled him in her arms, and carried him to an entrance where zookeepers could actually retrieve him.

1338.   Studies conducted by the global commission on aging at Transamerica Center for Retirement Studies show that traveling is good for you. It promotes brain health and decreases your risk of heart attack and depression.

1339.   Compared to one cigarette, one hookah session delivers about 25 times the tar, 2.5 times the nicotine and 10 times the carbon monoxide.

1340.   In 2009 three masked burglars unknowingly broke into Swedish actor Dolph Lundgren's home, tied him up and then threatened his wife. But they immediately fled when they found a family photo and realized who owned the home.

1341.   It took Ronda Rousey a total of only 25 minutes and thirty-six seconds to win all of her 12 fights.

1342.   Bowhead whales are amongst the longest-living mammals. In 2007, a specimen caught off the Alaskan coast was found to have a 35-inch-long head of an explosive harpoon embedded deep in its neck. The projectile was manufactured in Massachusetts around 1890, suggesting that the whale survived a hunt over a century ago.

1343.   Humpback whales often let dolphins hitch a ride on their head for the sheer fun of it.

1344.   The difference between terror and horror is that terror occurs in anticipation of the horrifying experience, while horror occurs after.

1345.   Your eyebrows renew themselves every 64 days.

1346.   Five high school students and their teacher from a small town in Sicily, Italy, created a prototype of a vending machine that turns your plastic recyclables into phone cases. It grinds down the plastics into tiny pellets which are then melted and then used to create 3D printed phone cases. The project was created to encourage other youths to recycle more.

1347.   Retired NBA All-Star basketball player, Yao Ming, has his own winery in Napa Valley. Yao Family Wines opened in 2009 and makes ultra-premium wines and is open from 10 to five for tastings.

1348.   In late 2016, the world's second tallest building, the Shanghai Tower, built the world's fastest elevator. According to manufacturer, Mitsubishi, the elevator moves as fast as 4,035 feet (1200 metres) per minute. That's 46 miles (76 km) per hour.

1349.   Steven Tyler, from the band Aerosmiths, birth name was Steven Victor Tallarico.

1350.   Sushi is actually meant to be eaten with your hands and sashimi with chopsticks.

1351.   Before Saladin, the first Sultan of Egypt died in 1193. He had given all of his wealth to his poor subjects. His final estate consisted of a single piece of gold and 40 pieces of silver, not even enough to pay for the funeral.

1352.   KevJumba, a YouTuber, created a second YouTube channel and donated 100% of its ad revenue to a community in Kenya which used that money to construct the first secondary school in their community and named the school after him.

1353.   Breastfeeding allows the baby to give germs to the mother so her immune system can respond and synthesize antibodies for her baby.

1354.   Jason Padgett was a jock who never made it past pre-Algebra, but, after being attacked outside of a bar, he started seeing the world in pixelated, geometric shapes. He soon understood the concept of pi, and had a sudden ability to hand draw complex fractals and is now a renowned math genius.

1355.   A Florida woman named Sara Barnes accidentally burned down a 3,500-year-old cypress tree. It was the fifth oldest in the country, and she did it because she was smoking meth under it and lit a fire so that she could see her meth better.

1356.   The town of Tikrit in Iraq erected a two-meter-tall monument to the shoe that was thrown by the journalist at George W. Bush during his final visit to Iraq.

1357.　A bear named Wojtek, which means he who enjoys war, fought in the Polish army in World War II. He carried shells to the front line and was taught to salute and even became a mascot for the soldiers. Although he developed a habit for drinking beer and smoking cigarettes, he survived the war and lived the rest of his life in the Edinburgh Zoo.

1358.　Limbo queen Shemika Charles had been training six hours a day since she was a teenager. She set a world record in 2010 and is now so flexible that she could actually limbo under a car.

1359.　In 2015, Adidas released a shoe made entirely from ocean trash, including gill nets and beach litter. The company stated that there is no shortage of material to produce this line.

1360.　When the mummified remains of Ramses II was transported in 1974, it was issued an Egyptian passport, which listed his occupation as king deceased.

1361.　A study done in 2011 shows that the brain responds to emotional pain the same way that it does to physical pain. So when people say rejection hurts, it's quite true

1362.　When Thor: The Dark World came out, a movie theater in Shanghai accidentally used a fan-made photo as the official poster for the film.

1363.　UK brothers Jeff and John Bitmead created a grown-up version of the red and yellow Little Tikes toy car. It's road legal, fully functional, and can go up to 370 feet (113 kilometers) an hour.

1364.　Mice can sing just like birds. It's simply inaudible to human ears.

1365.　Queen Elizabeth II has owned more than 30 Corgis over her reign.

1366.　Steve Jobs had a high school GPA of 2.65.

1367.　Hummingbirds have such a high metabolism that they are always hours away from starving to death.

1368.　In France, it is illegal for grocery stores to throw away edible food. Stores have to donate edible, unused food to charity or facilities that process it into animal feed or compost.

1369.　A survey conducted by 'Buy T-Shirts Online' says that those who wear black are seen as serious and reliable. Almost 50% of women and 64% of men agree that black exudes confidence.

1370.　Lois Gibson is the world's most successful police sketch artist. By being patient and talking to victims she's able to coax out realistic descriptions of the suspects. At last count back in 2007 she'd helped solve over 1,000 cases in Texas alone, in the 30 years that she'd been in the police force.

1371.　In 1893, the first graduating class of New Mexico State University had one student. His name was Sam Steele and he was murdered before graduation.

1372.   In developing countries, beehive fences are used to deter elephants by taking advantage of their natural fear of bees, and they worked. They have reduced conflicts between humans and elephants by over 80%.

1373.   The University of Oxford is so old that one of its constituent colleges New College was actually established in 1379.

1374.   Bamboo is the fastest growing plant in the world. It can grow up to 91 centimeters in a single day.

1375.   Because he didn't like to sign autographs, Marlon Brando's personal checks became collector's items. People often didn't cash Brando's checks because his signature was worth more than the checks were made out for.

1376.   There is an environmentally friendly spray-on coating for pavements called Star Path that makes pavement glow in the dark. Not only that, but it even adjusts to the level of natural light available and the darker it is the brighter it glows.

1377.   Ducks have accents. Just like humans they're influenced by their environment and this affects their communication making them quack in regional accents.

1378.   At 52, Rolling Stones bassist Bill Wyman married 18 year old Mandy Smith, but divorced after a year. Bill's 30 year old son Stephen then married Mandy's mother, age 46. If Bill and Mandy had remained married, Stephen would have been his father's father-in-law, and his own grandpa.

1379.   The Gobi chimpanzee war was a conflict between two communities of chimpanzees in Tanzania that lasted four years and included violent skirmishes, numerous deaths, and kidnappings.

1380.   If your friend has a hard time waking up, there's a sonic grenade alarm clock that might just do the trick. Just pull the pin, toss it into their room, and run for cover. It emits an ear splitting noise that they can't turn off until you decide to put the pin back in.

1381.   Voyager II was launched on August 20, 1977, and Voyager I was launched September 5th. They were sent on different trajectories and Voyager I was put on a path to reach Jupiter and Saturn ahead of Voyager II.

1382.   Canada is larger than the entire European Union. In fact, it's 33 times bigger than Italy and 15 times bigger than France.

1383.   If you have a fear of cheese, you have something called turophobia.

1384.   In order to get street view of a desert, Google hires camels to carry its trekker camera. The term Captcha stands for Completely Automated Public Turing Test to tell Computers And Humans Apart.

1385.   Scorpions glow a bright blue green when under ultraviolet light.

1386.   According to National Geographic, there used to be 100,000 wild tigers in Asia a century ago; now due to poaching, sadly there are only about 3,200.

1387.   According to a report by Michael Gibson Light, a doctoral candidate in the University of Arizona's School of Sociology, ramen noodles are now more popular than tobacco as currency in U.S. prisons.

1388.   The owner of the Gin Tub in Brighton, England had a Faraday cage built into its ceiling to block cell phone reception. He wants his patrons to socialize the old-fashioned way.

1389.   There are no natural lakes in the state of Maryland. All of the lakes are man-made by damming rivers.

1390.   According to Guinness World Records, the only man to be struck by lightning seven times was ex park ranger Roy C. Sullivan. He suffered a lost toenail, lost eyebrows, a shoulder injury, leg burns, an ankle injury, chest and stomach burns, and had his hair set on fire twice. Unfortunately, he ended up taking his own life after being rejected in love.

1391.   Jupiter's largest moon, Ganymede, has a saltwater ocean buried under 95 miles (152 km) of ice. Scientists estimate that it's 60 miles (96 km) thick, which is about 10 times deeper than our oceans.

1392.   After trick photography was developed in 1856, creating headless portraits became a trend that swept through the Victorian era.

1393.   The box jellyfish's venom is among the most deadly in the world. Human victims sometimes drown of heart failure from the pain and shock and survivors can continue feeling considerable pain for weeks after. They also often have significant scarring where the tentacle made contact with their bodies.

1394.   Flowers from bamboo are rarely seen. Some species can develop flowers after 65 to 120 years. But, what's most fascinating, is that if they do flower, all plants of that one bamboo species develop flowers at the same time no matter where they're located in the world.

1395.   Gasoline, kerosene, benzine, and turpentine all used to be used to cure head lice. References to it appear in medical journals as far back as 1917.

1396.   Antarctica has no reptiles. Reptiles need heat to keep their bodies functioning, so they cannot survive in severe, extended cold temperatures. They would literally freeze solid.

1397.   There's an island in Brazil that is untouched by humans because it is covered in deadly snakes. The Ilha da Queimada Grande, or Snake Island, has up to five golden lancehead snakes per square meter. The golden lancehead is responsible for 90% of snake bite related fatalities in Brazil. The snakes are so dangerous that the Navy has forbidden anyone from landing there.

1398.   There's an underwater museum off the coast of the Spanish island of Lanzarote called Museo Atlantico. It contains the sculptures of British artist, Jason deCaires Taylor, and depicts our changing, and sometimes destructive, role in the modern world.

1399.   Mark Spitz, 9 time Olympic champion, jokingly told the Russian swim team coach in 1972 that his mustache increased his speed in the water, deflecting water away from his mouth. The next year every Russian swimmer was sporting a mustache.

1400.   There's an aquarium in Japan called Keikyu Aburatsubo Marine Park, where they let you shake hands with otters.

1401.   Greenland allows its inmates huge liberties as part of its open prison system, aimed to rehabilitate prisoners. Inmates are allowed to leave the premises during the day for work or school and even go hunting with rifles. Believe it or not, some of them even hold the key to their own cell.

1402.   The world's ugliest animal is the Blobfish. A deep-sea fish that can live anywhere between 2000 and 4000 feet (600 and 1200 meters) below water, because of its lack of flesh and muscle structure.

1403.   According to a study conducted in 2012, people who complain actually live longer by about two years. This is because by complaining they release their tension which increases their immunity and boosts their health.

1404.   In 2014 an entrepreneur named Muchi Tsung developed a facial recognition software for cats. It's aimed to help cats maintain their goal weight by recognizing their faces and tracking their food intake.

1405.   In 2008 as part of a fundraiser, Father Adelir de Carle of Brazil, tied 1,000 balloons to an armchair in an attempt to break the world record for the most hours flying with balloons. Unfortunately the winds blew him off course and he lost contact with the ground.

1406.   Studies show that just one week of camping outdoors with only natural light is enough to reset the body's biological clock to normal sleep rhythms.

1407.   The tesla model S car aced all of its national highway traffic safety tests. In fact it's so safe that it actually broke the crash testing gear.

1408.   Lillian Weber is a woman from Iowa who makes a dress from scratch every single day so that a child in need can have something beautiful to wear. She has made over 840 dresses in the last several years for an organization called little dresses for Africa.

1409.   In 2014 scientists at MIT designed a device to help the blind read without braille. It's called the finger reader, and wearers can use it to scan a line of text with their finger and receive audio feedback of the words.

1410.   In order to advertise their services, prostitutes in ancient Greece wore sandals that left the words follow me imprinted in the dirt as they walked.

1411.   On the evening of September 11, 2001, hundreds of Iranian people gathered in Madar Square, Tehran, in a candlelight vigil to express sympathy and support for the American people.

1412.   There are more neurons lining your stomach than there are in your spinal cord, so your digestive system can work without needing your brain. In fact when you're flooded with emotion the neurons react and you get a gut feeling.

1413.   29 year old Alasan Dixon from Ireland has mastered the art of the animal selfie. Though they appear very casual he sometimes spends hours gaining an animal's trust before a shot.

1414.   Despite being a millionaire Steve Jobs only paid $500 a month in child support to his daughter Lisa. That's the same girl that he named the computer after, but still attempted to deny paternity for.

1415.   In 1986 Soviet pilot Alexander Kliuyev made a bet with a copilot that he could land an airplane blind. He curtained the cockpit windows and crashed the plane into a landing strip killing 70 out of 87 passengers.

1416.   There's a battery powered bell at Oxford University that has been continuously ringing for over 175 years. Nobody knows what the battery is composed of and no one wants to take the device apart in order to figure it out.

1417.   The 'Like-A-Hug' jacket gives you a hug whenever a friend likes one of your Facebook posts.

1418.   In World War II nine airmen escaped from their planes after being shot down during bombing raids. Eight out of the nine men were captured, tortured, beheaded and eaten. The ninth man was George W. Bush.

1419.   In 2015 a man named Torkel Kristoffers was arrested for kidnapping when his neighbors didn't recognize him with his new beard that he grew while taking time off of work.

1420.   Studies have suggested that gifted people often have bad handwriting because their brains are often working faster than their hand.

1421.   There's a biological reason why we can't resist puppy dog eyes. Sustained eye contact significantly raises oxytocin levels in both humans and dogs, which in turn encourages trust, love, and bonding. This response isn't found in even hand raised wolves, which suggests that humans and dogs may have co-evolved to share this trait in order to be companions.

1422.   In Finland, speeding tickets are calculated on a percentage of the person's income. This causes some Finnish millionaires to face fines of over $100,000.

1423.   Nobody has died from a confirmed spider bite in Australia since 1979. Deaths by spiders actually occur more from being surprised by them, like while you're driving.

1424.   Psychopaths are immune to contagious yawning and are less likely to be startled.

1425.   Yunessun Spa House in Hakone, a southeastern town in Japan, is now offering ramen noodle baths. The bath, consisting of ramen pork broth and synthetic noodles allegedly helps improve patient's skin.

1426. Colonel Sanders would often make surprise visits to KFC restaurants. If he was dissatisfied with the food, he would throw it on the ground and curse at the employees.

1427. Alzheimer's disease does not affect emotional memory as strongly as informational memory. As a result, Alzheimer's patients, when given bad news, will quickly forget the news but will remain sad and have no idea why.

1428. There is a popular tourist destination in Chongqing, China, where part of the pavement is devoted to cellphone users who are too busy looking at their screens to bother looking where they're going. Right beside it is another section of the road that completely bans the use of cell phones.

1429. There's an island in Alaska that's reflected in such a way that it looks like it's just floating in air.

1430. Route 50 in the United States is also known as the loneliest road in America because of the large desolate areas the road goes through.

1431. The most important organism in the world is marine algae because it produces about 70 to 80 percent of our oxygen.

1432. The word electrocute comes from the combination of electro and execute meaning death by electric shock. So technically if you survive an electric shock you aren't electrocuted but just shocked.

1433. When filming Mission Impossible, Tom Cruise vandalized the world's tallest building. He climbed to the top of the Burj Khalifa and etched his then wife's name, Katie Holmes, into the spire.

1434. Peacock flounders are masters of camouflage and can match the color of a checkerboard if they are placed on one.

1435. The FedEx logo has won over 40 design awards and was ranked as one of the 8 best logos in the last 35 years. And in case you never noticed it, the white arrow in the logo was an intentional design choice, crafted by blending two different fonts together.

1436. Steve Jobs' biological father was a Syrian immigrant.

1437. Women have twice as many nerve receptors as men, causing them to feel pain more intensely. However, they also have a higher tolerance for it.

1438. Meteors were initially only referred to as comets, a name given from the Latin word "comes" meaning hair, and were given their name for the flowing golden tail of hair that flashed through the sky.

1439. According to studies conducted at Turkey's Ataturk University and the University of Manchester, dogs and cats are right and left pawed, just like humans are right and left handed.

1440. If you could dig a hole through the earth and jump through it without dying, you would not come out the other side. You would fall down for 20 minutes until you reached the center, then technically, you would be considered falling up until you made it to the opposite surface. However, if no one was there to catch you, you would fall down again over and over forever.

1441.   Prior to the invention of rubber erasers in 1770 by Edward Nairne, people would use moist bread to erase pencil marks. In fact, the invention of the eraser, which fixes mistakes, was discovered by accident by Edward thinking that he had grabbed bread.

1442.   Henry Cavill almost missed the call for the role of Superman from Zack Snyder because he was playing World of Warcraft.

1443.   A study published by the Journal of Transportation found that people are in the best mood when they are bicycling compared to any other mode of transportation.

1444.   There exists a variation of soccer where three teams face off against each other at the same time.

1445.   The tallest outdoor elevator in the world is the Bailong Elevator, also known as the Hundred Dragons Elevator. It carries tourists 1,083 feet (330 metres) up the side of a massive sandstone column in a mountain range in China's Hunan Province. It's so big that it can carry 50 people at a time.

1446.   Britain is responsible for creating the lie that carrots improve eyesight, to distract the Nazis of a new technology that they made for night raids.

1447.   Frank Hayes, an American jockey, suffered a fatal heart attack in 1923 and died mid-race. His body remained on the horse and crossed the finish line in first place. He had never won a race before in his life.

1448.   Studies from the University of Chicago concluded that lonely people spend more time in their beds regardless of whether they're tired or not. Chronic loneliness can cause insomnia as well as the need to get in bed without feeling tired.

1449.   Rick Astley became an Internet phenomenon in 2007 with his video "Never Gonna Give You Up" when it became part of an Internet prank known as "Rickrolling". Sadly, he forgot to claim ownership of his work, and earned only $12 in royalties off of his nearly 150 million YouTube views.

1450.   In the Vietnamese version of Cinderella, "Tam Cam", Cinderella dismembers her stepsister, puts the body into a jar of food, and sends it to her stepmother to eat, who enjoys it until she finds a skull at the bottom of the jar, and then dies out of shock.

1451.   A "gut feeling" is actually a chemical signal that your stomach creates to warn your brain of danger.

1452.   Starting in 1979, the residents of Naco, Arizona and Naco, Mexico began an annual tradition of having a volleyball match over the fence of the border that divides them.

1453.   Thomas Jefferson proposed in 1784 to end slavery in all the territories, but his bill was lost in Congress by a single vote.

1454.   In Texas, it is against the law for anyone to have a pair of pliers in their possession.

1455.   Praying mantises can turn their heads 180 degrees. They use this ability to scan their surroundings using two large, compound eyes and three other simple eyes located between them.

1456.   When minimum wage first became a law in the U.S. back in 1938, it was 25 cents an hour and if you adjust that for inflation, it would be $4.31 cents an hour today.

1457.   New York's first Saint Patrick's Day parade was held on March 17th, 1762.

1458.   On March 13th, 1781, astronomer William Herschel discovered the planet Uranus. It was the first discovery to be made in modern times and also the first to be made using a telescope.

1459.   On July 16th, 1935, the world's first parking meter, known as the Park-O-Meter, was installed on the southeast corner of what was then First Street and Robinson Avenue in Oklahoma City.

1460.   Panama hats are actually made in Ecuador, not Panama.

1461.   Actor Tommy Lee Jones and Vice President Al Gore were freshmen roommates at Harvard.

1462.   Adidas will cancel any sponsorship deal that they have with a player if it turns out he has anything to do with Scientology.

1463.   "Puppy Pregnancy Syndrome" is an illness where the sufferer believes that they are pregnant with puppies after being bitten by a dog.

1464.   The Yakuza, Japan's largest organized crime syndicate, provided food, water, blankets, diapers and more during both the 1995 and 2001 Japanese earthquakes. They even had a faster response time than the Japanese government.

1465.   Doodlebug is an orphaned baby kangaroo that was found abandoned on the side of the road when he walked up to a human, held up his arms and asked to be picked up. The rescuer later gave him a teddy bear, and he wouldn't stop hugging it.

1466.   Jets leave a white trail across the sky for the same reason that you can see your breath in the winter. It's carbon dioxide and water creating visible moisture.

1467.   The sixth-tallest pyramid in the world is a Bass Pro Shops mega store, located in Memphis, Tennessee.

1468.   White supremacist and racist Craig Cobb said that he would take a genetic test and receive the results on live television. He was found to be 14% Sub-Saharan African.

1469.   A man named László Polgár developed a method to raise child prodigies. He wrote a book on it, married a language teacher, and they raised the world's best and second-best chess players.

1470.   In 2014, a fan was waving a flare at a Polish soccer game when a security guard used pepper spray on him, not knowing that the substances were combustible, causing him to burst into flames.

1471.   German canoeist Oskar Speck kayaked from Germany to Australia between 1932 and 1939, only to arrive to be declared as a prisoner of war due to the outbreak of World War II.

1472.   Scientists at the University of South Denmark have created "Aquaman crystals" that can actually absorb a roomful of oxygen and store it for later use. This discovery might actually be the key to underwater breathing. A handful of crystals could pull oxygen from the water and provide divers with air.

1473.   Killer whales that live in captivity with dolphins can learn their complicated language and they eventually actually begin to use it.

1474.   Harvard is officially free for those with less than $65,000 in annual family income. You still need to get the marks to get in however.

1475.   If a catastrophe or hacking group caused the Internet to crash, there are seven people in the world who have key cards that can reboot the system when five of the keys are used together. They literally hold the keys to the worldwide Internet security.

1476.   Researchers at Ohio State University have discovered something that they're calling experience talking. It's where, while reading a book or story, people actually change their behavior or thoughts to match those of a fictional character in a book or story that they can identify with. They subconsciously become that character.

1477.   The life expectancy of people with Down syndrome has increased from 25 in 1983 to 60 today.

1478.   According to research done by Aric Prather, assistant professor of psychiatry at The University of California, you are four times more likely to get a cold if you get less than six hours of sleep per night.

1479.   Actor Tom Cruise is only 5.6 feet tall.

1480.   Biologists led by Koji Nishida at Osaka University in Japan have discovered a new way to grow parts of the human eye, like the retina, cornea and lens just by using a small sample of adult skin.

1481.   According to a study done in 2013 by researchers at The Harvard School of Public Health, drinking several cups of coffee daily appears to reduce the risk of suicide in men and women by about 50%.

1482.   U.S. politician, Henry Kissinger, was the person who convinced Brazilian soccer great Pele, to play in The United States.

1483.   In 1140, when King Conrad III of Germany captured a castle, the women of the castle were granted free departure and allowed to take what they could carry on their backs. Thinking quickly, the women often carried the men on their backs. The king kept his word and let the men leave that way.

1484.   The female loggerhead turtle will sometimes travel thousands of kilometers to return to the beach where they hatch their eggs.

1485.   In 1978, serial killer Rodney Alcala, who murdered four women and a child, appeared on a game show The Dating Game and won.

1486.   White house physician, Admiral Joel T. Boone, invented a game called Hoover-Ball for President Hoover. It was a combination of tennis, volleyball and medicine ball created to help keep President Hoover physically fit.

1487.   All 10 of the documented people that lived the longest are all women, each range from 116 years old to 122 years old.

1488.   The plane that crashed in the movie The Dark Knight Rises with the use of computer generated special effects actually did crash the next year, killing two people on board.

1489.   The word emoji is the Japanese term for picture characters. Emojis were actually born out of necessity back in 1999, when mobile carriers were struggling to support the messaging needs of 80 million users of a rapidly growing technology of cell phones, and their hopes were that an emoji would reduce the need for multiple text messages or even picture messages.

1490.   Blue jays and cardinals go bald in the late summer and fall. Usually they lose all of their feathers and replace them gradually when they mount, but sometimes they lose them all at once, creating a bald head. They're only bald for about a week though, and their feathers grow back.

1491.   Actress Carrie Mulligan and singer Marcus Mumford of Mumford & Sons were childhood pen pals who lost contact. Each individually found fame and were reintroduced to each other as adults and fell in love.

1492.   Results from an online survey revealed that 11% of Americans think that HTML is a type of STD.

1493.   In 1859, English settler Thomas Austin released 24 rabbits onto his property in Australia, stating the introduction of a few rabbits could do little harm and might provide a touch of home in addition to a spot of hunting. By the 1920s, the rabbit population had reached 10 billion.

1494.   There's a place in California called glass beach, where years of people dumping garbage into an area of the coastline has resulted in the development of smooth sea glass. Believe it or not tourists in the area like to collect the glass, so now there's actually been a movement to replenish the beach with discarded glass.

1495.   Architects in Australia design a concept home called the cliff house. The concept shows a five-story house hanging off a cliff on the australian south west coast with amazing views of the Indian ocean.

1496.   Germany is a graveyard for unexploded bombs left over world war two. Disturbingly, an average of 2,000 tons of buried munitions are discovered there annually.

1497.   The Charbonnet Labatt funeral home became famous in 2014, for displaying the bodies of the deceased in upright poses. Disturbingly the phenomenon of the sitting dead actually first appeared in 2008 in Puerto Rico.

1498.   Apple generated $43.7 billion in sales in the first quarter of 2014 which was more than Google, Amazon, and Facebook combined.

1499.   The Hawaiian island Niihau is also known as the forbidden island. Elizabeth Sinclair bought it in 1864 and now her descendants the Robinson family own it. The island is completely off-limits to everyone except the islands owners, relatives, and invited guests.

1500.   Even though we're laughing when we're being tickled, it's actually our body's defense mechanism kicking into gear in responding to panic and anxiety.

1501.   Madagascar houses some of the most exotic organisms on the planet. About 90% of all plant and animal species found in Madagascar are endemic, meaning that they're unique to a specific geographical location

1502.   During the first world war, there was a Christmas truce in 1914. In the week leading up to Christmas German and British soldiers had a series of cease-fires where they entered No-man's land to mingle and exchange seasonal greetings. That truce is seen as a symbolic moment of peace during one of the most violent events in history.

1503.   In 2012, more than 30% of all deaths in Russia were attributed to alcohol.

1504.   Herders in Finland spray reindeer's antlers with a reflective paint, so that they won't cause as many traffic accidents.

1505.   In 2011, after four years of planning, in two months, working every night from 10 PM to 5 AM, a team of hackers at MIT actually turned their Earth and Planetary Science Department building into a giant, multicolored, playable Tetris game.

1506.   During the Vietnam War, American troops would eat small amounts of C4 plastic explosive in order to get high.

1507.   Virtually all of the eyewear industry is controlled by one Italian company: Luxottica SpA, which owns brands such as Ray-Ban, Persol, and Oakley. They also make glasses for Chanel, Prada, Armani, Burberry, Versace, Dolce Gabanna, and a lot more. They also own retail brands like LensCrafters and Sears Optical.

1508.   The very first message sent between two computers over the Internet was back in 1969, and it was "lo". It was supposed to be "login", but the computer crashed after the first two letters.

1509.   Skeleton flowers have such delicate petals that they become transparent when it rains.

1510.   Having bridesmaids in a wedding wasn't originally for moral support. They were actually intended to confuse evil spirits or those who wished harm on the bride.

1511.   About 70% of the world's spice production comes from one country, India.

1512.   New York City has the area code 212 because rotary phones were used at the time, and the number uses the shortest dialing time.

1513.   In January of 2013, the finance minister of Zimbabwe announced that his country had only 217 dollars left in its bank account.

1514.   Mike Tyson was arrested a whopping 38 times by the time that he was 13 years old. He was sent to a boy's home where he found out that he could box and he started training professionally with a former boxer and the rest is history.

1515.   There's a charity organization called Food for the Poor that gives over 95% of their proceeds to the poor. Ironically their CEO's name is Robin Mahfood.

1516.   Marie Antoinette's last words were, Monsieur, I beg your pardon. She was apologizing to her executioner after she accidentally stepped on his foot on the way to the guillotine.

1517.   Humans are the kings of the planet when it comes to long-distance running. We can outrun every animal on the planet and run in conditions that no other animal can run in.

1518.   Forty-two-year-old Russian fisherman Igor Vorozhbitsyn was brutally attacked by a bear, but he was suddenly saved when his ringtone, that his granddaughter installed on his phone, Justin Bieber's 'Baby', went off, sending the bear running back into the woods.

1519.   The word "outlaw" originally meant outside the protection of the law, so you could rob or kill them without legal consequences.

1520.   At the Nuremberg trials, several Nazi leaders achieved genius level scores of an IQ test.

1521.   When 70-year-old farmer Winston Howe's wife of 33 years Janet died suddenly he decided that he wanted to create a lasting tribute to her, so he planted thousands of oak saplings in a six acre field and left a heart shaped point facing towards her childhood home.

1522.   Villagers in the Indian village of Marottichal began playing chess as an alternative to drinking after a ban on alcohol. The village is now known as Chess Village due to its near 100% chess literacy.

1523.   Japan keeps a defunct train station called Kyu-Shirataki on the island of Hokkaido running just for one girl, so that she can attend school every day. The train only makes two stops. One when the lone high-school student leaves for school and the other when she returns.

1524.   A typical Rihanna hit single costs around $75,000 to make, another million to promote it, but the lyrics are usually written in about 15 minutes.

1525.   In 539 BC, Persian king Cyrus the Great issued the first ever decree on human rights. He freed the slaves, declared that all people had the right to choose their own religion, and established racial equality.

1526.   Crack dealing is one of the most dangerous jobs in America, and the salary on average is only about $3.30 an hour.

1527.   Hitler actually had a pet alligator named Saturn, now aged 85 that Russians were gifted by the British government. Saturn is actually still alive and well, and can be seen at the Moscow Zoo.

1528.   There are a total of 15 countries with absolutely no military force including Costa Rica, Liechtenstein and Samoa.

1529.   Author Peter Benchley, who wrote Jaws, was the first-ever host of Shark Week. In the years since, MythBusters star Adam Savage, Dirty Jobs host Mike Rowe, late night host Craig Ferguson and former SNL star Andy Samberg have all filled the role.

1530.   Colorado-based company Apollo Peak has created a wine for cats. It actually contains no alcohol and is made of catnip with beets to give it that red wine color. It comes in flavors like pinot meow and moscato. Single serving bottles are $5, and eight-ounce bottles are $12.

1531.   In July of 2016, monks from Prince Edward Island, Canada, went all around the island buying up to 600 pounds of lobster just to release them back into the ocean. The purpose was to cultivate compassion for the lobsters and for all beings.

1532.   You can buy a fan just for your armpits. Japanese gadget-maker Thanko has developed the wacky gadget. It's a battery-run small fan that clips onto your sleeve to deliver cool air to your armpits for five to nine hours, but if that isn't long enough, you can actually connect it to your PC or a battery pack.

1533.   Since 1996, Harold Hackett from Prince Edward Island, Canada, has launched 4,871 messages in a bottle into the ocean and has actually received 3,100 responses. That's a 63.6% response rate.

1534.   Paris only has one stop sign. Every intersection in Paris is basically a mad free-for-all where you enter at your own risk.

1535.   In German there's something called Street Pong where there are touch screens installed on traffic lights so you can play pong with people across the street from you.

1536.   Research shows from 2014 that sleep patterns are linked with important character traits and behavior and that people who stay up late tend to take more risks than early risers.

1537.   Only one person has ever been killed by armed police in Iceland since it became an independent republic in 1944.

1538.   Anything that a duckling meets within the first 10 minutes after it's born will consider its parent forever.

1539.   Early on in Beyoncé's career, she was managed by her father, Matthew Knowles. He would make his daughter and the other members of Destiny's Child run a mile while singing so that they could perform on stage without getting exhausted.

1540.   In 1969, Bill Cosby won a Man of the Year Award and jokingly suggested renaming the award to "The Nice Guy As Far As We Know Award".

1541.   In 2007, Harry Potter star Daniel Radcliffe wore the same clothes home from a theater in London for six months in a row so that the paparazzi would end up with the same photos every day and therefore not be able to publish the pictures.

1542.   Sometimes female lions can develop manes. Such masculine females likely occur when the embryo is disrupted either at conception or while in the womb.

1543.   Engineers in Canada receive an iron ring to remind them to have humility. It's in memory of a bridge that collapsed twice due to incorrect calculations involving iron.

1544.   The 'your mother' insult is found in nearly all cultures and is as old as humanity itself, with examples in Shakespeare and the Bible.

1545.   Mobile phone throwing is a sport in Finland.

1546.   Dwayne "The Rock" Johnson released a motivational alarm clock. He created the app to help you get out of bed and meet your personal goals and the best thing is that there is no snooze button. There are 25 ringtones to choose from that were created by The Rock himself. For example, there's one that's just a mash up of sounds that come from his dog, a couple where he just keeps repeating the words beep and ring-ring, and another where he smashes a harp.

1547.   The world's biggest tire graveyard is in Sulaibiya, Kuwait. Every single year, gigantic holes are dug into the desert and filled with old tires. There are seven million tires there already and the dump is so large that it's actually visible from space.

1548.   There's a monument in Israel called the "9/11 Living Memorial Plaza" that was initiated and designed by Eliezer Weishoff. It was completed in 2009 for $2 million and sits on a hill overlooking Jerusalem's largest cemetery. It's a 30-foot bronze American flag that forms the shape of a flame to commemorate the flames of the Twin Towers. The base of it is made from melted steel from the wreckage of the original World Trade Center. Surrounding the monument are plaques with the names of the victims of 9/11.

1549.   In 2015, Disney banned the use of selfie sticks in their parks due to safety concerns. Gadgets were already prohibited on rides, but selfie sticks themselves pose a unique concern, as the long arms could collide with a ride's mechanism or stick another guest.

1550.   Swindon, England, is home to what may be the most confusing-looking intersection ever created. The 'Magic Roundabout' was designed by engineer Frank Blackmore of the British Transport and Road Research Laboratory back in 1972 to help alleviate traffic jams. The interchange consists of five separate smaller roundabouts supporting clockwise traffic; all situated around one larger central roundabout that runs counterclockwise. Believe it or not, traffic jams were greatly reduced.

1551.   The biggest stadium in the world is the Rungrado May Day Stadium, located in Pyongyang, North Korea. Completed on May 1st, 1989, it's used for sporting events but is more famous for being the place where the annual Mass Games are held, an artistic and gymnastic event with over 100,000 participants in it.

1552.   Some of the world's oldest sunglasses were discovered on North Baffin Island in northern Canada. They were created by the Eskimo or Inuit of the Arctic. Also referred to as snow goggles, they were created from bone, leather, or wood, with small slits to see through, designed to protect the eyes from snow-blindness caused by the sun.

1553.   'Hatebeak' is a black metal band whose lead singer is a parrot.

1554.   Wild dogs operate under a strict hierarchy while wolves will actually cooperate and communicate with each other to make decisions as a group.

1555.   In 1990, disabled activists got out of their wheelchairs and crawled up the steps of the Capitol, inconveniencing senators to encourage a vote on the Americans with Disabilities Act.

1556.   According to a study done in 2014 by St. Michael's Hospital, almost half of homeless men who took part in the study have suffered from at least one traumatic brain injury in their life. 87% of those injuries occurred before they lost their homes.

1557.   Until 1992, it was not required for electrical appliances in Britain to be sold with plugs on the end of them. Often, consumers had to attach them themselves.

1558.   Phil Collins' song 'Sussudio' was based on a completely made up word. When he couldn't think of actual lyrics to fill the line, he just left it in as the chorus and title.

1559.   Troll dolls were originally created in 1959 by Danish fisherman and woodcutter Thomas Dam. Dam could not afford a Christmas gift for his daughter Lila and decided to carve a doll out of his own imagination. Other children in the Danish town of Gjøl, saw the troll doll and decided that they wanted one and the rest is history.

1560.   Napoleon once removed the Mona Lisa from the Louvre so he could hang it on his bedroom wall.

1561.   Coral is actually an animal, not a plant.

1562.   Australian researchers at the Commonwealth Scientific and Industrial Research Organization discovered that drinking a cup of Asian pear juice before drinking alcohol resulted in fewer and/or diminished hangover symptoms the very next day.

1563.   A stowaway Greek cat once flew in the undercarriage of an Airbus A321 from Athens to Zurich. It had shock and hypothermia but unbelievably it survived.

1564.   The "PT" in PT Cruiser stands for Personal Transport.

1565.   Samsung, the manufacturer of TVs, home appliances, and of course cell phones, started off as a grocery store.

1566.   According to the National Severe Storms Laboratory, the part of lightning that we can see actually comes from the ground up, not the sky down.

1567.   In 2011, a cafe opened in Istanbul called the Down Cafe. They only hire staff between the ages of 18 to 25 with Down syndrome.

1568.   In 1891, Dr. James Naismith from Almonte, Ontario, Canada, invented the game of basketball. He cut out the bottom of a peach basket and hung it 10 feet in the air, and thus the game was born.

1569.   In 2014, the International Space Station had to be moved three separate times in order to avoid being hit by lethal-sized space debris.

1570.   Oregon's Mount Angel Abbey Museum houses the world's largest pig hairball. It's the size of a football.

1571.   According to the New England Journal of Medicine, a 30-year-old man from India developed an unusual flower-shaped cataract with 10 petals after sustaining a concussion from a bike accident.

1572.   In March of 2012, Israel adopted a law called the Photoshop Law, stipulating that fashion and commercial models should have a body mass index, or BMI, of at least 18.5. For context, a healthy BMI is between 18.5 to 24.9.

1573.   Adding cold cream to your coffee actually keeps it warmer longer when compared to just black coffee.

1574.   One in every 3,000 babies is born with a tooth.

1575.   A study done in 2007 by the Bayer College of Medicine determined that magnesium, not calcium is the key to healthy bones.

1576.   The Louvre Museum in Paris was the most visited museum in the world in 2014. There were 9.3 million visitors, almost the same amount of people as the population of Sweden.

1577.   Approximately 1500 earthquakes are recorded in Japan every year.

1578.   Seahorse babies eat as much as 3000 pieces of food a day. They have such a voracious appetite because they have no stomach and their digestive system has been described as inefficient, meaning that they must eat a lot in order to stay properly nourished.

1579.   A frog's tongue is about a third of the length of its entire body. In comparison, if a human had the same sized tongue, it would reach our belly button.

1580.   Researchers at the University of Oxford and the University of Queensland discovered that the small tropical archer fish can be taught to accurately recognize human faces. When the researchers display two faces side by side on a screen over a fish tank, one familiar and one unknown, the fish was able to recognize the same face 81% of the time in color and even more accurately in black and white images.

1581.   Donald J Trump is the oldest U.S. president in history at almost 71 years old.

1582.   Dolphins can't chew their food. Their teeth are only used to grip food and they'll shake and rub it on the ocean floor to tear it into smaller more manageable pieces.

1583.   The Moomin House Cafe in Bunkyo, Tokyo offers coffee, treats, and companionship of an enormous stuffed animal. They will actually seat you with a stuffed animal so that you don't have to dine alone.

1584.   In Singapore, the importation or sale of gum is illegal unless you have a medicinal reason for needing it.

1585.   There's a solar facility at Walt Disney World in Lake Buena Vista, Florida that is comprised of 48,000 solar panels and is in the shape of Mickey Mouse.

1586.   Researchers exploring the Northwestern Hawaiian Islands aboard the Okeanos Explorer came across the world's largest sea sponge. It was found 7000 feet (2100 feet) below the ocean surface and measured 12 feet long and seven feet wide.

1587.   In 2015, in the French city of Valenciennes, a couple actually named their baby 'Nutella'. A judge ruled that it was contrary to the child's best interest to bear that name, as it was the name of a spread. When the parents failed to appear in court, they renamed the child 'Ella'.

1588.   The average human scalp has 100,000 hair follicles.

1589.   According to the American Psychological Association's 2014 survey, the most stressed out people in America are millennials, which are people between the ages of 18 and 35, women, parents with kids under 18, and low-income households. The main source of stress was money.

1590.   The world's largest indoor beach is called the "Tropical Island Resort" in Krausnick, Germany. Built inside an old airplane hangar, it contains a 50,000-plant forest that spans over a 107,639-square-foot area, a spa, a waterfall, a whirlpool, and a water slide. In fact, it's big enough that you could fly a hot air balloon inside.

1591.   There are hundreds of stone slabs dotting the coastlines of Japan that give advice. This advice includes "high dwellings are the peace and harmony of our descendants", "remember the calamity of the great tsunamis", "do not build any homes below this point" and also "if an earthquake comes, beware the tsunamis". Some of these markers are more than 600 years old.

1592.   A handful of British companies are now offering "Pawternity", paid time off to take care of a pet in need.

1593.   Over 3200 confirmed new planets have been discovered by telescope.

1594.   London based ice cream company The Licktators, teamed up with breastfeeding campaigner Victoria Hilly to celebrate the birth of the royal baby number two by launching their breast milk flavored ice cream. The ice cream is called Royal Baby Gaga. It's made of donated breast milk that has been screened with hospital standards, and Madagascan vanilla.

1595.   If you are caught injuring or killing a swan, or stealing one of their eggs in the UK, you could be fined or could be sent to jail for up to six months.
1596.   South African architect Clara da Cruz Almeida has designed a little portable house that can be packed into a 258 square foot pod and shipped anywhere.
1597.   Gladiators were for the most part, vegetarians. Their diets consisted of barley and vegetables. This enabled them to put on weight to protect them during fights and make them appear more spectacular to the crowd.
1598.   Even though George Washington chose the site for the White House, he never actually lived there. In fact, he's the only president who did not reside in the White House.
1599.   There's a gang of women called the Gulabi Gangor Pink Gang in India, who stand up to abusers in the country. The gang was founded in 2006, and is based in Badousa. It has a whopping 400,000 members, and helps bring rapists, abusers, and corrupt policemen to justice. The women that join the gang are registered, given a small ID card, and wear a distinctive pink uniform, a pink sari. And for 500 rupees a year, they also get a stick to carry.
1600.   Lady Gaga has a whole genus of ferns named after her, a DNA sequence spells out Gaga, and the ferns have Gaga-like qualities. Some of them resemble her elaborate stage costumes, and one of them is even called the Gaga monstraparva.

1601.   According to a team of astronomers and geologists led by J. Alexis Rodriguez, at the Planetary Science Institute in Tucson, Arizona, there is evidence that there were two massive tsunamis on Mars billions of years ago. They were both triggered by meteor impacts and were millions of years apart. They created waves as high as 150 feet (45 metres).

1602.   The Hunger Games is banned in Vietnam. The movie was originally just delayed, but according to a member of the Vietnamese National Film Board, the board considers the film to be too violent, and unanimously voted for it to be banned.

1603.   Buzz Lightyear from Toy Story was actually named after astronaut Buzz Aldrin, the second astronaut to walk on the moon.

1604.   The first Ferris Wheel was invented in 1893 for the Chicago World's Fair by George W. Ferris. It was 260 feet (79 m) high, cost 50 cents per ride, and could carry 60 passengers in each of the 36 cars. That's a total capacity of 2,160 passengers.

1605.   In Alaska, it's against the law to look for a moose from an airplane.

1606.   The two abbreviated letters 'OK' first appeared in the Boston Morning Post in March 23rd, 1839 as a joke. When it appeared in print, it was intended to be a shortening of "Orl Korrekt", the then humorous misspelling of all correct. It appeared in newspapers and in the 1840 presidential campaign, and after that, we continued to use it to this day.

1607.   The highest flying bird in the world is the Ruffles Vulture. There is confirmed evidence of one flying at an altitude of 37,000 feet (11,300 meters) above sea level during which it collided with an aircraft.

1608.   The Indianapolis 500 has claimed more than 60 lives, at least one of them being an innocent bystander. In 1931, a wreck by Billy Arnold sent a stray tire flying out of the race track and across the street where it struck and killed an 11 year old, Wilbur Brink, while he was playing in his front yard.

1609.   In 1872, Victoria Woodhull was the first woman to vie for the presidency. She ran as an equal rights party nominee against Ulysses Grant. This was nearly 50 years before the 19th amendment gave women the right to vote.

1610.   There's an exhibition at the Isle of Wight Zoo in the UK dedicated to poop. It features feces from the animal world and the human world. It also features fossilized poop called coprolites that dates back 140 million years.

1611.   Up until 1564, the French celebrate New Years between March 25th and April 1st; but when the new Gregorian calendar was introduced, the festival was moved to January 1st. Those who resisted the change became victims of pranks, including invitations to non-existent New Year's parties on April 1st; and this is why we celebrate April Fool's Day on April 1st.

1612.   According to a study done in 2007 by Marshall McCue, a researcher in the department of biological sciences at the University of Arkansas, intense snake hunger can cause snakes to actually digest their own heart muscle; however, immediately following a nutritious meal, snake hearts can actually quickly rebuild themselves.

1613.   Some marine birds, like the penguin, have a supraorbital gland located just above their eyes that can remove sodium chloride from their blood stream. It works just like our kidneys, removing salt, which allows the penguin to survive without access to fresh water. The penguin excretes the salt byproduct as brine through its bill.

1614.   In 2016, according to the brand management firm Interbrand's annual ranking of the best global brands, Apple was number one for the fourth year in a row, with a brand value of 178 billion, and Google was number two with a brand value of 133 billion.

1615.   According to the Guinness World Records, the largest mouth in the world belonged to the bowhead whale. It can measure up to 16 feet long, 13 feet high, and eight feet wide. Its tongue alone weighs almost 2,000 pounds.

1616.   The fastest recorded avalanche in history was the volcanic explosion of Mount St. Helens on May 18th, 1980. The velocity reached was 250 miles per hour.

1617.   A study recently published in the journal of Neurobiology of Aging shows that the more flights of stairs a person climbs and the more years of school a person completes, the younger the brain physically looks. Researcher, Jason Steffener, a scientist at Concordia's PERFORM Centre, found that the brain age decreases by .95 years for each year of education, and it decreases 0.58 years for every daily flight of stairs climbed.

1618.   Cornell University discovered that the tiger beetle runs so fast, it can no longer see where it's going. It actually has to use its antennae to avoid obstacles.

1619.   New research published in the Journal of meteoritics and Planetary Science confirmed that the blade on the dagger found in Tutankhamun's tomb is made with materials from a meteorite. Scientists performed X-ray fluorescence spectrometry on it, which is a method used to learn more about elements of an object and what they're composed of. It was found to contain iron, nickel and cobalt; all materials found in chunks of space rocks.

1620.   A Yoctosecond is one-trillionth of a trillionth of a second and is comparable to the time that it takes light to cross an atomic nucleus.

1621.　There is such a thing as "braille tattoos". They're not like normal tattoos in that they're not made of ink, but instead are made of metal beads that are put under the skin to create designs of braille messages.

1622.　The smallest crocodile in the world is the dwarf crocodile. It grows to 1.7 meters in length and weighs only six kilograms.

1623.　Shakespeare used about 17,677 words in his plays, sonnets, and narrative poems. He invented about 1,700 or nearly 10% of those words by simply changing the prefixes and suffixes, connecting words together, borrowing from a different language, or simply inventing them altogether.

1624.　Former child rock stars Hanson have released a beer called 'Mmmhops'.

1625.　The result of a 40-year-long study published in Developmental Psychology points to a correlation between childhood defiance and success later in life.

1626.　Most of Wikipedia's entries are written by 1,400 individuals who do little, but contribute to the site, and over 50% of the edits are done by only 524 users.

1627.　The KGB once tried to blackmail the then Indonesian president Achmed Soprano with tapes of him having sex with russian women disguised as flight attendants. Except the president was not upset by being blackmailed and in fact, asked for more copies of the video to show back in his country.

1628.　In the 13th century, in order to discover which language humans would speak naturally, Frederick II, Emperor of Germany, placed 50 newborns in the care of nurses who would only feed and bathe the babies but not speak or hold them. The emperor never got his answer because all of the infants died.

1629.　The fin whale produces an average of 257 gallons (970 litres) of urine each day.

1630.　There's a toilet made by Kohler called the numi that has a heated seat, foot warmers, lights, and Bluetooth technology.

1631.　Salt and pepper actually comes in liquid form in space. If astronauts tried to sprinkle regular salt and pepper, it would just float around.

1632.　Cheese making artists at Dublin Science Gallery made cheese using bacteria from several artists and scientists that were collected using sterile cotton swabs from various parts of their body including a belly button, a mouth, and even tears.

1633.　Grand Banks, Newfoundland, Canada, is the foggiest place in the world with 206 foggy days every year.

1634.   The California condor is the largest flying bird in North America. Its wingspan can be as wide as 10 feet (3 metres) from tip to tip, and they can fly as high as 15000 feet (4600 metres) if the in the air by catching air currents.
1635.   The duck billed platypus and the echidna are the only two mammals to lay eggs.
1636.   More twins are born in Nigeria than any other place on earth.
1637.   The landscape arch in Arches National Park, Utah, has the longest natural rock span in the world, spanning 290 feet (88 metres).
1638.   The peacock spider does a little mating dance to attract a partner. Each type of peacock spider has its own style of dance.
1639.   Elephant Island, located off the coast of Antarctica has elephant moss growing on it that is over 5500 years old.
1640.   The Nile crocodile rolls and squeezes her eggs in her mouth to help her hatchlings emerge.
1641.   The White House, the Empire State Building, the Sears Building, and Dodger Stadium are so large that they have their own zip codes.
1642.   There are over 10 million weddings in China every year. Couples spend an average of $12,000 on each, and it's estimated that the wedding industry there will reach $120 billion by 2020.
1643.   A service dog named Opal not only leads her blind owner around; she's also become a guide dog to the family's previous guide dog, Edward. The previous dog had taken care of the owner for six years until he had his eyes removed after developing cataracts.
1644.   In the original book The Wizard of Oz, Dorothy's magical slippers were actually silver. They were changed to ruby red for the technicolor movie because it was believed that they'd stand out better against the yellow brick road.
1645.   Angela Stogner of the University of Vienna Austria discovered that giraffes can hum. The hum is a low frequency sound at about 92 hertz.
1646.   There's a restaurant called "Subsix" located at the Per Aquum Niyama Restaurant in the Maldives that is located 20 feet below the surface of the Indian Ocean. You can sit near floor to ceiling glass windows and watch schools of fish and more than 90 coral reef species while you eat.
1647.   The Dwarf lantern shark, according to the Guinness Book of World Records, is the world's tiniest shark. Male measures only about 6.3 inches in length.
1648.   There's a phenomenon known as "heteropaternal" superfecundation that is so rare that there are only a handful of documented cases in the world. The phenomenon is when two twins have two different fathers.

1649.   The gadget was the first atomic bomb ever made and was tested at Trinity Site, New Mexico on July 16th, 1945. The test code named Trinity was a success, unleashing an explosion with the energy of about 20 kilotons of TNT.

1650.   Punt guns is a type of gun that was first used in the 1800s. They were used in commercial waterfowl hunting and these guns fired almost one pound shots that could kill 50 to 100 birds in a single shot. The barrels had opening upwards of two inches in diameter and weighed over 99 pounds (44 kg) and measured almost 10 feet (3 metres) long.

1651.   One of the richest men of all time, J. Paul Getty, an oil and gas tycoon had a pay phone installed in his house after visitors racked up his phone bill.

1652.   The Bohemian Grove is a 137 year-old secret exclusive camp, only open to the rich and powerful men of the world. Richard Nixon was once a member, but cheerfully referred to it as "the most faggy goddamn thing you'll ever imagine."

1653.   There's a phenomenon called "Crown Shyness" where in some tree species, their crowns, when fully grown, don't touch each other. The tree canopy ends up with channel-like gaps and the weirdest thing is that scientists aren't sure why it happens.

1654.   In the 1996 movie Twister, a recording of a camel's moan was slowed down and used as the sound for the tornado.

1655.   Scorpions can survive being frozen and thawed and extreme heat up to 122 degrees Fahrenheit (50 degrees celsius).

1656.   Tulips used to be the most expensive flower. In the 1600s, tulips were more valuable than most people's homes and cost almost 10 times what the average working man would earn in a year.

1657.   On January 1st, 1976, the day that relaxed marijuana laws came into effect in California, Danny Finegood, an art student at Cal State, Northridge, and some of his friends took $50 worth of fabric to the Hollywood sign and changed it to read "Hollyweed". They used the gag as a school project, earning them an A.

1658.   In 2002, O.J. Simpson was charged and fined $65 for creating a wake in a manatee zone in his boat in a bay in Florida. He decided to plead innocent instead of paying the fine.

1659.   The island on the TV show Gilligan's Island was created in Hollywood in the middle of an artificial lake in CBS's studios. The set cost $75,000 to construct and had artificial palm trees mixed in with real plants and flowers.

1660.   When howling together, no two wolves will howl on the same note. Instead, they actually harmonize to create the illusion that there are more of them than there actually are.

1661.   The consumption of poppy seeds can actually cause positive results on drug screening tests.

1662.   The Darwin's bark spider is small and inconspicuous, but it can spin a web 25 meters across that's able to span an entire river and it's stronger than Kevlar.

1663.   In the Miombo Woodland area of Central Africa, scientists discovered an abandoned termite mound that is more than 2,200 years old.

1664.   According to the Guinness World Records, the smallest dog in terms of length is Brandy, a female Chihuahua from Florida. She measures only 6 inches (15.2 centimeters) from the nose to the tip of her tail as of January 31st, 2005.

1665.   The most lightning-prone place in the world according to NASA is Lake Maracaibo in Venezuela. Storms light up the skies almost 300 nights each year.

1666.   The holes at the top of pen caps are there to prevent you from choking if swallowed.

1667.   Scientists in Sweden have developed transparent wood that can actually be used as windows.

1668.   The restaurant Chomp Eatery in Los Angeles is offering a rainbow grilled cheese sandwich. In fact, the blue tastes like lavender, the green like basil, the red like tomatoes, and the yellow tastes like plain cheese.

1669.   According to research done in 2012, published in the journal of Chemosensory Perception, people who scored high on a test for psychopathy had more problems being able to tell different smells apart, and also identifying smells.

1670.   San Francisco is the first major U.S. city to require that all new buildings have solar panels installed on the roof.

1671.   According to a study done by The University of New South Wales, good manners go a long way. The study found that going out of your way to say thank you makes people see you as a person with greater interpersonal warmth. It can also make you a happier person.

1672.   The world's oldest lighthouse is the Tower of Hercules in Spain. It was erected in the first century and is still operational.

1673.   Pakistan's parliament is the first parliament in the world to be completely powered by solar energy.

1674.   President Calvin Coolidge had a pet raccoon named Rebecca. She was originally supposed to be eaten at their 1926 White House Thanksgiving dinner, but the Coolidge family found her to be friendly and docile and decided to keep her as a pet instead.

1675.   It's possible to be allergic to the cold. This allergy, called "cold urticaria", is an allergic response to cold temperatures triggering hives, swelling and itching and if the allergy is severe enough, it can actually result in fainting, shock, or even death and there is no cure.

1676.   In a new study published in the Journal of Entomology, a research team from the University of Florida and Union College found that bed bugs love the colors black and red and hate yellow and green.

1677.   Evel Knievel, the pioneer of motorcycle long jumping exhibitions, suffered 433 fractured bones and holds the world record for the most bones broken in a lifetime.

1678.   The world's largest specie of earthworm can be found in Gippsland in southeastern Australia. The giant Gippsland can get as big as 10 feet (3 metres) long.

1679.   In 1972, a few years after being elected to congress, Shirley Chisholm became the first black woman to run for the presidency. She never expected to win, but she ran to prove that Americans could vote for a black woman.

1680.   Queen termites have a really long lifespan and they are the oldest termite in the colony. They can live up to 50 years long and produce eggs for up to 10 years.

1681.   Melba toast and Peach Melba are both named after the most famous opera singer of the late Victorian era, Dame Nellie Melba.

1682.   According to researchers at the Washington University School of Medicine in St. Louis, moms who are supportive and nurturing during their children's preschool years can actually boost the growth of their kids' brains. They found that kids who were nurtured in their early years had a larger hippocampus, the part of the brain tied to learning, memory, and emotion control.

1683.   Tokyo has the world's first hedgehog cafe. It has 20 to 30 friendly hedgehogs of different breeds that you can actually spend time with and even take home.

1684.   Ukrainian drivers are converting their cars into being fueled by wood burners to save money on expensive gasoline.

1685.   Oklahoma man Paul Phillips loves fishing so much that he actually dug up his own pond and then built a house over it. There's a trap door in his living room that he can fish whenever he wants.

1686.   The Japanese spider crab has the largest leg span of any Arthropod, reaching over 12 feet (3.6 meters) in length.

1687.   For months, after returning from trips to space, many astronauts report letting go of objects in mid-air, still fully expecting them to float.

1688.   Margaret Anne Cargill left all of her stocks to be split between two charities after her death, totaling six billion dollars. This made her the most generous philanthropist in the world in 2012, even though she died in 2006.

1689.   Robert Gleason Jr was a convicted murderer who vowed to continue killing his fellow inmates until he was given the death penalty. He finally got his wish in 2013.

1690.   John Shepherd-Barron the inventor of the ATM originally intended them to have PINs that were six digits long, but his wife could only remember four digits at a time, so that became the standard.

1691.   In 2009 the Nigerian police force arrested a goat on suspicion of attempted armed robbery.

1692.   In Russia there's a capsule that's used to treat alcoholism that's implanted under the skin and causes a chemical reaction resulting in shortness of breath, nausea, and mental confusion if the person drinks alcohol. On an unrelated note, about 25% of Russian men die before they hit the age of 55, mostly due to alcohol.

1693.   The Kuru-Kuru Nabe is a pot developed in Japan that can stir its own contents when the water inside the pot gets hot enough.

1694.   Vin Diesel got his first acting break when he was only 7 years old when he and his friends broke into a theater to vandalize it. A woman stopped them however and offered them a script and 20 dollars each on the condition that they'd attend rehearsal everyday after school.

1695.   Ruth Lawrence is a child prodigy who passed the Oxford University Entrance Exam when she was only 10, coming first out of 530 candidates. She graduated after only two years in the bachelor's degree program and she earned a doctorate degree by the time she was 17 years old.

1696.   You can actually take a ride on the Hogwarts Express! It's a real train in Scotland called The Jacobite, and has been named for the most beautiful railway route in the U.K.

1697.   Male kangaroos flex their biceps and wrestle other males to attract female kangaroos.

1698.   Since 2005 Utah has reduced its rate of homelessness by 78% by providing homeless people with apartments and social workers, which actually cost less than the annual ER visits and jail stays.

1699.   Finland has the highest rate of recycled bottles in the world. With a return rate of over 90% for plastic bottles and cans and almost 100% for glass bottles.

1700.   Danny Lloyd, the actor who played the creepy little kid in 'The Shining', stopped acting as he grew up and went on to actually become a professor, teaching biology in Louisville.

1701.   The Anglo-Zanzibar War lasted only 38 minutes, making it the shortest war in history.

1702.   The word 'tsunami' means "harbor wave" in Japanese.

1703.   The scent of freshly-mowed grass is the lawn actually trying to save itself from injury. Plants release a number of volatile organic compounds called green leaf volatiles. When plants are injured, these emissions increase like crazy.

1704.   The still-beating hearts of live cobras are eaten as a delicacy in Vietnam.

1705.   Sea otters have skin pockets where they keep their favorite rocks to keep for cracking open mollusks and clams.

1706.   The praying mantis can actually camouflage itself by changing color. It can vary from dark brown to green to blend in with tree bark and leaves. This enables it to hide from predators and also sneak up on prey.

1707.   Steven Spielberg named the shark prop used in the 1975 movie Jaws "Bruce" after his lawyer.

1708.   Back in the 1920s, there were beach police that actually went around measuring women's swimsuit lengths to ensure that no one was wearing a swimsuit with a questionable length. If a woman was found violating the code, they would be forced to cover up or sent home or, in some cases, actually arrested.

1709.   Research from the Chinese Academy of Medical Sciences shows that people who ate spicy foods six to seven times per week had a 14% lower risk of premature death for all causes, rather than people who ate spicy food less than once a week.

1710.   On June 10th, 1986, two and a half year old Michelle Funk from Salt Lake City fell into a creek near her home. When rescuers finally pulled her out of the creek over an hour later, she had no pulse and wasn't breathing. Doctors put her on a heart-lung bypass machine and rewarmed her blood. Unbelievably, when her blood finally warmed to 77 degrees Fahrenheit, she woke up and is still living to this day.

1711.   The smallest commercial flight in the world is from the Westray Airport to Papa Westray Airport between two small Orkney Islands north of Scotland. It's only a distance of 1.7 miles and if the wind is ideal, it can take as little as 47 seconds from start to finish.

1712.   There's a Burger King in Finland with an in-house sauna. The 10-person sauna can be rented for $285 US for three hours and can be used for birthday parties or work events.

1713.   KFC in Hong Kong is offering lickable edible fingernail polish in two different flavors, original and hot and spicy.

1714.   Amsterdam has a houseboat that is a sanctuary for rescued cats. It's actually become a tourist attraction that receives about 4,500 visitors a year.

1715.   According to the World Health Organization, worldwide, up to 5 million people are bitten by snakes every year. The majority of these occur in Africa and Southeast Asia.

1716.   According to the World Health Organization, the number of people with diabetes has risen from 108 million in 1980 to 422 million in 2014.

1717.   September 10th, 1977, was the very last time that someone was executed by a guillotine.

1718.   Uruguayan architect Rafael Vinoly designed a ring-shaped bridge on Uruguay's southern coast, called the Laguna Garzon Bridge, to encourage people to slow down and take in the view.

1719.   There are some turtles, such as the Australian Fitzroy River turtle and the North American Eastern Painted turtle that can breathe through their butts as well as their mouths.

1720.   The Vermont Novelty Toaster Corporation introduced the toasted selfie. All you have to do is send it a selfie and they'll print it for you on a selfie toast-producing gadget in just 10 days.

1721.   Only female mosquitoes bite humans and animals. Male mosquitoes only feed on flower nectar.

1722.   Up until the late 1960s, long-haired male visitors to Disneyland were actually turned away because they didn't meet the unwritten dress code.

1723.   Bill Gates received an honorary knighthood from Queen Elizabeth, but because he's American, he cannot use the title, sir.

1724.   According to the Guinness World Records, the first human cannonball was a woman named Rosa Zazel Richter in 1877. She was shot at a distance of about 20 feet at Westminster Aquarium in London, England.

1725.   Rockefeller Center receives an average of 470,000 visitors on any given weekday, and almost 800,000 during the holiday season. The warehouse scene in Raiders of the Lost Ark was actually a matte painting created by artist, Michael Pangrazio. It took him three months to create, was painted on glass, and the live action shots were actually done through a hole in it.

1726.   Robert Behnke, a Wisconsin dairy farmer owns the queen cow of milk production. His cow, Gigi, has produced more milk in one year than any other cow, at 8,700 gallons. That's three times the national average for a dairy cow to produce in a year.

1727.   According to Professor Charles P Gerba of The University of Arizona's Department of Soil, Water, and Environmental Science, 20% of office coffee mugs carry fecal bacteria.

1728. In 1952, Albert Einstein was actually offered the presidency of Israel. However, he politely declined the offer.

1729. Mountain Dew is an old slang term for moonshine.

1730. The longest highway in the world is Highway 1 in Australia with a total length of 9000 miles (14,500 kilometers).

1731. When Anglerfish mate, they actually fuse together into a single fish.

1732. Emperor penguins can dive to 1850 feet (565 meters) underwater which is deeper than any other bird and can stay under for over 20 minutes.

1733. Steve Jobs once gave a secretary a brand new Jaguar after she told him that she was late because her car wouldn't start.

1734. While we have leap years, we also have leap seconds. Which are added every few years to adjust to the Earth's speed of rotation.

1735. All swans in England are the legal property of the queen.

1736. Scientific research from the London School of Economics and Political Science in 2010, shows that men who are unfaithful tend to have lower IQs.

1737. All surface water of the Atlantic Ocean is significantly saltier than the Pacific Ocean.

1738. The TV-show 'All in The Family' was the first primetime show to have a sound of a flushing toilet. For much of television's history, it was actually taboo to even show a bathroom, let alone have any sort of bathroom sound.

1739. Author J.K. Rowling, who wrote the Harry Potter series, also writes crime novels under the name Robert Galbraith. Books that she's published under her fake name include "The Silkworm and Cuckoo's Calling."

1740. WD-40 was invented by Norm Larsen back in 1953. He was attempting to concoct a formula to prevent corrosion, a task that's done by displacing water. WD stands for water displacement, and the 40 is because he finally gained success on his 40th attempt.

1741. The band 'Nickelback' got its name from Mike Kroeger's cashier experience at a Starbucks. Customers would pay $1.50 for a coffee that always only cost $1.45, so he would always have to give them a nickel back.

1742. In 1998, Kevin Warwick, a professor of cybernetics at Reading University became the world's first technical cyborg. He had a radio frequency ID implanted in his arm and could turn on the lights by snapping his fingers.

1743. In ancient Rome, women thought that if you wore leather pouch containing a cat's liver on their left foot during sex that it would prevent pregnancy.

1744. In 2014, the United States Department of Agriculture reported that the average American consumes up to 170 pounds of refined sugar every year.

1745. Pablo Escobar, the infamous colombian drug lord, collected exotic animals for his personal zoo. When his house was raided his hippos were released into the wild and now Colombia has the largest hippo outside of Africa.

1746.   Instead of keeping your departed loved one in an urn on the fireplace mantle, now, thanks to the company Bios Urn, you can keep them in the form of a tree. Bios Urn created 'Bios Incube', which is an incubator that monitors and cultivates trees from human ashes in people's homes.

1747.   Back in 1994, a man named Tony Cicoria was struck by lightning while standing next to a public telephone, and was resuscitated by a nurse who was waiting to use that phone. Not long after his recovery, he noticed that his head became flooded with music, so he went out and bought a piano, and is now a successful composer and performer.

1748.   Dinosaurs often used to swallow large rocks. These rocks stayed in their stomach and helped them grind up food.

1749.   Ann Hodges from Alabama is the only confirmed person in history that has ever been hit by a meteorite. On a clear day in November of 1954, she was having a nap on her couch when a softball sized hunk of black rock broke through her ceiling, bounced off a radio, and hit her in the thigh, leaving a pineapple shaped bruise.

1750.   On January 21st, 1977, in his first day in office, President Jimmy Carter fulfilled a campaign promise by granting unconditional pardons to hundreds of thousands of men who had evaded the draft during the Vietnam War by fleeing the country or failing to register.

1751.   Researchers that were training monkeys to recognize themselves in mirrors found that the first thing that the monkeys did was check out all the places on their bodies that they've never seen before, especially their genitalia area. The researchers found them contorting and spreading their legs in front of the mirror to get a better look at previously unseen corners of their bodies.

1752.   In Sweden, blood banks send texts to blood donors to notify them whenever their blood helps save a life.

1753.   Spain's national anthem, 'Royal March', has no lyrics.

1754.   American company Cabot Guns has made the first gun made almost entirely from a piece of Gibeon meteorite that crashed on earth approximately 4.5 billion years ago. The meteorite was originally found in Namibia in the 1830s.

1755.   Bison may look slow and not very agile, but they can run at 35 miles (56 km) per hour and jump as high as six feet off the ground.

1756.   There's a new contact lens invented by Canadian optometrist Dr. Garth Webb that can improve human vision beyond 20/20. The bionic lens replaces the natural lens of the eye in a painless eight-minute procedure. It takes effect in only 10 seconds and enhances eyesight for life.

1757.   Research conducted at the University of North Carolina concluded that loving someone and being loved in return makes wounds heal faster, due to the release of oxytocin in the blood.

1758.   Bruce Wayne, aka Batman, is part owner of the Daily Planet where Clark Kent, aka Superman, works, so essentially, Batman pays Superman's salary.

1759.   In 2003, a Coca-Cola employee was fired because he was drinking Pepsi on the job.

1760.   Ryan Gosling and Rachel McAdams hated each other when filming 'The Notebook'. However, after finishing the film, they actually fell in love and dated for four years.

1761.   The African Union intends on having a single, continent-wide currency modeled after the Euro. The most popular proposed name for the currency as of right now is the Afro.

1762.   In ancient Rome, women tried to dye their hair blond with pigeon dung. In Renaissance Venice, they used horse urine.

1763.   The word, 'stewardesses', is the longest word that is typed with only the left hand.

1764.   New Zealand doesn't have a single land snake, but it does occasionally get visited by sea snakes.

1765.   The California grizzly bear was designated as the official state animal of California in 1953, more than 30 years after the last one was killed. It was also honored on the state flag.

1766.   Studying the earwax of a blue whale can tell scientists the story of its life. The technique, described in the proceedings of the National Academy of Sciences, can be used as a tool to understand the whale's hormonal and chemical biography. It can also be a window into how pollutants, long discontinued, can still pervade the environment today.

1767.   On October 18, 1963, French scientists launched the first cat into space on a Veronique AGI Sounding rocket number 47. The cat, named Felicette, was successfully retrieved after a parachute descent.

1768.   Sweden was the first nation to make it illegal to strike a child as a form of punishment known as corporal punishment back in 1979. Since then, many other countries in Europe have also instituted this ban as well as New Zealand and some countries in Africa and the Americas.

1769.   According to the Guinness World Records, the largest chocolate bar, by weight, was created by Thorntons in Alfreton, Derbyshire, U.K., on October 7, 2011. The bar measured 12 feet by 14 feet by one foot thick and weighed a whopping 12,700 pounds (5500 kg).

1770.   It's illegal except in extreme circumstances to neuter your dog in Norway. They believe in social neutering and training.

1771.   The puffer fish or blowfish has enough toxin in it to kill 30 adult humans, and there is no antidote, but amazingly, the meat of some pufferfish is still considered a delicacy.

1772.   None of the members of The Beatles could read music. Music was a discovery process for them and did not involve any books.

1773.   Mathematician Katherine Johnson is known as the 'computer'. Her obsession with counting allowed her to skip ahead in high school at the age of 10, and in 1961, she calculated the trajectory of NASA's first trip into space and was correct.

1774.   The only domestic animal not mentioned in the Bible is the cat.

1775.   Nicholas Cage once woke up to a naked man wearing a leather jacket eating a Fudgesicle in front of his bed. After that, Cage could no longer live in that house and moved to the Bahamas.

1776.   A man with a Liverpool FC tattoo with the club motto "You'll never walk alone" had his lower leg amputated after a combat injury in Afghanistan. Unbelievably, the surgeon unknowingly cut his tattoo so it now reads "You'll never walk". However, in reality, luckily, the man now has a prosthetic leg and competes in marathons.

1777.   The indigenous Sami people of Norway have a tradition of castrating reindeer with their teeth.

1778.   Military commandos in Lebanon eat live snakes, a tradition that displays their strength and daring.

1779.   Thousands of condoms were issued to soldiers for D-Day. Most of them were used to keep their rifles dry.

1780.   Snow monkeys in Japan entertain themselves by making snowballs.

1781.   Russian criminals used to get tattoos bearing the images of Lenin and Stalin because it was a commonly held belief that Communist firing squads were not permitted to shoot at an image of their leaders.

1782.   Gabe Belfiore of Cortez, Colorado built the 'Dog Gone' vacuum truck. It's used to suck prairie dogs out of their burrows.

1783.   Scientists estimate that a single ragweed plant can release one-billion grains of pollen over the course of a single season and can travel hundreds of miles on a gentle breeze.

1784.   The great white shark is an example of an apex predator, which means, as an adult, it has no natural predators in its ecosystem.

1785.   The pope has his own vehicle that he uses at public appearances called the popemobile. It has bulletproof glass that surrounds him, as well as a handrail for him to hold on to while he stands and waves at the crowd in order to get in and out. It's designed to protect him and still allow him to be visible to the crowds.

1786.   Every year, London holds the Great British Duck Race, where people purchase rubber ducks to help support various charities. The ducks are raced more than half a mile down the River Thames, and the first one over the finish line wins a cash prize.

1787.   In 2009, they set a world record for the largest plastic duck race with over 205,000 ducks.

1788.   The vampire fish impales their prey with their long, sharp fangs. Their fangs can grow as long as six inches.

1789.   All NHL hockey pucks are frozen before the game because they glide smoother and faster when frozen.

1790.   The trap-jaw ant from Central and South Africa can snap its jaw shut at a speed of up to 145 miles (233 km) per hour. To put that into context, that's 2300 faster than the blink of an eye.

1791.   According to a study led by Igor Malyshev, a zoologist at St. Petersburg State University in Russia, the Australian red kangaroo and the eastern gray kangaroos are almost always left handed.

1792.   Bellandur Lake in Bangalore, India, is so toxic that it's covered in froth and sometimes bursts into flames. The foam on it is the result of toxic water which has a high amount of ammonia and phosphate, and very low dissolved oxygen because of decades of untreated chemical waste going into it. Because of the amount of grease, oil, and detergent in the froth, it often catches fire.

1793.   According to researchers at the Donald O. Perelman Department of Dermatology at The New York University School of Medicine, the higher up you are in altitude, the higher your risk of getting sunburned, and it's quite a bit more, approximately 60% higher.

1794.   During the opening ceremony of the Olympic Games, the procession is always led by the Greek team, followed by the other teams in alphabetical order, and the last team is always the team of the hosting country.

1795.   There's an isopod called the Cymothoa Exigua that eats fish tongues and then becomes the fish's tongue.

1796.   Researchers at McGill University in Montreal, Canada raised a fish called the Polypterus. It can breathe air and walk on land using its front fins.

1797.   When lobsters fight or flirt with each other, they actually squirt urine at each other's faces from little urine release nozzles under their eyes.

1798.   In 2006, the Hao Sheng Hospital in Japan decorated their maternity ward with all Hello Kitty-themed murals and items to help calm anxious mothers. The cartoon image is on everything, from walls to newborn baby blankets. A giant Hello Kitty figure is dressed in a pink doctor's uniform that even greets visitors in the lobby.

1799.   Teratoma tumors can grow hair, teeth, organs, and limbs, and scientists have no idea why they form.

1800.   The average person blinks about 12 times per minute. That's about 10,000 blinks on average, per day.

1801.   A kitchen faucet would need to be turned on all the way for at least 45 years to equal the amount of blood pumped by the heart in the average lifetime.

1802.   The University of Southern Queensland found that facial hair can block up to 95% of the sun's harmful UV rays.

1803.   An ostriches' powerful long legs can cover ten to sixteen feet (three to five meters) in a single stride. Their legs can also be formidable weapons. In fact an ostrich kick can kill a human or a potential predator like a lion.

1804.   The deepest lake in the world is Lake Baikal in Siberia. It's over 5383 feet (1,641 meters) deep, and is also the most voluminous freshwater lake on Earth, containing nearly 20% of the world's unfrozen fresh water.

1805.   On October 2nd, 1954, Elvis Presley made his first and last Grand Ole Opry appearance. Apparently, his gyration-filled performance was not well received and one of the officials there reportedly told him not to quit his day job, which was driving trucks.

1806.   Actor Brad Pitt's first acting job was playing a chicken. He wore a chicken suit to attract customers to an El Pollo Loco restaurant in Hollywood. Today, the 55-year-old actor has been in more than 70 movies, won an Academy Award out of five nominations, and more.

1807.   While editing his biggest movie, the Titanic director James Cameron taped a razor blade to the side of the computer with instructions that says, "Use only if the film sucks." But he didn't need to worry very much because the film went on to gross a total of $1.84 billion worldwide.

1808.   An underground fire in the coal mines beneath Centralia, Pennsylvania, has been burning since 1962. Astonishingly, nobody knows how the fire even started, but one theory is that burning trash from a nearby landfill accidentally ignited coal beneath the old entrance to the mine. From there, the fire spread wildly through all the mines.

1809.   There is a scented cup that tricks your brain into thinking that regular water is actually flavored with citrus, apples, berries, peaches, or cola. The invention, called The Right Cup, was launched on Indiegogo in early 2016 in hopes that people will drink more water if it has a more exciting taste.

1810.   The word canvas was derived from the Latin word 'cannabis'. Canvas made from hemp was quite popular among artists who needed a cheap writing material, right up until the end of the 18th century.

1811.   Boa constrictors have an innate ability to sense its prey's heartbeat. If it senses a heartbeat, the snake will actually add more pressure until it feels no heartbeat.

1812.   There is a humpback whale that has been tracked by Greenpeace since 2008 called Mr. Splashy Pants.

1813.   About half of Australia's koalas have chlamydia. In fact, their strain of Koala chlamydia can also infect humans.

1814.   You can pay to go on expeditions with National Geographic to exotic places like Antarctica.

1815.   There's a golf course in Brisbane, Australia with full grown bull sharks living in the water hazards.

1816.   The Pineberry is a white strawberry that tastes like a pineapple.

1817.   A study published in the Journal of Neuroscience found that anxiety disengages the prefrontal cortex, a region of the brain that plays an important role in flexible decision making.

1818.   The Japanese company YKK makes approximately half of the world's zippers.

1819.   Tug of War was once an Olympic sport in the early 1900s.

1820.   Two of the world's largest rivers, the Amazon, and the Rio Negro, meet but do not mix and are visually distinct but occupy the same body of water. This is due to the river's different speeds, density, and temperatures.

1821.   Research shows that others see you as 20% more attractive than you think you are. This is because when you look in a mirror, all that's reflected are your looks, not your personality.

1822.   The world mortgage is derived from French, meaning death pledge. Referring, of course, to the death of a loan because you amortize a mortgage.

1823.   It is theoretically possible to get addicted to cuddling. Couples that cuddle a lot can actually, experience oxytocin withdrawal when they are apart from each other.

1824.   Dogs don't feel guilt or shame. However, they do feel sadness when their owners yell at them.

1825.   In Japan's Brazilian Washuzan Highland Park, there's a scary roller coaster called the Sky Cycle. On it, people actually pedal to propel themselves forward through the track.

1826.   It is easier to get into Harvard than it is to get a job at Apple's newest store in New York. Harvard's acceptance rate is 7%, while Apple's is only 2%.

1827.   In 1979 a woman named Elvita Adams attempted suicide by jumping off the 86th floor of the Empire State Building. She survived when a gust of wind blew her back onto a ledge on the 85th floor.

1828.   Pike County farmer and loyal Democrat, Valentine Tapley, vowed to never trim his beard again if Abraham Lincoln was elected president in 1860, and he kept his word. His beard grew to 12.5 feet (3.8 meters) long.

1829.   In 1964, a pair of Australian scientists, Isabel Joy Bear and RG Thomas, did a study to determine what causes that powerful, wonderful scent of fresh rain.

1830.   They determined that it's a mixture of plant oils that are secreted by some plants after an arid period, bacterial spores, and ozone.

1831.   On March 29th, 1867, The United States bought 586,412 square miles of land at the northwestern tip of the North American continent, which is the current state of Alaska from Russia. They paid 7.2-million dollars, which amounted to about two cents per acre.

1832.   Disney Parks can actually refuse you access to their parks if they find that you have an objectionable tattoo.

1833.   Cats can actually get something called whisker stress from eating or drinking out of a bowl that's too small. Whiskers are very sensitive to pressure, and any time they come close to something, it triggers a sensation in your cat. If you see your cat trying to scoop out food with their paw, it might mean that they have whisker stress.

1834.   If you consumed coconut oil or coconut meat lately, there's a reasonable chance that it was imported from Thailand. Thailand has been raising and training pig-tailed macaques to pick coconuts for around 400 years. In fact, a male monkey can collect an average of 1,600 coconuts a day and a female can get around 600. A human can only collect around 80 maximum a day.

1835.   Narwhal skin is an important source of Vitamin C for the Inuit people. Ounce for ounce, there is almost as much Vitamin C in Narwhal skin as than there is in an orange.

1836.   Our urge to breathe is not because of our need for oxygen but our bodies wanting to get rid of carbon dioxide.

1837.   David Hasselhoff has a 14 foot (4.27 meter) tall replica of himself from the SpongeBob Squarepants movie.

1838.   Cockroaches are not the toughest insect when it comes to resisting nuclear radiation. Insects like the flower beetle have been proven to have higher nuclear radiation resistance.

1839.   People who live in Estonia have been able to vote via the internet since 2005.

1840.   It has actually snowed in the Sahara desert, in 1979 and 2012.

1841.   The trombone was originally called the sackbut.

1842.   Port Lincoln, Australia holds an annual festival called the Tunarama. The main event is the world championship tuna toss competition where the winner is the one who can throw their tuna the farthest.

1843.   There is a sauna in Norway that can house 150 people. It's a large timber construction set on a beach overlooking the Arctic Ocean.

1844.   The bowhead whale, which lives exclusively in the Arctic, has the thickest blubber of all of the whales. It can get as thick as 28 inches (71 cm).

1845.   Hurricane Patricia, from 2015, is the strongest hurricane recorded in the Western Hemisphere. It had winds as high as 200 miles (321 km) per hour.

1846.   Owls are unable to roll or move their eyes, so they have to turn their heads to look sideways.

1847.   Australians are the world's biggest meat eaters. They consume about 200 pounds (90 kg) per year, and the United States is right behind them, consuming just under that at 198 pounds (89 kg) a year.

1848.   According to a study published in the South African Journal of Science, traces of cannabis were detected on pipes that were found in William Shakespeare's garden. Scientists examined 24 pipes using advanced gas chromatography methods and found cannabis on eight fragments, four of which were confirmed from the Bard's garden.

1849.   There are little tiny holes or pores in chicken and other bird eggs that allow baby birds to breathe in oxygen and get rid of carbon dioxide. A chicken egg has more than 7,000 pores.

1850.   Prince Charles is actually a descendant of Vlad the Impaler, the cruel 15th century Romanian warlord who helped inspire Bram Stoker's 1897 vampire novel, Dracula.

1851.   In the 1940s, there was a remote control for the Ga rod TV set that was attached to the set with a 20-foot cable. When you pushed the button.

1852.   There's an animal called a wholphin, which is a cross between a false killer whale and bottlenose dolphin. They are hybrids that are believed to live in the wild but have also been born in captivity.

1853.   The Nazis had a plot to kill Sir Winston Churchill with a bar of exploding chocolate during the Second World War. Hitler's bomb makers coated explosive devices with a thin layer of dark chocolate and packaged it in expensive-looking black and gold paper, but luckily, the plot was foiled by British spies.

1854.   Henry Ford's estimated net worth would have been 200 billion dollars today if he were still alive.

1855.   Super Mario was originally known as "Jumpman".

1856.   The sea anemone looks like a beautiful flower, but it is really a sea creature that uses venom-laden tentacles to stab passing victims with paralyzing neurotoxin, rendering them helpless.

1857.   The word 'prolly', the informal pronunciation of probably originated in the 1940s.

1858.   Unlike other planets that take their names from Greek mythology, Uranus' moons are named after characters in Shakespeare's plays. These include Umbriel, Cordelia, and Ariel.

1859.   In rural China, hiring strippers to perform at funerals was a common practice in order to attract mourners. It wasn't until 2015 that it was finally banned.

1860.   Thousands of microscopic mites live on your face right now. There are two species, Demodex Folliculorum that reside in your pores and hair follicles and D. Brevis that settle deeper in the oily sebaceous glands in your face.

1861.   An average elephant can hold and store four liters of water in its trunk.

1862.   Large dogs age faster and die younger than small dogs and scientists are still uncertain why this is.

1863.   According to vet Joyce Armen, horses can safely drink alcohol because of their huge mass.

1864.   Mickey Mouse has a brand recognition of 97% which is higher than Santa Claus.

1865.   Spain offers citizenship to the descendants of those who came to the Americas to flee the Inquisition.

1866.   There is a reverse color blindness test that exists, where only people who are colorblind can see what the hidden image is.

1867.   On April 14th, 1986, Bangladesh was hit by the biggest hailstones ever recorded, weighing in at over 1 kilogram each, killing 92 people.

1868.   Before mating, the female giraffe will urinate in the male's mouth. From the taste of her urine, the male can determine if she's in heat or not.

1869.   The original Twinkie filling was actually banana-flavored. It wasn't until World War II that there was a banana shortage, so vanilla became the standard flavor.

1870.   One in two million lobsters is blue; but one in every three million can be yellowy-orange; and even rarer are white lobsters. Each of these colors only shows up about once every few years.

1871.   It is possible to cry in outer space. However, your tears never fall; they just sort of sit there like a blob under your eye.

1872.   In 2009, in the jungles of the Philippines, scientists discovered a new species of pitcher plant. It's the largest carnivorous plant ever discovered. It's called the "se-Nepenthes attenboroughii", named after Sir David Attenborough. Other meat-eating plants eat things like insects and spiders, but this one's so big that it actually eats rats.

1873.   McDonald's Hamburger University trains students in restaurant management skills, and has over 275,000 graduates with a selection rate of one percent at its Shanghai Campus; this intense week-long training program is more exclusive than Harvard.

1874.   After years of campaigning by conservationists, in May of 2016, President Obama signed a National Bison Legacy Act into law, making the North American bison the official mammal of the United States. It's the first official mammal recognized by the federal government.

1875.   On May 15th, 1809, Connecticut woman Mary Kies was the first American woman to receive a patent. Her innovation was to make a hat by weaving silk or thread into straw, creating a pleasing appearance that became a fashion fad.

1876.   The Pacu fish, native to South America, was found in New Jersey in June of 2015. It's a relative of the flesh-eating piranhas and is known for its distinctive teeth, which bear an eerie resemblance to human teeth. Luckily, the Pacu fish is not going to bite your face off because it primarily eats plants and is considered mostly harmless to humans.

1877.   United Kingdom-based horticulture company Thompson & Morgan has developed a plant that grows both cherry tomatoes and potatoes. It was developed in Canada and is being called the ketchup and fries plant and can be bought in Canadian Costco retailers and even in some independent garden centers.

1878.   Some children in southwest China between the ages of 6 and 15 have to scale a cliff about 2600 feet (800 meters) high multiple times a month in order to get to their school. The school, located in Atule'er village, takes about 90 minutes to get to.

1879.   At the 2008 Olympics in Beijing, China, visitors could buy seahorse kebabs and deep-fried scorpion. It's estimated that up to 40,000 restaurants ended up adding crazy twist menu items such as this.

1880.   Ellen Church was the first female flight attendant who began flying in 1930. She implemented a plan that required all flight attendants to be a registered nurse, which was a great idea, except when World War II began, all of the nurses enlisted in the war, so most airlines were forced to drop the requirement in order to find any workers.

1881.   The esophagus of a leatherback sea turtle is lined with papillae, sharp prongs that enable the turtle to dine on jellyfish.

1882.   In 2011, Tom Pearcy, a farmer from York, England, created a maze by carving two football-field sized portraits of Harry Potter into a corn field.

1883.   If you have an irrational fear of being near, or in the company of teenagers, you have what's called ephebiphobia.

1884.   In ancient Egypt, people were paid for their services in bread and beer. They were also paid in grain, meat and cloth rations, which were considered the necessities of life. But bread and beer were the most basic of the Egyptian diet.

1885.   In 2016, the Ed Rolf family from Turkey got food poisoning from eating food that was prepared to celebrate getting out of the hospital for food poisoning.

1886.   Ancient Greeks valued political participation and collective governance. The term idiot was used in Ancient Greece to describe someone who did not contribute to politics or the community.

1887.   The state of Alaska has over three million lakes. In fact, 86,000 square miles (222,000 square kilometers) of Alaska are covered by water.

1888.   Hawks have vision that's about eight times more accurate than humans. They have up to one million photoreceptors in the retina compared to only 200,000 in humans.

1889.   The first garbage disposal was invented by architect John W. Hammers in 1927. He wanted to make cleaning up for the kitchen easier for his wife.

1890.   In Fairbanks, Alaska, the Aurora Borealis can be seen an average of 240 nights a year. On those nights, the sky is lit up with colors ranging from yellow and greens to reds, purples and blues.

1891.   The black and white patterned undersides of a humpback whale are distinctive for each whale. The shape and color patterns on their dorsal fins and flukes are like fingerprints for humans.

1892.   In 2013, Navy Veteran Lonnie Bedwell became the first completely blind kayaker to paddle the entire length of the Grand Canyon, 226 miles (363 km) in a solo kayak. It took him 16 days.

1893.   There are numbers on the lampposts in New York City's Central Park to help people navigate where they are if they get lost. The first two or three numbers indicate the closest cross street, and the last number indicates what side of town that you're closest to. If you're an odd number, that means you're on the west side, and if you have an even number, that means you're on the east.

1894.   There's a beaver dam located in Wood Buffalo National Park in northern Alberta, Canada, that is so large, it can be seen from outer space. It spans 2,789 feet (850 meters) across.

1895.   Personal finance website Finder.com has launched a programmable handbag designed to help you monitor and curb your impulsive spending. Using GPS tracking, it can be programmed to lock if you enter your pre-programmed danger zones. It will actually vibrate and flash lights to indicate how many times you've taken out your wallet. It will also flash yellow lights and vibrate every two hours to remind you to put on sunscreen.

1896.   In August of 2016, 323 reindeer were killed with a single lightning strike in the Hardangervidda National Park in Norway. They were huddled together because of a heavy storm and were killed because of ground current that had stopped all of their hearts.

1897.   A man named Mbah Gotho of Indonesia claims to be 146 years old, and there is a photo of his government ID card to prove it. The card shows his birth date as December 31, 1870. He has outlived all 10 of his siblings, four wives and his children.

1898.   The Lithuania village of Ramygala holds an annual beauty pageant where the contestants are goats. Around 500 people brave the summer heat to attend the parade in honor of the goat, a traditional symbol of the northern village.

1899.   According to a survey done by Pew Research in 2016, of 1,520 adults living in all 50 states and the District of Columbia, just over one in four people didn't read a single book within the last 12 months.

1900.   On May 17th, 2016, a woman named Mary Anne Noland had her obituary published in the Richmond Times which stated that faced with the prospect of voting for either Donald Trump or Hillary Clinton, she literally chose to die.

1901.   On May 19th, 2004, a boa constrictor triggered a 15-minute nationwide blackout in Honduras when it got itself trapped between two enormous generation units. The boa was electrocuted and the resulting short circuit caused the emergency system to shut down the entire plant, which shut down the country's electricity.

1902.   Rhinotillexomania is the scientific word for picking your nose. "Rhino" means "nose", "tillex" means "habitual picking", and "mania" means "rage or fury".

1903.   It's actually possible to cause your eyeball to pop out of its socket, known as exophthalmos, by blowing your nose too hard, vomiting, or coughing excessively. The good news is if you're brave enough, you can just pop it back in.

1904.   Arachibutyrophobia is the name for the fear of peanut butter sticking to the roof of your mouth.

1905.   The children's ring game 'Ring Around the Rosie' refers to the Great Plague of London back in 1665. The 'ring around the rosie' refers to the rosy red rash in the shape of a ring that someone with the plague would develop. The 'pocket full of posie' refers to the fact that people filled their pockets and pouches with sweet-smelling herbs or posies because they believe that the disease was transmitted via bad smells and the 'ashes', that refers to the 'cremation of the dead bodies'.

1906.   The word 'Exocannibalism' refers to when you eat someone outside your own family or tribe. 'Endocannibalism' is when you eat someone from the same community or tribe.

1907.   Back in 2013, PayPal accidentally put over $92 quadrillion into PR executive Chris Reynolds' account. PayPal admitted their error and offered to donate money to a cause of Reynolds' choice.

1908.   Jessica Cox, born in 1983 in Sierra Vista, Arizona, was born without arms due to a rare birth defect. She ended up being the first pilot ever to fly with no arms.

1909.   There's a museum in Croatia filled with 507 stuffed frogs. 'Froggyland' shows off the work of 20th century Hungarian taxidermist Ferenc Mere, who spent 10 years stuffing and meticulously arranging the frogs.

1910.   The LG in LG Corporation stands for "Lucky-Goldstar", which is its former name and is the abbreviation of the company's tagline, "Life's good."

1911.   There is a giraffe sanctuary in Kenya called "Giraffe Manor". It's also a hotel where guests can hang out with giraffes and feed them from their windows.

1912.   Viagra was originally developed to treat high blood pressure. The fact that it enhances erections was discovered purely by accident.

1913.   Pigs have the ability to be purposefully manipulative. They're intelligent enough to pinpoint a weak spot, remember it, and use it to their advantage later on.

1914.   The 'Free Little Library' is a nonprofit organization that was started back in 2009 that offers free books in many little libraries in communities all over the world. Today, there are over 50,000 book exchanges worldwide.

1915.   Bedbugs don't have wings and they can't fly or jump. They can, however, live for months without food.

1916.   The world's largest snake, an eight-meter-long, approximately 250-kilogram reticulated python, was captured at a Malaysian construction site. The snake ended up dying just three days later after its discovery while laying an egg.

1917.   Japan is about to build a 123-meter Ferris wheel and it's going to have see-through floors. The Redhorse Osaka Wheel will be the fifth-tallest Ferris wheel in the world and the tallest in Japan.

1918.   Fruitarianism is a subset of veganism. It's a diet that consists primarily of fruit and possible nuts and seeds. In fact, some fruitarians will only eat what falls or what would naturally fall from a plant.

1919. A study published in the journal 'Brain Structure and Function' found that after monitoring mice under the effects of both silence and different types of noise, that two hours of silence per day promoted cell growth in the part of the brain that controls memory, emotion, and learning.

1920. According to the National Institution of Health, one out of every 2,000 to 3,000 babies born is born with teeth. They're called natal teeth.

1921. In Tennessee, a law exists that prohibits the sale of bologna on Sunday.

1922. City birds use cigarette butts to line their nests in order to drive away parasites, as the nicotine in the cigarettes act as a natural pesticide.

1923. Every single president Egypt has ever had has either left the position by being arrested into military custody, or died in office.

1924. There's an animal native to east Asia called the raccoon dog. It looks like a raccoon, but is actually a dog.

1925. The little brown myotis bat can consume up to 1,000 mosquitos in one hour.

1926. Dolphins actually have two stomachs, one for storing food, and the other for digesting it. Basically, they're water cows, except way smarter and a little prettier. Dinosaur fossils have been found on every major continent in the world. They've been found in Antarctica, Australia and India, and in the far north of Canada. The Goliath frog is the largest frog in the world. It can reach up to 12.5 inches in length and weigh 7.2 pounds (3.27 kg).

1927. On May 31, 2014, according to the Guinness World Records, 104 volunteers at the Deer Run Camping Resort in Gardners, Pennsylvania, made the largest s'mores ever. It weighed a whopping 267 pounds (121 kg).

1928. Because camels live in conditions where there is little water, their digestive systems wring their food dry of almost all of its moisture. In fact, their poop is so dry, you can actually use it to start a fire.

1929. The Pagoda in Japan is the oldest wooden building in the world. It was built using trees from 600 AD.

1930. The planet Jupiter has a total of 63 moons that have been discovered to date.

1931. Gummy bear candies were originally called dancing bears. Hans Riegel originally created them back in 1920, which were originally made out of licorice.

1932. There's a building near Newark, in Ohio, shaped like a picnic basket. It was built by Dave Longaberger, owner of Longaberger Basket Company in 1997 to be used as his head office.

1933. The United States has had two presidents who were both peanut farmers, Thomas Jefferson and Jimmy Carter.

1934.   In Tanzania, almost two out of every five girls get married before they turned 18. That's almost 15 million girls a year.

1935.   The hagfish has no jaws, no bones in its body and is able to tie itself into a knot.

1936.   In August of 2016, the first documented case of twin dogs were born via C-section at Rant en Dal Animal Hospital in Mogale City, South Africa.

1937.   To stay cool in hot temperatures, kangaroos lick their arms until their fur and skin is sopping wet. The wind hitting their arms causes the saliva to evaporate and cool them off.

1938.   Movie theaters are forbidden in Saudi Arabia and have been banned since the 1980s.

1939.   According to Guinness World Records, Anthony Victor from India has the longest ear hair ever. It measures over seven inches at its longest point.

1940.   The Chinese have recorded solar eclipse sightings all the way back since 720 BC.

1941.   The Hammetschwand lift in Switzerland is the highest exterior elevator in Europe. It connects a rock path with the lookout point Hammetschwand on a plateau overlooking Lake Lucerne. It takes passengers 502 feet (153 meters) up the summit in less than a minute.

1942.   The Slinky was accidentally invented by Richard James. Richard was a naval engineer, and while working with tension springs in 1943, discovered that when one of the springs fell, it kept moving. He thought it would make a great toy, and the Slinky toy was born.

1943.   In the 1980s, a musician named Daryl Davis befriended members of the KKK in Maryland, causing them to disband in that state because they learned all about the misconceptions of black people from Davis.

1944.   To this day, 4% of the sand on Normandy beaches is made of shrapnel from the original fight on D-Day.

1945.   It is illegal in many countries to perform surgical procedures on an octopus without anesthesia due to their intelligence.

1946.   Hugh Jackman didn't know that Wolverines were actual animals until he started filming X-Men.

1947.   According to the World Health Organization and UNICEF, hand washing with soap is a more effective way to prevent disease than any vaccine out there.

1948.   Jason Lewis journeyed around the world between 1994 and 2007 by biking, roller blading, kayaking, and pedaling and became the first person to circumnavigate the globe by pure human power.

1949.   After Seth Rogen released the parody to the Bound 2 music video, Kanye West, actually, invited him to give feedback on every new song off his new album.

1950.   According to statistics, most missing children are abducted by relatives and parents.

1951.   Shockingly, most energy drinks don't contain as much caffeine as coffee. A Grande coffee at Starbucks has 320 milligrams of caffeine, which is four times the 80 milligrams of caffeine that can be found in an average can of Redbull.

1952.   Clint Eastwood was the mayor of Carmel, California, from 1986 to 1988. His salary was $200 a month.

1953.   IKEA in Australia once gave away cribs to couples that could prove that their babies were born on November 14th, exactly nine months to the day from Valentine's Day.

1954.   There's an umbrella called the "Oombrella" that can actually predict when it's about to rain and send an alert to your smartphone reminding you to bring your umbrella along. Not only that, but if you forget it in a restaurant, it can send you a notification via Bluetooth that you forgot it before you get too far.

1955.   Ancient Egyptian pharaohs made slaves fan their wine all night to cool it down.

1956.   Jellyfish are the ocean's most efficient swimmers. They consume 48% less oxygen than any other swimming animal.

1957.   Scientists from Tufts University have created worms with the heads and brains of other species of worms by manipulating cell communication. Instead of altering their DNA, the scientists manipulated proteins that control conversations between cells.

1958.   According to the Guinness World Records, the oldest message in a bottle spent 108 years, four months, and 18 days at sea. It was put in the sea by the Marine Biological Association in the United Kingdom in November of 1906. It washed ashore on Amrum Island in Germany on April 17, 2015.

1959.   The Shin-Yokohama Ramen Museum in Yokohama City, Japan, is a museum dedicated to the ramen noodle.

1960.   Bees in Ribeauville, France started producing honey in different shades of blue and green. When the beekeepers investigated, they actually found that instead of collecting nectar from flowers, the bees were feeding on remnants of colored M&M candy shells that were being processed by a plant 2.5 miles (4 km) away.

1961.   The largest meteorite and largest piece of iron ever found is the Hoba meteorite. It was discovered in 1920 in Namibia, by a farmer who was plowing his field. The meteorite weighs 66 tons and measures 8.9 feet (2.7 metres) long and wide and about 3 feet (1 metre) thick. Experts estimate that it fell to earth about 80,000 years ago.

1962.   Cows, sheep and goats all have a tough dental pad below their top instead of front teeth. This dental arrangement helps ruminants gather great quantities of grass and fibrous plants.

1963.   When the Krakatoa volcano in Indonesia erupted in 1883, the sound it made could be heard thousands of miles away in Australia and the island of Rodriguez. It was the loudest sound ever recorded on the planet.

1964.   The microscopic tardigrade, also known as water bear, or moss piglets, is one of the world's toughest creatures. It can go a decade without water, and can withstand temperatures as low as -459 degrees Fahrenheit (-272 celsius) as well as highs of 304 degrees Fahrenheit (151 celsius).

1965.   Adult rats can fit through a hole as small as a quarter, or a gap less than one inch wide. This is how rats can infest your home without your knowledge.

1966.   According to researchers at the National Hansen's Disease Program in Baton Rouge, Louisiana, the armadillo is one of the few mammals that harbor the bacteria that cause leprosy.

1967.   There is a musical road in Lancaster, California. It was created as a TV ad for Honda. The road is cut into groves that when traveling about 50 miles (80 km) per hour, it will actually play William Tell's Overture.

1968.   From 1956 to 1958 Chrysler offered a record player in its new cars called the Highway Hi-Fi. But it was short lived because they had a tendency to break.

1969.   Author, American sex therapist, and media personality, Dr. Ruth, was trained as a sniper when she was just 16 years old by the underground Jewish military organization Aganah in Israel.

1970.   In 1992, locals from Zernikow, Germany discovered a 100-tree swastika during an aerial survey. The swastika was made up of a group of large trees only visible from the air and was almost 7 square miles (19 square meters). In autumn, the yellowing trees stand out against the surrounding evergreens. Nobody knows who planted these trees, but it is known that it was created during Hitler's peak in the 1930s.

1971.   The world's largest pool is in the seaside resort of San Alfonso del Mar in Chile. It was built in 2006 and is 114 feet (35 meters) deep and is filled with 65 million gallons (249 million liters) of water.

1972.   Scientists at Duke University have developed a device that allows monkeys to control robotic wheelchairs by sending signals with their brains. They're hoping that one day it will help people with disabilities.

1973.   Chiayi, Taiwan, built a 55 foot (17-meter) glass structure shaped like a giant high heel shoe. It's used as a wedding hall and a tourist attraction. It was built in honor of women who suffered from arsenic poisoning from well water that caused gangrene, a condition sometimes known as black feet disease.

1974.   36-year-old Wang Xiaoyu is a Chinese hair stylist trained in the art of kung-fu. He cuts hair while standing on his head.

1975.   Not only does the Earth spin on its axis, it also moves around the sun at a speed of about 66,000 miles (107,000) kilometers an hour.

1976.   In 1984, Jack Lalanne, sometimes referred to as the 'Godfather of Fitness', towed 70 rowboats with passengers in them from Queensway Bridge to the ship Queen Mary while shackled, handcuffed, and fighting winds and currents.

1977.   'Happy hour' has been illegal in the Republic of Ireland since 2003 under the Intoxicating Liquor Act.

1978.   Rodents are incapable of vomiting. They can't puke because of anatomical constraints. In other words, they simply aren't built with the ability to.

1979.   On the Norwegian island of Spitsbergen sitting inside a mountain is the Svalbard Global Seed Vault, which holds over 850,000 copies of seeds from across the planet just in case of a global catastrophe.

1980.   A tiger's tongue is so coarse it can actually lick flesh down to the bone.

1981.   Bhutan, the world's most eco-friendly country, once planted 108,000 trees to celebrate the birth of its new prince.

1982.   A group of bears is called a "sloth of bears."

1983.   Steven Tyler estimates that he spent at least five to six million dollars on cocaine in his lifetime.

1984.   In the 1950s, psychologist Fredric Wertham wrote a book called "Seduction of the Innocent" that accused Batman and Robin of being homosexual and Superman of being a fascist right-wing fantasy.

1985.   When it was first released, there was a lot of debate over the identity of the unknown wizard at the back of the Harry Potter and the Philosopher's Stone first edition. The illustrator, Thomas Taylor, later revealed he based it on his father after being told to draw a wizard to decorate the back cover.

1986.   Pigeons actually produce milk to feed their young.

1987.   Jackie Chan is the highest paid actor in Asia.

1988.   Pablo Escobar used to cheat at Monopoly games with his kids, hiding extra money ahead of time near where he planned to sit.

1989.   Amazonian butterflies drink turtle tears in order to receive mineral sodium from them.

1990.   When a cat rubs their face on an item, they're not merely scratching themselves; they're actually leaving their own scent behind. Cats have glands located around their mouths, chins, inside of their face, neck and ears. This is called "bunting."

1991.   People throw away approximately $4.5 million into fountains and wishing wells every single year.

1992.   Big Bang Theory and Two and a Half Men creator Chuck Lorre wrote The Teenage Mutant Ninja Turtles theme song.

1993.   Michigan judge Hugh Clarke actually held himself in contempt after his own smartphone rang in court.

1994.   A mosquito's proboscis, or nose, has 47 sharp edges on its tip to help cut through skin, and can even cut through protective clothing.

1995.   There is a drug called "Truvada", which has been shown to prevent HIV infection at a 92% success rate for gay men, and a 70% success rate for intravenous drug users, but unfortunately less than 1% of at-risk people currently take the drug, and only 1/3 of primary care doctors have even heard of it.

1996.   Many Japanese bathrooms have a button that when pushed, plays the flushing sound to mask the sound of your own "business".

1997.   In 2015, Croatia launched a program called "Fresh Start" which wiped away debt for 60,000 low income Croatians who had been struggling to pay their bills, in an effort to boost consumer confidence and spending. The state, along with firms and banks, agreed to forgive up to 60,000 Kuna or 8,830 dollars per individual.

1998.   According to astronomers at the Australian National University, there are ten times more stars in the night sky than there are grains of sand in the world's deserts and beaches.

1999.   Even though the Church of Scientology has been in Germany since 1970, the German government doesn't recognize it as a religion and sees it instead as an abusive business masquerading as a religion.

2000.   Alpacas can get sick or even die from loneliness, so it's always best to have them in pairs or more.

2001.   About 90% of the world's population lives in the northern hemisphere. This means that only about 700 million people live in the southern hemisphere.

2002.   According to biologists working at Newfoundland's Memorial University, bread is junk food for ducks because it makes them fat and disease-ridden.

2003.   Dogs watch more TV now than they did before because of flat screen televisions which flicker at a rate that a dog's eyes are actually able to process.

2004.   The Bororo people are an indigenous race in Brazil and all share the same blood type. Type O.

2005.   Beethoven began losing his hearing at the age of only 28, so he cut the legs off his piano so that he could sit on the floor and compose music by feeling the vibrations of the piano.

2006.   The Greater Honeyguide bird guides people to beehives and after the honey is taken out the bird eats what's left of the hive.

2007.   After the Second World War, crystal meth was prescribed as a diet aid and remained legal right up until the 1970s.

2008.   The Second Chance Coffee Company in Illinois conducts FBI background checks to make sure that those seeking employment in the company have actually been to prison, because the company only hires ex-inmates.

2009.   Rabbits eat their own poop every day. They produce special poop called "Cecotropes", or night feces, which are nutrient rich and are passed out of the body like normal stool, but are a little different. They can later be re-ingested by the rabbit safely so that important nutrients can be reabsorbed.

2010.   The menstrual pad, when it was first invented, used to be held up by a belt.

2011.   A Cornell food and brand lab study of 497 diners showed that patrons who order their dinner from a heavy server ordered significantly more food, were four times more likely to order dessert, and ordered 17% more alcohol.

2012.   In November of 2015, Nestle admitted that they used slave labor in the production of its 'Fancy Feast' cat food brand in Thailand.

2013.   Coffea charrieriana, discovered in 2008, is the first known coffee plant that contains no caffeine.

2014.   Haagen-Dazs ice cream was founded in 1961 by Reuben and Rose Mattus, two Jewish-Polish immigrants, in the Bronx of New York. They invented the Danish sounding name as a tribute to Denmark's exemplary treatment of the Jews during the Second World War, and included an outline map of Denmark on early labels.

2015.   In 2002, actor Vin Diesel saved an entire family from a burning car wreck.

2016.   The Muppets creator Jim Henson believed in allowing a character to grow organically. His guiding philosophy was that each Muppet had a distinct personality. In fact, he believed that it was the job of the puppeteer to uncover it.

2017.   It can take anywhere from 90 to 120 minutes just to hard-boil an ostrich egg.

2018.   The saying 'Bless You' after a sneeze comes from the 14th century Pope Gregory VII who asked for it to be said after every sneeze in order for it to protect him against the plague.

2019.   Mosquitoes survive the impact of raindrops using a zen-like approach of non-resistance.

2020.   The legendary horror writer R.L Stine got his start by writing comics for Bazooka Joe bubble gum under the pen name Jovial Bob Stine.

2021.   Nintendo 64 wasn't always called 'Nintendo 64'. It began as Project Reality and then it was renamed to Nintendo Ultra 64 before they finally shortened it to simply Nintendo 64.

2022.   Pentheraphobia is the fear of your mother-in-law. The origin of the word 'penthera' is Greek, meaning "mother-in-law", and 'phobia', in Greek, meaning "fear".

2023.   The game bingo was originally called "Beano" because players used beans to cover the numbered squares.

2024.   The most commonly broken bone is the clavicle, more commonly known as the collarbone.

2025.   The first person to ever go over Niagara Falls and survive was 63-year-old schoolteacher Annie Edson Taylor back in 1901.

2026.   In 1848, an ice jam up the river from Niagara Falls caused the falls to stay bone-dry for nearly 48 hours. Some people actually took it as a sign that the world was ending and attended special services at local churches. Normally, it has the highest flow rate of any waterfall in the world and provides 4.4 gigawatts of energy to the region.

2027.   In 2008, Burger King introduced a new product for the Christmas season called "Flame", meat-scented cologne for meat-loving men. It was promoted as the scent of seduction with a hint of flame-broiled meat.

2028.   Newborn giraffes stand at about 6 feet (1.83 meters) tall, making them taller than most humans.

2029.   The food coloring known as "carmine" is extracted from the female cochineal insect shells boiled in ammonia or sodium carbonate solution, and it's in more things than you might think. It actually makes ice cream, yogurt, candy, and red fruit drinks.

2030.   It's a faux pas in Russia to give your date a dozen roses. You give an odd number of flowers for a happy occasion and an even number for condolences.

2031.   Expiration dates for bottled water is actually for the bottle, not for the water in it.

2032.   An elephant can actually die of a broken heart if their mate dies. They may refuse to eat or lay down, shedding tears until they starve to death.

2033.   There is specie of orchid that only grows at high elevations in certain mountainous areas of Ecuador, Colombia, and Peru, that looks just like a monkey.

2034.   According to the National Retail Federation, the four most common grocery items shoplifted are cigarettes, energy drinks, high-end liquor and infant formula.

2035.   The farthest flight on a hoverboard was 900 feet (275 meters) and was achieved by Alexandru Duru in Quebec, Canada, on August 25th, 2014.

2036.   A U.K. woman named Tess Christian claims that she has not smiled or laughed in 40 years, all in an effort to prevent wrinkles.

2037.   On May 8th, 2010, actress Betty White, who was 88 at the time, became the oldest person to host Saturday Night Live.

2038.   Indonesian scientists have created a birth control pill for men by using a plant called the gendarussa. It's 99% effective.

2039.   The urine from a Maned Wolf smells like marijuana.

2040.   Indonesia's Kawah Ijen volcano burns blue along with its lava because of the high amounts of sulfur gas contained within it.

2041.   Crocodiles can hold their breath underwater for up to two hours if they need to. The colder the water, the longer that they can stay under because a cold crocodile uses less energy and oxygen than a warm one.

2042.   The 1925 released film, Ben Hur, was the most expensive silent film ever made. Costing between four to six million dollars at that time.

2043.   Actress Margaret Hamilton, who is most remembered for her scary portrayal of the wicked witch in The Wizard of Oz, and terrifying children everywhere, was actually a kindergarten teacher before she got into acting.

2044.   In Spain and France the tooth fairy is a mouse. Known as the la bonne petite souris, the tiny mouse will procure teeth left under pillows replacing them with either cash or sweets.

2045.   In 1985, Lynette Woodard became the first woman to play for the Harlem Globetrotters. Since then, she has played in the WNBA and has been inducted into the Basketball Hall of Fame and Women's Basketball Hall of Fame.

2046.   If you have delusions where you think you're a wolf or another wild animal, you suffer from what's called lycanthrope.

2047.   India has 23 official languages. While Hindi is the official language of the central government in India, with English as a provisional official sub language. Individual state legislatures are free to adopt any regional language as the official language of that state.

2048.   There's an annual sidewalk egg frying contest on the Fourth of July in Oatman, Arizona. Contestants are given 15 minutes to fry two eggs using only solar power. They can use mirrors, magnifying glasses, and aluminum to help speed up the process.

2049.   Pablo Picasso's full name was, Pablo Diego Jose Francisco de Paula Juan Nepomuceno Crispín Crispiniano María Remedios de la Santísima Trinidad Ruiz Picasso.

2050.   The library of Congress is the largest library in the world. It has more than 162 million items, over 838 miles (1350 km) of bookshelves, more than 38 million books and print materials, 3.6 million recordings, 14 million photos, 5.5 million maps, 7.1 million pieces of sheet music, and 70 million manuscripts.

2051.   Baby hedgehogs are born with quills but they are soft and flexible.

2052.   In the early days of the Indie 500, most of the cars had two seats. One for the driver and one for the onboard mechanic. The mechanic monitored the gauges, made repairs, and sometimes would even massage the driver's arms and neck. The onboard mechanic was mandatory from 1912 to 1922, and then again from 1930 to 1937.

2053.   Boxer and olympic gold medalist George Forman has five sons and he named all of them George.

2054.   There's a hotline in Germany called "Schimpf-los", which means "swear away", where people can call to let off steam after a stressful day at work.

2055.   In 2013, Mark Zuckerberg spent 30 million dollars buying four houses that surround his home, just to make sure that he has privacy.

2056.   In 2012, a Swedish man named Peter Skyllberg survived for two months in a snowed in car by eating snow and staying warm in a sleeping bag.

2057.   In 1993, a lawyer named Garry Hoy in Toronto decided to show off to a group of law students just how durable his office's windows were by bodychecking one. Unfortunately, the window didn't shatter and instead popped out of its frame and he ended up falling 24 stories to his death.

2058.   The coldest village on earth is Oymyakon in Russia. The average temperature in January averages negative 123 degrees fahrenheit (51 degrees Celsius), and their all-time low is negative 91 degrees fahrenheit (71 degrees Celsius) in February.

2059.   In Crater Lake in central Oregon, there is a floating tree trunk known as the "Old Man of The Lake" that has been bobbing completely vertically in the lake for well over a hundred years. It's been referenced in writing as far back as 1896.

2060.   The octopus, squid, and the salmon all die soon after giving birth. For the most part, males die soon after fertilizing the females' eggs, and the females only live long enough to birth their young before dying.

2061.   The Amazon rainforest is home to 427 mammals, 1,300 birds, 378 reptiles, and more than 400 amphibians.

2062.   Google was originally named "Backrub".

2063.   In 2006, an analysis of cat's tongues showed that they do not have the taste receptors that react to sweet-tasting things. Every feline from lions to tigers down to the domestic housecat cannot taste anything sweet.

2064.   There's a resort in Finland called Kakslauttanen Arctic Resort, where your accommodations are a glass igloo.

2065.   The recessed dip on the facial structure of your skull between your eyes and above the bridge of your nose is called the nay-see-an. Cosmetic surgeons rely heavily on the type of nay-see-an a person has when planning a rhinoplasty, a.k.a. "nose job".

2066.   August 13th is officially Left Handers Day.

2067.   In some African countries, albinos' body parts are believed to bring wealth and good luck. Disturbingly, as a result, attackers chop off their limbs and pluck out their organs and sell them to witch doctors.

2068.   Elephants are now being trained for bio detection in South Africa. They are being tested to see if they can utilize their heightened sense of smell to look for poachers, land mines, and explosives. Elephants have 1,948 genes dedicated to smelling, whereas dogs only have 811 and humans only have just under 400.

2069.   In 2006, Evel Knievel sued Kanye West for his video in the song Touch the Sky, in which Kanye takes on the persona of Evel Knievel and jumps a motorcycle over a canyon.

2070.   Singer Barry Manilow wrote the 'State Farm like a Good Neighbor' jingle. He was paid a flat fee of $500.

2071.   Researchers at Norway's University of Bergen have found a link between being addicted to work and anxiety. They looked at more than 16,000 workers across the country and found that nearly 8% of workaholics were more likely to suffer from ADHD, OCD, depression, and anxiety. They also found that people who work more than 55 hours per week were at a higher risk of heart attack and stroke.

2072.   On November 14, 1969, the Apollo 12 was struck by lightning just 36 seconds after liftoff. And moments later, it was struck again. The second strike tore through the ship, and wiped out many of its electrical systems. One of the flight controller's remembered how to switch the spacecraft's signaling conditioning equipment to auxiliary, and the Apollo 12 was able to actually continue onto successfully land on the moon.

2073.   Actress Megan Fox suffers from papyrophobia, which is the fear of dry paper.

2074.   In the 16th century, up until the 1960's, Egyptian mummies were actually ground and used to produce a brown paint color called Mummy Brown. The powder was mixed with white pitch and myrrh to produce a rich brown pigment.

2075.   During the Vietnam War, U.S. Fighter jets would drop their external fuel tanks over Vietnam when they were empty or the pilot needed more maneuverability. Vietnamese farmers would then repurpose them and use them as canoes.

2076.   A 68 year old grandmother from West Wales had her car followed and swarmed for two days by 20,000 bees. They were actually trying to rescue their queen bee, which unbeknownst to her, had hitched a ride in her Mitsubishi Outlander. Beekeepers were brought in to safely remove them.

2077.   The hood ornament on a Rolls Royce car is actually called the Spirit of Ecstasy.

2078.   In 1974, Gerber baby products tried marketing singles by Gerber, which were meals in a jar like creamed beef and beef burgundy. Marketing was aimed to college students and young adults. The product failed!

2079.   Believe it or not, Nintendo was originally a playing card company, founded in late 1889. It was based in Kyoto, Japan, and produced and marketed a game called "Hanafuda". In fact, Nintendo continues to manufacture playing cards in Japan and even organizes its own tournament called the Nintendo Cup.

2080.   According to a study done in 2002 by Daphne Soares from the University of Maryland, an American alligator can orient themselves to the ripples created by a single drop of water, even in complete darkness. This is because their faces and bodies are covered with tiny bumps that are far more sensitive than our own fingertips.

2081. During the filming of 'Wolf of Wall Street', actor Jonah Hill snorted so much fake cocaine, which was vitamin D powder, he ended up being sick for six weeks with bronchitis.

2082. According to a study done in 2015 by Common Sense Media and CEO James Steyer, the average teen spends up to nine hours a day on social media.

2083. There are actually three different types of tears. Basal tears keep your eyes lubricated. Irritant or reflex tears are produced when you get something in your eye and emotional tears, of course, are produced during moments of intense feeling.

2084. The Mutter Museum in Philadelphia has an exhibit of a woman's body that was naturally converted into soap due to the chemicals in the soil where she was buried.

2085. The average sloth travels only 123 feet (37 meters) per day. That's less than half the length of a football field.

2086. Chewing gum causes increased saliva, which increases swallowing, which increases the amount of air that you swallow, which makes you pass gas more.

2087. Gangsta's Paradise is one of the few Coolio songs to not feature any profanity because it was the only way that Stevie Wonder would authorize the sampling of his song, Pastime Paradise.

2088. Leopards are solitary animals that prefer to hunt and live alone and only get together with other leopards to mate. Also, they can eat things that are twice their size.

2089. The sound of Velociraptors talking back and forth to each other in the movie Jurassic Park was actually the sound of mating tortoises.

2090. The founder of IKEA, Ingvar Feodor Kamprad, started his career at age six, selling matches. At the age of 10, he was going around the neighborhood on his bike, selling Christmas decorations. Then, at the age of 17, he was getting money from selling fish and pencils. Finally, after his father gave him a small sum of money for doing well in school, he started IKEA.

2091. New York City's 9-1-1 systems handle more than 11 million calls per year, making it the largest of its kind in the nation.

2092. There's a religion called Dudeism, based on the movie "The Big Lebowski", which advocates the practice of going with the flow, being cool headed, and taking it easy.

2093. Created in Italy, "Let's Pizza" is the world's first pizza vending machine and can deliver fresh pizza with custom toppings in only three minutes.

2094.   Maryana Naumova is a 16 year old Russian powerlifter who can bench press 370 pounds (170 kilograms).

2095.   City raccoons are very intelligent and have learned to adapt to their urban environment by opening doors and trash bins.

2096.   In 1986 a French woman named Nadine Vaujour was so determined to get her husband out of jail that she learned how to fly a helicopter and flew over the prison where he was at to pick him up off of a roof. And she did! But was arrested shortly after.

2097.   The Maruyama Zoo in Japan spent four years trying to mate two hyenas before realizing that they were both male.

2098.   In 2014 the Journal of Neuroscience found that brain patterns synchronize when people have conversations, as our brains are constantly trying to predict what the person is trying to say next.

2099.   As of July 2015, 600 billion LEGO parts have been produced. Which is about 86 pieces for each person on the planet.

2100.   In Thailand people text 555 to each other instead of "hahaha" because the number five is pronounced "ha" in Thai.

2101.   The Citarum river in Indonesia is considered the most polluted river in the world. Full of dyes, chemicals, and a lot more nasty stuff.

2102.   There was an ancient Chinese custom where girls would have their toes and arches broken, tied, and bound underneath their feet before the arch of the foot could develop. This was done so that their feet could fit into tiny little shoes. Back then, small feet in China represented the height of female refinement.

2103.   There is a phobia called "Koumpounophobia" where sufferers have a paralyzing fear of buttons. The specific fear varies from person to person, but some people feel that buttons are dirty and some are afraid of the texture of certain buttons.

2104.   A woman named Vesna Vulovic from Yugoslavia holds the Guinness World Record for the highest fall survived without a parachute. On January 26, 1972, she was working as a flight attendant when she fell over 32,000 feet (10,000 meters) over the Czech Republic. Unbelievably, the plane that she was working aboard blew up and she fell inside a section of the tail unit. After being in the hospital for 16 months and emerging from a 27 day coma, she had multiple broken bones but miraculously survived.

2105.   Ontario, Canada, has more than 250,000 lakes and contains about one-fifth of the entire world's fresh water.

2106.   NASA scientists have discovered that about 4.3 billion years ago, Mars may have had enough water to cover its entire surface in a liquid layer about 137 meters deep. This primitive ocean would've held more water than the Arctic Ocean. However, over time, it lost about 87% of that water into space.

2107.   Researchers from the French university, Universite Libre de Bruxelles found that cockroaches have their own personalities and even display different character traits. They are simple animals, but they can make complex decisions on survival, and one cockroach's decision can actually sway others.

2108.   In 2008, a man named Ian Usher from Perth, Australia, sold his entire life on eBay for $399,000 following the breakdown of his marriage. The sale price included his home, his car, his motorcycle, a two-week trial in his job, and an introduction to his friends.

2109.   There's a disorder called "Congenital Amusia" where people can't recognize common songs from their culture, can't tell when notes are out of tune, and sometimes say that music sounds like banging to them.

2110.   In ancient Greece, the apple was thrown at someone to symbolically declare one's love for them. This is because in Greek mythology, the Greek goddess Eris became disgruntled after she was excluded from a wedding; and in retaliation, tossed a golden apple inscribed with "For the most beautiful one" into the wedding party. At that point, it was claimed by Aphrodite, and thus became a symbol for love.

2111.   According to the World Health Organization, an estimated 350 million people globally suffer from depression. It's also a leading cause of disability worldwide, and is a major contributor to the overall global burden of disease.

2112.   Koalas have human like fingerprints; in fact, they're almost identical to human ones. Not even careful analysis under a microscope easily distinguishes the loopy, whorled ridges on koala's fingers from our own.

2113.   For five years, a woman named Oxana Malaya from the Ukraine lived with dogs and survived on raw meat and scraps. She walked on all fours, panted with her tongue hanging out, and whined and barked. After she was abandoned by her alcoholic parents, she was actually raised by a pack of dogs on a run-down farm in the village of Novaya. When she was finally discovered in 1991, she had almost forgotten how to speak.

2114.   During the first three years, a child's brain triples in weight and establishes about 1,000 trillion nerve connections.

2115.   Road traffic crashes are the leading cause of death among children ages 10 to 19.

2116.   Omphalophobia is the fear of the belly button. Sufferers of this are actually afraid to have their belly buttons touched or to touch another persons.

2117.   Some baby whales are actually born with hair. Most species born with hair usually lose it over the first several days or weeks of birth.

2118.   According to a study done by Nick Wolfinger, a sociologist at the University of Utah, people have a better chance of not getting divorced if they get married between the ages of 28 and 32.

2119.   Abu Dhabi has the largest falcon hospital in the world. In fact, it houses over 6,000 falcons.

2120.   North Yungas Road in Bolivia has the nickname, "Death Road," because it's estimated that between 200 to 300 people per year die on it.

2121.   The Starbucks logo in Saudi Arabia is just a floating crown. This is because, believe it or not, the original logo featuring a mermaid is far too raunchy to be displayed in the deeply religious and conservative part of the world.

2122.   Apple Computers was actually formed by three people, not two. Ronald Wayne was the third co-founder, but in less than a couple weeks, he pulled out of the company, and on April 12th, 1976, Wayne sold his 10% equity in the company for $800. Today, that stake in the company would be worth 62.93 billion dollars.

2123.   There are white strawberries with red seeds in Japan called "The Scent of First Love". They are amazingly sweet and rich, but also ridiculously expensive at about $4.10 American per berry!

2124.   In 2012, John and Frances Canning invited Queen Elizabeth to their wedding in Manchester as a joke. But astonishingly, the queen surprised them by actually showing up.

2125.   Elvis Presley once tipped a limo driver by buying him the same limo that he had been driving him around in.

2126.   A businessman named Armand Hammer coincidentally served on a board of directors for Arm & Hammer.

2127.   Paul McCartney is the only musician to ever top the charts as a solo artist, and in a duo, trio, quartet, and quintet.

2128.   In the music industry, for every $1000 of music sold, the average musician only gets about $23.40.

2129.   The IOS game "Clash of Clans" was making an astonishing 1.5 million dollars a day in its peak.

2130.   Habitat 67 is a model community and housing complex in Montreal and is considered an architectural landmark as well as being the most recognizable buildings in the city.

2131.   Facebook has over one billion users and more than 10,000 of them die every day. Meaning that dead Facebook users will soon outnumber the living ones, which also means that it could become a digital graveyard by the year 2065.

2132. A 20 year old gallon of McDonald's barbecue sauce that was used for the McJordan Burger in the early 1990's sold for almost $10,000 in 2012.

2133. While filming "I am Legend", Will Smith got so attached to his co-star Abbey the German Shepherd, that he asked if he could keep her, but the owner refused.

2134. During World War two, the Soviets built an A-40 Krylya Tanka, a tank with wings. It didn't actually work.

2135. If humans had eagle vision, we'd be able to see an ant crawling on the ground from the roof of a ten story building. In fact, everything would also be brilliantly colored and objects in our line of sight would be magnified.

2136. Phytophotodermatitis, often referred to as "margarita dermatitis", or lime disease, not to be confused with Lyme disease with a Y, is a toxic reaction resulting from citric acid mixed with sunlight. It can cause second degree burns and is very painful.

2137. The distance from Mars to the Sun is 128 million miles (206 million km) at its closest point. And 154 million miles (250 million km) at it furthest.

2138. According to National Geographic, the Beelzebufo Ampinga, or the "devil frog", may be the largest frog that ever existed. These extinct beach ball sized amphibians grew to almost half a meter long and weighed approximately 10 pounds (4.5 kilograms).

2139. Novice climbers are not allowed to climb Mount Everest according to joint-secretary of Nepal's Ministry of Tourism. In order to qualify to climb it, you are required to have reached the peak of at least one 21,000 feet (6,500 meter) mountain in your lifetime.

2140. Scientists have discovered that there are actually five tastes or senses that your tongue and recognize. They are sweet, sour, salty, bitter, and umami. Parmesan cheese is an example of umami.

2141. From 2010 to 2015, taco bell secretly reduced the sodium content in 33 menu items by 33%, and nobody noticed.

2142. The opposite of deja vu is Jamais vu. It's a French word meaning "never seen." It's a feeling or experience when a person knows or recognizes a situation, but still feels very unfamiliar and unknown to them.

2143. In 1965, Mattel released Slumber Party Barbie. Apparently, one of her slumber party essentials was a pink scale that was permanently set to 110 pounds (50 kg).

2144. Makoto Igarashi from Tokyo developed a Hizamakura Lap Pillow, which is a cushion shaped like a woman's legs wearing a mini-skirt, that you can lay your head down on for maternal feelings.

2145. During World War II, Germany used guns that had a curved barrel device that was clamped onto the end of an MP44 rifle that allowed soldiers to shoot over obstacles without exposing themselves to return fire.

2146. Sea scallops have about 60 eyes. They can be a bright blue color and help the scallop detect light, dark, and motion.

2147. Boxer Muhammad Ali's star on the Walk of Fame is on the wall, not on the pavement because he didn't want the name of Muhammad to be stepped on.

2148. Writer and director Oliver Stone received a Purple Heart and Bronze Star for his service in the Vietnam War.

2149. Breast fed babies poop more than formula fed babies because breast milk contains immunoglobulins, substances produced by the body's immune system which works like a natural laxative.

2150. According to the Centers for Disease Control and Prevention, or the CDC, as of 2014, one in 68 children, or more specifically, one in 42 boys and one in 189 girls, has autism spectrum disorder, which includes a wide range of symptoms, skills in different levels of disability.

2151. In 2014, scientists discover the earliest evidence of human footprints. These were outside of Africa on the Norfolk coast in the east of England. The footprints were found on the shores of Happisburgh and were more than 800,000 years old.

2152. Every single spring, Sweetwater, Texas, has a rattlesnake round-up. For three days, snake hunters bring in their catches, which end up being 1000's of snakes, for which they're paid five dollars for every pound. The junior Chamber of Commerce began the tradition back in 1958 to address the overpopulation of snakes.

2153. In Indonesia, whole smoked bats are considered a delicacy.

2154. When important Vikings died, they were put into a burial ship along with their clothes and jewelry, where they were either buried or set on fire and pushed out to sea.

2155. The fear of clowns is called "coulrophobia", and has increased significantly over the last 20 years due to their portrayal in popular culture and the recent scary clown phenomenon where people have been dressing up as clowns to scare others.

2156. If your parents or grandparents have a history of multiple cavities or dentures at an early age, you have a higher risk of the same thing due to genetics.

2157. Frogs can't swallow with their eyes open.

2158.   On March 26th, 1976, Queen Elizabeth sent her first email. The message was transmitted over ARPANET, the forerunner for the modern internet. She is considered the first head of state to have used electronic mail.

2159.   Tony Iommi started down-tuning his guitar after an accident that cut the end of his two fingers off, thus creating Black Sabbath's signature sound.

2160.   Elle King, singer of 'Ex's and Oh's' is actor Rob Schneider's daughter.

2161.   Michael Jordan's number 23 was retired by the Miami Heat, even though he has never played for them.

2162.   Dogs feel most vulnerable when they're pooping, so they look to their owners for protection, which often results in awkward staring.

2163.   The name LEGO was an abbreviation for the two Danish words "leg godt", meaning "play well."

2164.   In 1989, Disney forced three daycare centers to remove a mural of Mickey, Donald, and Goofy, under threat of legal action.

2165.   The reality show 'The Voice' has yet to create any new singing stars, but has effectively rejuvenated the careers of its celebrity judges.

2166.   It's estimated that the Mexican Drug Cartel Caballeros Templarios, or 'The Knights Templar', makes $152 million a year from growing and selling avocados.

2167.   Mexican jumping beans get their jump from moth larvae inside the pod that twitches when abruptly warmed.

2168.   In 1723, French Naval Officer Gabriel de Clieu carried a single coffee seedling all the way from France to Martinique, a Caribbean island, where it spread and birthed 18 million trees over 50 years. Eventually, those trees made it to South and Central America.

2169.   Elephants have the longest known pregnancy of any animal, lasting up to 680 days. In addition to being born with an advanced level of brain development, they also have a unique cycle of ovulation and hormone levels that are unlike any other animal.

2170.   Dr. Wuzong Zhou of St. Andrews University found that about 1.5 million diamond nanoparticles are created in a candle flame every second that it burns. Unfortunately, they're burned away during the process; however, it's believed that this discovery could lead to research into how diamonds could be created more cheaply.

2171.   Because the main purpose of marriage to ancient people was to produce children, they used to shower the new bride with fertility symbols like wheat grain. The Romans used to bake this wheat into small cakes to be eaten in a tradition known as "confarreatio", meaning "eating together". The guests of the ceremony used to throw handfuls of honey-eyed nuts and dried fruits called confetto; and this was how the tradition of throwing confetti at weddings started.

2172.   The origin of the game hopscotch began in ancient Britain during the Roman Empire. The original courts were 30 meters long and were used for military training exercises. Soldiers actually used to run in full armor and field packs to improve their footwork. Roman children drew their own, smaller courts and added a scoring system; and thus, hopscotch was born and spread throughout Europe.

2173.   The 2011 Japan earthquake was so powerful, that it actually changed the Earth's rotation on its axis, and shortened the 24 day that we know by 1.8 milliseconds.

2174.   The largest hidden Mickey Mouse is in Mickey's forest. A 60-acre forest near Walt Disney World, containing over 50,000 pine trees.

2175.   The letter Q is the only letter in the alphabet that doesn't appear in any U.S. territory or state name.

2176.   Australia has the largest resource of uranium in the world at 31%. At around 12% of the world's annual production, they are the world's third-largest producer behind Kazakhstan and Canada.

2177.   Up until 2013, if you were found to be trafficking drugs in Singapore, you were given a mandatory death sentence. As far as harsh drug laws are concerned, Singapore had and still has some of the toughest out of any country in the world.

2178.   There's a hotel in Bolivia called the "Palacio de Sal Resort" that is made up of one million 14-inch blocks of compressed grains of salt. Even the furniture is made out of salt.

2179.   Mahatma Gandhi never won the Nobel Peace Prize, despite being nominated five times between 1937 and 1948, this despite being one of the strongest symbols for nonviolence in the world and being one of the most respected.

2180.   Horses can actually sleep while standing up. This is because of the way that their legs are built. They have ligaments and a structure that allows them to doze off without collapsing.

2181.   Believe it or not, fishing was the activity that accounted for the most lightning strikes and deaths between 2006 and 2012. In fact, there were a total of 26 fishing deaths because of it.

2182.   Vultures with GoPros and GPS trackers are used to find illegal trash dumps in Peru.

2183.   27 animals died on set throughout the filming of 'The Hobbit' trilogy. Some animals fell into sink holes, while other smaller ones such as chickens, and were killed by unsupervised dogs. The events led to PETA to have a global protest of the trilogy.

2184. In the late 1990s, the Coca Cola Company began testing a vending machine that could automatically raise prices for its drinks in hot weather.

2185. Recycling one aluminum can saves enough energy to run a television for three hours.

2186. There is a 30-foot replica of a 1951 Canadian nickel in Sudbury, Ontario, Canada.

2187. At birth, baby kangaroos or joeys can be as small as a grain of rice or as big as a bee.

2188. 3.5 billion years ago, a mega-asteroid that was likely 30 miles across slammed into Earth in Australia.

2189. As of May 10th, 2016, the Endangered Species Act of 1973 listed 1,367 species of animals and 901 species of plants as endangered or threatened.

2190. The horned lizard has blood-filled sinuses within the eye sockets that squirt blood in self-defense by swelling and rupturing.

2191. In 2012, the street artist, Megx converted an old bridge in Wuppertal, Germany into a giant Lego structure using colored panels to create the illusion of the underside of Lego bricks.

2192. In most European countries, including Britain, declawing your cat is illegal. If you're caught declawing a cat in Israel, you can actually be sent to jail for a year and be fined 20 thousand dollars. Scotland, Italy, New Zealand, and over 30 other countries have also followed suit.

2193. In New Zealand, it's illegal to own just one guinea pig because they are very lonely and social creatures. In fact, they have matchmaking companies to match up your guinea pig if their partner dies, which is part of a sweeping animals' rights legislation that was first introduced in 2008.

2194. If you live in Australia, you are 20 times more likely to drown than be bitten by a shark. In fact, to put it into perspective, you're significantly more likely to win the top prize in the lottery than even being involved in a shark accident of any kind.

2195. According to the World Health Organization, there are 360 million people in the world with disabling hearing loss. That's around five percent of the entire world's population with 32 million of them being children between the ages of zero and 14.

2196. On July 13th, 1955, nightclub owner, Ruth Ellis was the last woman to be executed for murder in Great Britain. She was hanged for killing her boyfriend, and it wasn't until 1965 that the death penalty for murder was banned in England, Scotland, and Wales.

2197.   A study in the Journal of Current Biology found that those people who exercise four hours after learning something new, retained the information better two days later than those who exercise immediately or not at all.

2198.   Ringling Bros Barnum and Bailey Circus have retired all elephants in their show as of May 1st, 2016. All of the elephants will go to Florida conservation, where they can help with cancer research, as they possess a special P53 gene, which helps fight cancer.

2199.   There is something called "geographic tongue", which is actually a real health condition, with a map-like feature across your tongue, and in some cases, entire mouth.

2200.   The mineral Jadarite, discovered in a Serbian mine, has the same chemical composition as Kryptonite that has been described in the Superman movies.

2201.   Every week, about 50 cats and dogs are transported from Houston to Colorado in order to avoid euthanization.

2202.   Male platypuses have venomous spurs, and can even sense electromagnetic fields just like a fish.

2203.   Sir Isaac Newton predicted that the world would end in 2060.

2204.   The animated film 'Sleeping Beauty' took so long to make, that Walt Disney grew bored of it, and actually redirected his energy into the creation of Disneyland. In fact, the iconic Sleeping Beauty's castle was built at the center of the park as promotion for that film's eventual debut just four years later.

2205.   As a 12 year old, Shia LaBeouf found an agent in the Yellow Pages, and was taken on after pretending to be his own manager.

2206.   Originally, the traffic and train light for go was white, and caution was green. The choice of white light for go turned out to cause a lot of problems. For example, back in 1914, one of the red lenses fell out of its holder while leaving a white light behind it exposed. This ended up with a train running a stop signal and crashing into another train; so the railroad changed it so that the green light means go, and yellow was chosen for caution mostly because it's the most distinct color from the other two.

2207.   Over the past decade, our complete obsession with bacon has led to some seriously strange bacon products. Some examples of this include bacon ice cream, bacon lollipops, bacon mayonnaise, bacon chocolate bars and, yes, bacon gumballs.

2208.   Netflix has actually made a Netflix and chill button called "The Switch," when you activate it, The Switch dims the lights, activates your phone's do-not-disturb feature, and gets Netflix ready for streaming.

2209.   Spiders cannot digest solid food. Before they can eat their prey, they must turn their meal into a liquid form. They exude digestive enzymes from their stomach onto the victim's body. Once the enzymes break down the tissues of the prey, they suck up the liquid remains.

2210.   The national animal of Scotland is the unicorn.

2211.   There is an island in the Bahamas known as Pig Beach, which is populated entirely by pigs. Visitors can actually arrange to swim with them.

2212.   It is against the law to disrupt a wedding or funeral in South Australia.

2213.   A Swedish tourism agency created The Swedish Number, 46 771 793 336, a single phone line that connects international callers to randomly-selected Swedish volunteers to chat about whatever's on their minds.

2214.   iPhone owners unlock their device, on average, about 80 times per day.

2215.   Slash didn't actually purchase his iconic top hat. He shoplifted it from a store. He just put it on his head and walked out.

2216.   Qatar Airways allows you to travel with and keep a falcon in the cabin, provided that there aren't already six falcons aboard.

2217.   The orange stitching on the back pockets of Levi jeans is called "arcuate". Since the design has literally no function, it was painted on during World War II rationing.

2218.   President John Quincy Adams had a pet alligator. He kept it in the bathtub in the East Room of the White House.

2219.   Back in the mid-2000s, Kim Kardashian used to be Paris Hilton's personal assistant.

2220.   About 25% to 40% of people have motion sickness. According to the University of Maryland Medical Center, women are more susceptible than men and Asians are more susceptible than white or black people.

2221.   According to the Guinness World Records, the longest videogame marathon playing World of Warcraft was 29 hours and 31 minutes. This was achieved by Hecaterina Kinumi Iglesias, a.k.a. Kinumi Cati, in Vigo, Spain, on the 29th to 30th of March, back in 2014.

2222.   There is an over-50-kilometer-long tunnel that connects the United Kingdom to Europe. It's called the "Channel Tunnel", or "Chunnel", and is located underneath the English Channel. The trip underneath through the channel takes only about 30 minutes and in fact, an entire trip to London to Paris is only two hours and 15 minutes.

If you enjoyed this book and learned anything it would mean the world to me if you could please leave a review so others can easily find this book and itch their curiosity!

Interesting, Fun and Crazy Facts of America

1.   The largest employer of the U.S. is the U.S. Department of Defense which employs over three million people.

2.   Hawaii has the only royal palace in the U.S. that's still used as an official residence by a reigning monarch.

3.   In the 1990s the U.S. Air Force did research on creating a gay bomb, a non lethal bomb that contained intense pheromones that would make the enemy's forces attracted to each other.

4.   The Department of Homeland Security released a manual to help people prepare for a zombie apocalypse after they discovered a brain parasite that has the potential to hijack the host's nervous system effectively turning them into a human zombie.

5.   The smallest park in the world is located in Portland, Oregon and measures just two feet in diameter.

6.   The First Lady of the United States is actually a position and not just an honorary title and can be filled by the president's niece, daughter or sister and not just his wife.

7.   There is a skyscraper in New York City with no windows located at 33 Thomas Street. It's an extreme example of the brutalist architectural style.

8.   There are so many restaurants in New York that you could eat at one place every day and not go to the same place after 12 years.

9.   In Montana there's a place called 'The Shire of Montana' that's a replica Hobbit Village that anyone can stay in for $295 a night.

10.   There's a charity that exists in the UK and the States that called Project Prevention that pays drug addicts 300 dollars to get sterilized. As of today they have paid over 4000 clients.

11.   The U.S. can cut its military budget by 80% and still have the largest military budget in the world.

12.   The current American flag was designed by a 17 year old named Robert Heft as a high school class project that he got a b minus for.

13.   James W. Rogers was the last man to ever be executed by a firing squad in the U.S. His final request was a bulletproof vest.

14.   After the attack on Pearl Harbor, Canada was actually the first western nation to declare war on Japan. The United States followed the day after.

15.   When the Domestic Parcel Service was first introduced by the U.S. postal service in 1913, it was legal to ship children as long as they weighed less than 50 pounds.

16.   Monowi, Nebraska is the smallest incorporated municipality in the US. with a population of just one. It's sole resident is the town mayor and the librarian.

17.   In 2012 a nineteen year old teen secretly lived in AOL's headquarters for two full months in California. He ate free food, used the gyms and showers and even slept in the conference room while working on his own startup.

18.   While John F. Kennedy worked in the White House in 1961 to 1963 he never once collected his salary instead donating it all to charity.

19.   It is illegal to wear a bulletproof vest while committing a murder in New Jersey.

20.   Dalton Chisholm sued the Bank of America for $1784 billion trillion because he was unhappy with their service. He didn't succeed.

21.   There is a micronation located in the state of Nevada called Molossia that was founded by a man named Kevin Baugh that consists of his house, his front and his backyard.

22.   The Zombie Research Society or ZRS has declared the month of May, Zombie Awareness month in the U.S. with the goal of bringing awareness about zombies and the possibility of a future zombie apocalypse.

23.   The Statue of Liberty was originally meant to be a gift to the Egyptians from France but when it was refused it was given to America instead in honor of her centennial.

24.   The average annual salary of a professional NBA cheerleader is $56,000.

25.   In some cities in the U.S. such as Rialto in California, police officers are required to wear a camera in order to document their interactions with civilians. In those cities, public complaints against officers fell by 88 percent.

26.   In 2013 a homeless man named Billy Ray Harris returned an engagement ring to a woman who accidentally dropped it into his change cup. The owner of the ring, Sarah Darling was so overjoyed that she and her fiance set up a fundraising page and raised $187,000 from public donations which allowed Billy to get a house and a job.

27.   To save workers time during the construction of the new world trade center building, a mobile Subway restaurant was installed for their lunches that moved up the building as they completed each new floor.

28.   There's a restaurant in L.A. called Evarestaurant that gives 5% off the total bill to patrons if they give up their phones before being seated.

29.   The United States budget for nuclear weapons is not included in the Department of Defense spending but actually falls under the Department of Energy.

30.   Killing season as it's known in the UK or the July effect as it's known in the U.S. is used to describe the time around July and August when newly qualified doctors first begin their residencies.

31.   Eminem was offered the lead role in 2013 sci-fi movie Elysium and was interested but turned it down because the director turned down his one request, that the movie was shot in his hometown of Detroit.

32.   According to NASA, nuclear power presented an average of 1.8 million deaths between 1971 and 2009 as a result of lower air pollution from reduced coal usage.

33.   Dr. Dre made more money off his beats headphones than he did in his whole music career.

34.   There is no federal law that requires an expiration date on canned foods except for infant formula. Canned food in fact is potentially still good for years after its expiration date. The biggest reason that they exist is that companies hope that you'll throw the product out and buy more.

35.   Michael Crichton, author of Jurassic Park felt that his literature professor at Harvard was giving him unfair grades so to prove it, he turned in a paper by George Orwell and received a B minus.

36.   Stephen Hawking once tried to find potential time-travelers by holding a party and sending out invitations after the party.

37.   In 2014 a 39 year old man named Ferdinand Puentes survived a plane crash off the coast of Molokai, Hawaii capturing the whole thing on his GoPro.

38.   Hamburger University is a real institution in Elk Grove, Illinois where students can earn a degree in Hamburgerology. It was founded by one of the first owners of McDonald's, Ray Kroc, in 1961.

39.   The world's fastest and tallest water slide was opened in Kansas City, in July of 2014. It's named 'Verruckt', which is German for 'insane'. It's 168 feet and can reach speeds of 65 miles per hour and has a plunge longer than that of Niagara Falls.

40.   In 1927 several million people sent petitions to Congress urging them to adopt the metric system. The petition was opposed by the manufacturing industry citing the cost of conversion.

41.   A study conducted in 2014 of the happiest and least happy states in the U.S. using 26 key metrics. The number one happiest state was Utah while the least happiest state was found to be West Virginia.

42.   AT&T Stadium in Texas formerly known as the Cowboys Stadium uses more electricity in one day than all of Liberia does in a day.

43.   In 1997 there was a short-lived cable network in America called the Puppy Channel, and all it did was broadcast footage of puppies playing for three whole years.

44.   Seattle, Washington is home to Beacon Food Forest. A city park filled with hundreds of edible plants like vegetable plants, fruit trees and more. It's the largest free food forest on public land in America.

45.   American was the official language of the state of Illinois from 1923 all the way up to 1969.

46.   In 1918 a World War One homing pigeon named Cher Ami saved 194 American soldiers lives by continuing her journey after losing an eye, a leg and after having been shot through the chest.

47.   In 1962 the CIA tipped off South Africa's intelligent service about the location of Nelson Mandela that led to his arrest that put him in jail for 27 years.

48.   Former U.S. president Calvin Coolidge used to enjoy buzzing for his bodyguards and then hiding under his desk as they frantically searched for him.

49.   There is a squirrel whisperer student at Penn State University named Mary Krupa. She has the unique ability to not only attract squirrels but to put hats and earmuffs on them as well.

50.   A study conducted by the University of Wisconsin, Madison in 2012 concluded that people who appear to be constantly distracted have more working memory and sharper brains.

51.   According to the FBI the most common time for a bank robbery in the U.S. is between 9 am and 11 am on a Friday.

52.   In 1916 an amendment was proposed to the Constitution that the decision to go to war would be put to a national vote and anyone who voted yes would be forced to enlist in the United States Army. Luckily it did not pass.

53.   The manchineel tree native to Florida are one of the most poisonous trees in the world. In fact, just touching the rain water that drips off of its leaves will burn your skin.

54.   In 2012 Walmart abandoned a huge 124,000 square feet store in McAllen, Texas. The city turned it into the largest single-floor public library in the United States for which it has even won awards.

55.   In 2005 the Golden State Fence Company in Southern California was hired to build part of the fence that separates the U.S. and Mexico. Ironically, just one year later in 2006 they were fined five million dollars after it was discovered that they had hired illegal immigrant workers to build part of the fence.

56.   There are more tigers held in captivity in the United States at 5,000 than there are running wild in the rest of the world at only 3200.

57.   There's a city in Kansas called Gas that was named for the abundant amount of gas that was discovered in the area. The city's motto is don't pass Gas, stop and enjoy it.

58.   The U.S. embassy located in Baghdad Iraq is the largest and most expensive embassy in the world spanning more that 104 acres and costing more than $750 million.

59.   Researchers from the University of California in 2013 found that 29% of San Francisco's pollution comes from China. The hazardous air from China can travel all the way to the west coast of America within only days if the weather conditions are right.

60.   There's an amusement park in Las Vegas called 'Dig This' where you get to drive construction equipment over a giant sandbox.

61.   Peachtree City in Georgia has a 90 mile network of pathways dedicated to pedestrians and golf cart use. Most of the city owns golf carts that use them as an extra car to get around for local transportation.

62.   Switching from one dollar bills to one dollar coins would save American taxpayers approximately $4.4 billion over the next 30 years. This is because coins are significantly more durable than paper bills and have to replaced much less often.

63.   For the past three years, Ohio police have been on the lookout for a serial pooper, who has pooped on at least 19 cars.

64.   There's a town in Alaska called 'Whittier' where almost everyone lives and works under one roof. Inside of a 14-story building, there's a police station, school, two convenience stores, and also a bed and breakfast if you want to make a visit.

65.   In March of 2015, a Georgia teen was arrested for stealing a goat, later confessing he had planned on asking a girl if she would 'goat to prom with him'.

66.   Since 2011, there have been at least four incidents in America of people cooking meth inside of a Walmart.

67.   There exists a series of 69 foot concrete arrows from San Francisco to New York City designed to direct aerial traffic that exists from the pre-digital days, originally installed in 1924.

68.   Until 1974, it was actually illegal to appear in public in Chicago if you were ugly.

69.   There is a statue of famed inventor and electrical engineer Nikola Tesla that radiates free Wi-Fi located in Silicon Valley. Inside the statue, there's also a time capsule to be opened in the year 2043.

70. Since 2010, at least five Americans have shot off their penises by accident.

71. In the 1896 U.S. election, William Mckinley won despite the fact that he campaigned from the front porch of his home in Ohio while his opponent traveled extensively by railway speaking at over 600 events.

72. A parking meter official in Salem, Oregon got busted for stealing $90,000 in quarters in 2015. Bank staff became suspicious because he was regularly depositing large amounts of coins into his personal bank account while still wearing his parking enforcement uniform.

73. Some college students in Cleveland are living rent free in a retirement home. This unique living situation is beneficial for both parties as studies have shown that contact with younger people helps beats dementia while the students save on housing costs.

74. In 1944 a 16-year-old black student in Columbus, Ohio won an essay contest on the theme 'what to do with Hitler after the war' by submitting a single sentence. "Put him in black skin and let him live the rest of his life in America."

75. Every resident of Alaska receives an annual oil royalty check, a payment representing their share of revenue from Alaskan oil. In 2008 the payout reached a high of $2069, or $8267 for a family of four.

76. Virgil Griffith, an American software application writer, gathered information on students about their tastes in music and compared it with their SAT scores. It goes SOCA, gospel, jazz, hip-hop, pop, oldies, reggae, alternative, classical, R&B; rap, rock, country, classic rock, and techno in increasing order of SAT scores.

77. Alice Pick, a 35-year-old woman, tried to use a fake million dollar bill to buy $1675 worth of merchandise at a Wal-Mart in Atlanta, expecting the rest in change.

78. Thomas Jefferson argued that because no generation has the right to bind subsequent generations, the constitution should expire every 19 years.

79. Research conducted at Brooklyn College concluded that females are better at discriminating among colors, while males excel at tracking fast-moving objects. This is believed to be an evolutionary adaptation from our hunter-gatherer past.

80. Research conducted at the University of Chicago found that rats who were trained to press a lever for food stopped pressing that lever once they realized that it also caused another rat to receive an electric shock.

81. Although Donald Trump has described himself as an ardent philanthropist, he ranks among the least charitable billionaires in the entire world.

82.   Bill Gates continued to fly coach all the way until 1997, when his net worth was already, 36 billion dollars U.S.

83.   During construction of the Golden Gate Bridge, a safety net was suspended under the floor of the bridge from end to end, and it came in handy. The net actually saved the lives of 19 men, who became known as the Halfway to Hell Club.

84.   A man named Derek Amato from Denver, Colorado hit his head in a shallow swimming pool, and awoke with a condition known as Acquired Musical Savant Syndrome. What does that mean? Well, he simply became an amazing pianist, despite never having learned how to play the piano.

85.   In 2014, student loans hit a record $1.2 trillion in the U.S., the same size as the entire economy of South Korea.

86.   On June 16, 2014, Jeremiah Heaton of Abingdon, Virginia, claimed the only unclaimed habitable area left on Earth, Bir Tawil, as his kingdom, only so that his seven-year-old daughter, Emily, could be a real princess.

87.   A study by biologists at the University of North Florida concluded that male dolphins actually have a lifelong "bromance" with each other and team up to serve one another as a wingman, helping herd fertile females and sometimes even team up to keep females from mating with other males.

88.   UPS was started in 1907 by 18-year-old Claude Ryan and 19-year-old Jim Casey with one bike and $100 they borrowed from a friend.

89.   Throughout the 1990s, there was a homeless man in New York City named Gangaram Mahes who always purposefully got sent to prison, where he would receive three meals a day and a clean bed.

90.   In 2006, 84-year-old Edith Macefield from Seattle refused a $1 million offer from a shopping mall developer to move, so it was built around her house. In fact, Pixar's film "Up" was later modeled after her home.

91.   Approximately 27 people die every year using elevators in the United States. However, 1,600 die from taking the stairs.

92.   The United States is the most armed nation in the world with 88.8 guns per 100 people.

93.   There are two McDonald's in the U.S. that still serve 'McPizza'. One located in Ohio and the other in West Virginia.

94.   Michael Cicconetti is a judge in Ohio. He uses what he calls creative justice, sentencing guilty defendants with unusual punishments, like one woman who fled a cab fare, and was sentenced to walk 30 miles in 48 hours.

95.   If and when a woman becomes President for the first time in America, her husband will be called the first gentleman.

96.   Felix Kiprono, a lawyer in Kenya, has attempted to offer President Barack Obama 50 cows, 70 sheep, and 30 goats for their daughter, Malia's hand in marriage.

97.   There is a town in Texas called, Earth, and it's the only place on earth officially named, Earth.

98.   On December 16, 2002 during Yao Ming's first game in the NBA, the Miami Heat promoted the game by passing out 8,000 fortune cookies, but he wasn't offended because he had never seen a fortune cookie in China, and assumed that it was an American invention.

99.   A study conducted at Washington University found that rats not only enjoy being tickled, but high frequency recordings showed that they actually make the same laughing sound during a good tickle session than when they play with other rats.

100.   A team of researchers at Michigan State University have created a transparent solar panel that can be used in buildings to potentially power the entire building. It can also be retrofitted to older glass buildings to harness power.

101.   Scientists in Florida plan on releasing genetically modified mosquitoes into the wild in order to reduce cases of dengue fever and other diseases. The males still mate with females, but the hatchlings die before adulthood due to the presence of new genes.

102.   Approximately 7% of all potatoes grown in the United States are turned into McDonald's fries.

103.   There's actually a restaurant in Pittsburgh called the 'Conflict Kitchen', which only serves cuisine from countries that the U.S. is in conflict with. When they started serving Palestinian food, they received death threats.

104.   East St. Louis, Illinois, has a higher murder rate than Honduras, the country with the highest murder rate in the world.

105.   In 1986, the United Way released 1.5 million balloons in Cleveland as a publicity stunt. However, it clogged the land and waterways in northeast Ohio, shut down major airport runways and forced the Coast Guard to suspend search and rescue for two men who ended up drowning.

106.   In addition to being fluent in English, Greek, Latin, French, German and Spanish, Thomas Jefferson also studied Arabic. He also studied Gaelic and Welsh and remains the most multilingual president of the United States in history.

107.   In 1978, the U.S. Navy ship the U.S.S. Stein seems to have been attacked by an unknown species of giant squid. Almost all cuts on the sonar dome contained the remains of a sharp, curved claw that were found on the

rims of the suction cups of some squid tentacles, but the claw marks were much bigger than that of any discovered squid species.

108. A stroke-suffering cat owner from Ohio named Gary Rosheisen attempted to teach his cat Tommy how to dial 911. Unsure of whether the training stuck, the owner later fell over from a stroke in 2006, and the police actually received a silent phone call. When the emergency help arrived, they found the man incapacitated and Tommy by the phone.

109. If you're feeling blue, drawing a picture of your favorite comfort food can actually cheer you up. In 2013, a study by researchers at St. Bonaventure University in New York showed that people who drew pictures of pizza and cupcakes had up to a 28% increase in their moods.

110. A study conducted by the real estate website Movoto calculated population density, unemployment rates, hours worked, and other factors, and determined that Florida is currently America's most stressed-out state.

111. All U.S. astronauts are required to learn Russian as part of their extensive training. This is because they have to be able to run the International Space Station using Russian language training manuals if necessary.

112. On the St. Lawrence River between Canada and the U.S. there's an island called "Just Enough Room", where there's literally just enough room for a tree and a house.

113. After the film Fight Club was released, a bunch of fight clubs started popping up around the U.S. A gentlemen's fight club was started in Menlo Park with its members being from the tech industry only.

114. The ITT technical institute in the United States went under investigation in 2011 for inflating the students grades in order to get more money from the government. In fact, in one such instance a student received 100% on a computer forensics assignment even though all that he handed in was a noodle recipe.

115. There's a New York City hot dog vendor named Mohammad Mastafa who pays $289,000 a year for his location.

116. There are estimated to be nearly 14.5 million cancer survivors in the United States.

117. President Andrew Jackson managed to pay off the United States entire debt in 1835. It was the only time in history that the country was completely debt-free and it lasted exactly one year.

118. In both Canada and the U.S. the federal government requires money acquired through illegal means be reported and taxed just like legitimate income.

119.   The cost of a tourist visa for China is $140 for Americans, and $30 for the rest of the world.

120.   In 2002, a 'Hooters' in Panama City, Florida, offered employees a chance to win a Toyota, but when the winning waitress Jodee Berry was given a 'toy Yoda' action figure as a prank, she sued and won enough to pick out whatever type of Toyota she wanted.

121.   When their child was diagnosed with Xeroderma pigmentosum, a condition in which exposure to sunlight causes third-degree burns and cancer, a New York couple, Dan and Caren Mahar founded Camp Sundown, a summer camp for kids with the genetic disorder where all camp activities are held after sundown.

122.   In 2015, an advertising watchdog group called Truth in Advertising, or TINA, reportedly found that over 100 WalMart products were labeled made in the USA, that were actually made elsewhere.

123.   Just after her husband of 67 years died, a woman named Norma from Michigan was diagnosed with cancer. Instead of getting treatment, she told the doctor, I'm 90 years old, I'm hitting the road, and took an indefinite road trip across the U.S., with her retired son and his wife. The journey was documented on the Facebook page Driving Miss Norma.

124.   A golden retriever from Michigan, named Wesley, was outfitted with braces when he couldn't close his mouth or chew well, due to his crooked teeth.

125.   A study done by Iris Blandon-Gitlin, of California State University in Fullerton, showed that a lie will be more convincing if you have to pee while telling it. Because of a phenomenon called the inhibitory spillover effect, focusing on controlling your bladder also allows you to focus on hiding any signs you might have when fibbing.

126.   The US is the only nation that prints all of its currency in the same size and color. Because of this, 3.3 million blind and visually-impaired Americans depend on someone else, a family member, a friend, a cashier, or even a bank teller to identify the denomination of each bill.

127.   90% of U.S. media, TV, radio and news are owned by only six corporations, those being Disney, CBS, Viacom, News Corp, GE, and Time Warner.

128.   The current CEO of YouTube, Susan Wojcicki is the woman who rented her garage to Larry Page and Sergey Brin in 1998 when they were creating Google.

129.   The Shiawassee Police Department in Michigan staged a fake wedding on September 21, 1990. The bride and groom were undercover cops

who invited local drug dealers to their big day. At the reception, they busted them all at once.

130.   Panera and Chipotle are the only U.S. restaurant chains that have meat offerings that do not use antibiotics.

131.   In Nashville, Tennessee there's a five story, fully automated vending machine that dispenses real cars.

132.   There's a Santa Claus University in L.A. that teaches professional Santa Claus skills such as toy knowledge, poses, and how to avoid a lawsuit. A top level Santa Clause can actually make up to $100,000 a year.

133.   The U.S. Navy maintains a research vessel that is designed to be capsized vertically. As a result, most rooms on it have two doors, one to use when the ship is horizontal, another when vertical.

134.   The Empire State Building makes more money from observation decks than it does from renting office space.

135.   The University of Pennsylvania has produced 25 billionaires, the most of any college in the world.

136.   U.S. and European laws say that travelers must be compensated if their flight is cancelled or delayed but only a few of the eligible travelers try to claim their cash.

137.   A Starbucks in Saint Augustine, which is home to the Florida School for the Deaf and Blind, has employees that use sign language over a two-way video system so that people who are deaf can place their order at the drive-thru.

138.   In the United States sitting on a sea turtle is in fact a third degree felony.

139.   A fire hydrant in San Francisco that survived the 1906 earthquake and aided firefighters in saving the mission district was painted gold in memory of the event.

140.   According to tornado researcher, Tom Grazulis, about 75% of all tornadoes happen within the U.S.

141.   The very first attempt at assassination of a United States President was by Richard Lawrence, an unemployed house painter. However when he shot at Andrew Jackson his gun misfired.

142.   It gets so cold during Minnesota winters that Tom Grotting started sculpting frozen jeans to entertain his neighbors. The craze actually caught on throughout his town spreading to the northeast U.S. landing on the internet, and now the sculptures are popular worldwide.

143.   According to the U.S. Coast Guard Air Station in Traverse City, Lake Michigan can actually become so clear after the winter ice melts that you're able to see shipwrecks 91 meters below the water.

144.   Iowa and Montana will revoke your driver's license if you can't pay back your student loans.

145.   Researchers at Oregon State have patented a strain of seaweed that tastes like bacon when cooked and contains twice the nutritional value of kale.

146.   Up to 40% of tuna imported to the U.S. from Thailand is illegal or unreported, followed by up to 45% of pollock imports from China and 70% of salmon imports.

147.   During World War II, Japan launched balloons with bombs into the jet stream. The only known mainland attack in the U.S. occurred when five picnickers found a downed balloon and attempted to move it. The bomb went off and killed them. The locations of many of the balloons are still unknown.

148.   In 2012, a cat in Boston survived a fall from a 19-story window and survived. It literally only walked away with a bruised chest.

149.   In Jupiter, Florida, a man tossed a live alligator into a Wendy's drive-thru window after the server handed over his drink. He admitted to picking up the 1.07 meter long gator from the side of the road and was charged with aggravated assault, unlawful possession, and transportation of an alligator.

150.   Social anxiety disorder is the third most common mental disorder in the United States, right after depression and alcohol dependency.

151.   Pollution in China actually alters the weather in the United States. Once it gets into the atmosphere over the U.S., the pollution stops clouds from producing rain and snow, i.e., more pollution equals less precipitation. It also only takes just five days for the jet stream to carry heavy air pollution from China to the United States.

152.   Hawaii is the only state that is not geographically located in North America, is completely surrounded by water, and does not have a straight line in its state boundary.

153.   The original name of the USS Enterprise was the USS Yorktown, named after a World War II aircraft carrier.

154.   Air Force One is not the name of any one particular plane. It's the name given to any plane that the president of the United States happens to be traveling on at that particular time. Similarly, the Army aircraft that the president is traveling on is called Army One and their helicopter is called Marine One.

155.   Michael Jordan now makes more money each year than he earned in salary during his entire 15-year NBA career.

156.   According to new research published in the Journal of Computers and Human Behavior, the act of 'fubbing' or phone snubbing is a very real epidemic in the United States. Fubbing is the act of snubbing someone in a social situation by looking down at your phone instead of paying attention to

them, and can damage your relationships and even lead to severe depression and lower rates of life satisfaction.

157.   George Washington was so afraid of being buried alive that he asked his staff to wait two days after his death to bury him.

158.   In 2015, according to a nationwide survey released by Visa, the average American household with teens in it spent approximately $324 on asking a date to the prom.

159.   In 1936, the founder of Adidas, in an attempt to market his shoes, drove to the Olympics and persuaded U.S. sprinter Jesse Owens to wear them. Following Owens' win of four medals globally, letters came in from other national teams interested in buying their shoes. By World War 2, they were selling 200,000 pairs a year.

160.   In 1932, Winston Churchill received a prescription for alcohol in order to get around the American prohibition. After being hit by a car in New York City, his doctor concluded that the solution to what ailed the future prime minister was nothing less than six shots of alcohol at every meal. Although he was allowed to consume even more if he wanted to.

161.   Hundreds of thousands of books on Amazon have been written by bots. They include specialized technical and business reports, language dictionaries, and even crossword puzzle books for learning foreign languages. Philip M. Parker, a professor of marketing, created the computer system that can write these books in about 20 minutes.

162.   Earth Day was founded by U.S. Senator Gaylord Nelson as a way to promote the environmental movement. The first-ever Earth Day was held on April 22nd, 1970. It has been celebrated on that day every year since.

163.   In 2007, Kanye West ordered a curry dish for dinner to be delivered from Wales in the UK to NYC at a price of 3,900 dollars. The dish itself only cost 19 pounds. The rest was a delivery fee.

164.   In 1989, a Philadelphia financial analyst bought an old painting for four dollars at a flea market in Adamstown, Pennsylvania, just because he liked the frame. However, hidden behind it was an original Declaration of Independence which went on to sell at auction for 2.42 million dollars.

165.   Annual statistics reported from The American Cancer Society shows that the death rate from cancer in the United States has declined steadily over the past two decades. The cancer-death rate for men and women combined fell a whopping 23% from its peak in 1991, all the way up to 2012. That translates to approximately 1.7 million deaths averted.

166.   Most Americans are supposed to voluntarily declare and pay state tax on goods that have been bought online from out of state. Accountants and tax lawyers are some of the only people who actually pay it.

167.   According to the Center of Disease Control and Prevention, the number one cause of death in the United States in 2014 was heart disease, with over 600,000 deaths, followed by cancer, with 591,000.

168.   On August 4th, 1922, all phone lines were shut down for one whole minute across the United States and Canada in honor of Alexander Graham Bell's death.

169.   Rosemary Kennedy, John F. Kennedy's older sister, was lobotomized at the age of only 23, except that it failed and left her permanently incapacitated. However, that event inspired her sister, Eunice Kennedy Shriver, to launch the Special Olympics.

170.   State health department records over the past decade show that Hawaii's visitor drowning rate is 13 times higher than the national average and 10 times the rate of the number of its own residents.

171.   Inventor Joey Stein of Genius Ideas in New York City has invented a device that can communicate with fireflies. At the push of a button, it sends out a 'come hither' message that attracts fireflies and lets users observe them up close.

172.   The original Hollywood sign was erected in 1923 and was conceived as an outdoor ad campaign for a suburban housing development called "Hollywoodland". However, it was refurbished and shortened to just Hollywood in 1949.

173.   Pinball machines were actually banned in New York City back in 1976.

174.   Chocolate Avenue is a street in Hershey, Pennsylvania, that runs past the original Hershey's Chocolate factory. The streetlights are shaped like Hershey Kisses.

175.   Unifi, a manufacturer in Greensboro, North Carolina, recycles plastic bottles into polyester yarn to make t-shirts, shorts, or even graduation gowns. In fact, approximately 400,000 college students will actually accept diplomas this year while wearing these gowns.

176.   A survey done by Oxford University found that the average Facebook user has about 155 friends, but is only close enough with about four that they would be willing to turn to in a crisis.

177.   Motorized self-balancing scooters, a.k.a. "Hoverboards", are actually illegal in New York City.

178.   Two University of Washington undergraduates, Navid Azodi and Thomas Pryor, have actually created gloves called "SignAloud" that can convert sign language into spoken word via Bluetooth.

179.   In 2006, a flight from Washington to Dallas was forced to land in Nashville because passengers could smell burning matches. As it turns out, a

woman with a medical condition was lighting matches to cover her own body odor.

180.   Candace Payne, a Dallas mother of two, broke the Facebook Live video record as the most watched video on the platform ever. She shared a live video of herself in a Chewbacca mask laughing hysterically at the voice the mask makes and you may have seen this video because, as of the time of this recording, the video has gained over 164 million views and has been shared almost 3.4 million times.

181.   In May of 2016, President Barack Obama became the first active president to visit the Japanese city of Hiroshima since the bombing 71 years ago.

182.   In 1972, Curtis King built his son a spaceship house in the woods near Signal Mountain, Tennessee, where they lived. It has a drop down staircase and every detail channels futuristic living and it even cost $250,000 to build. It has three bedrooms, two bathrooms, a full bar, and an entertainment area. He eventually sold the house and it can now be rented for a futuristic vacation.

183.   Cincinnati surgeon Dr. Henry Heimlich, the man credited for developing the Heimlich maneuver, actually used it himself for the first time in his life on May 26th, 2016. He saved a woman that was choking at his senior center. He was 96 years old.

184.   If your name is Isabella, you get a free lifetime admission to the Isabella Stewart Gardner Museum in Boston.

185.   Budweiser changes its name to America for the summer of 2016. It literally changed the labels on all bottles and cans with images and phrases affiliated with the United States. The controversial campaign was called "America in Your Hands" and it was run from May 23rd to November of 2016.

186.   According to the U.S. Department of Treasury law, portraits of living persons are prohibited from appearing on government securities like money. This is why you never see living presidents on dollar bills.

187.   The burger with the most calories in the world can be found at the 'Heart Attack Grill' in Las Vegas. According to the owner, Jon Basso, the 'Octuple Bypass Burger' is 20,000 calories. The restaurant ended up making national headlines for literally killing its customers. The waitresses are all dressed as nurses.

188.   The world's longest yard sale, known as the "127 Sale", occurred between August 4th and 7 of 2016 and extended over 621 miles throughout four states. People selling goods lined the roadside along the U.S. Highway 127 and the Lookout Mountain Parkway all the way through Covington, Kentucky, Gadsden and Alabama.

189.   In 2008, a 57-year-old Chicago school bus driver and amateur artist Steve Kreuscher changed his name legally to "In God We Trust". He did this because it symbolizes the help that God gave him during tough times.

190.   American sprinter Forrest Smithson won a gold medal in the 110-meter hurdles in the 1908 Olympics. But what was really astonishing about it was that he was carrying a Bible in his hand. The common rumor is that he did this to protest against the decision to run the finals on Sundays. However, the truth is he was so religious that he often ran with a Bible.

191.   In 2016, Florida governor Rick Scott passed a bill making it legal to break into any locked vehicle in order to rescue a pet or vulnerable person that they believe to be in imminent danger of suffocation; and this was necessary, because as much as 32 people every year in Miami die in hot car deaths.

192.   The American College of Allergy, Asthma, and Immunology found that a bite from a lone star tick can cause you to develop an allergy to red meat, including beef and pork. If your nose ever gets stuffy and begins to run after eating meat, or you get nauseated or get a rash, you may have this allergy and a tick.

193.   A Silicon Valley-based company called "GotIt!" has developed an app by the same name. If you're a high school student, and you get stuck on a question, you can submit it to the app and get tutors to bid for an answer. When the student accepts the bid, which only usually costs about a dollar, he or she gets a 10-minute long tutoring session over text.

194.   It's estimated that poachers kill about 30,000 elephants a year to keep up with the global demand for ivory. As of July 2016 however, the United States has adopted a near-total ivory ban. In fact, more than a ton of ivory was crushed in New York City in 2015 as part of the U.S. government's plan to crack down on the illegal trade.

195.   In 2016, Mark Zuckerberg's Twitter and Pinterest accounts were hacked by a group called OurMine. Apparently, his password was "dadada".

196.   About 36,000 units of blood were donated to the New York Blood Center by New Yorkers wanting to help in the days following September 11th. Unfortunately, because blood can't be used more than a few weeks after donation, more than 200,000 of the 9/11 units had to be discarded.

197.   Gatorade was named after the Florida Gators. In 1965, a team of university physicians in Florida were approached by a University of Florida's assistant football coach because he wanted to find out why his players were being affected by the heat and heat-related illnesses. They ended up creating the drink Gatorade that balanced carbohydrates and electrolytes.

198.   It is illegal in Mobile, Alabama to possess confetti. It's also illegal to store, use, manufacture, sell, offer or sell, give away, or even handle it.

199.   There's a law in Pacific Grove, California that prohibits the molesting of monarch butterflies.

200.   The 31st president of the United States, Herbert Hoover, spent none of his salary on himself, and instead gave it away to charities, or as income supplements to his associates.

201.   On September 13, 1916, the town of Erwin, Tennessee hung an elephant, nicknamed Murderous Mary because she mauled one of her keepers to death. It required a massive crane to accomplish and was done because hangings and lynchings were a popular form of justice at the time.

202.   The automotive industry used to use sperm whale oil to lubricate new cars. In fact the stuff works so well that huge mammals were actually hunted almost to extinction, so the U.S. declared sperm whales an endangered species and switched to the new whale-free automatic transmission fluid.

203.   The first electric traffic light was installed on August 5, 1914 on the corner of Euclid Avenue and East 105th St in Cleveland, Ohio. Based on the design by James Hodge, who received a U.S. patent for his municipal traffic control system, it consisted of four pairs of red and green lights that served as stop and go indicators, each mounted on a corner post.

204.   The seven rays on the Statue of Liberty's crown stand for each of the seven continents. They each measure nine feet long and weigh as much as 150 pounds. In addition, it's overall height is 305 feet from its base, and it has a 35 foot waistline and weighs 225 tons.

205.   About 4.6% of the population of New York city has a net worth of over one million dollars, meaning that one out of every twenty one New Yorkers is a millionaire.

206.   Charlie Sheen once spent over $6500 to buy 2,615 seats at a baseball game so that he could catch a home-run ball. He went home empty handed that day.

207.   North Americans work more, take fewer vacations, and retire later than people in other industrialized countries.

208.   "Live Free or Die" is the official state slogan in New Hampshire and is written on all license plates. Ironically, prisoners in New Hampshire are the ones that make those license plates.

209.   If a baby with foreign parents is born on a plane flying above the United States, the baby is automatically granted American citizenship. However, if the baby is born while flying over the ocean, its nationality depends on the country in which the plane is registered.

210.   In 2010 Mark Haub, professor of nutrition at Kansas State University, went on an all junk-food diet where he ate Twinkies, Oreos, Doritos and other

junk-food for two months to teach his students that pure calorie counting is what matters the most in weight loss. He lost 27 pounds.

211.   In 1968, Samuel L Jackson attended Martin Luther King Junior's funeral as one of his ushers.

212.   Halle Berry was named after Halle's Department Store, a local landmark in Cleveland where she was born.

213.   During the building of the Hoover Dam, 96 people died from industrial fatalities, such as drowning, blasting, falling rocks or rockslides, falls from the canyon wall and truck accidents.

214.   The first ever product to be sold by scanning a barcode was a 10-pack of Juicy Fruit gum. The transaction took place at 8:01 AM on June 26th, 1974 at a Marsh Supermarket in Troy, Ohio.

215.   Almost one billion birds die each year in the United States due to collisions with glass. Although most people have seen or heard a bird hit a window, they often believe that it's an unusual event, but statistically, it's not.

216.   On May 20th, 2016, a man named Aaron Chervenak drove all the way from Los Angeles to a little Vegas chapel in Las Vegas to marry his love, his smartphone.

217.   Theodore Roosevelt was the youngest president in US history. He took office at just 42 years old in 1901, following the assassination of William McKinley, for whom he served as vice president.

218.   32 year old California native, Joey Jaws Chestnut, reclaimed his title by winning the 2016 Annual Nathan's Hot Dog Eating Contest, held at Coney Island. He wolfed down 70 hot dogs in just 10 minutes. That's one hot dog every 8.6 seconds.

219.   The longest tennis match in history was between Frenchman Nicolas Mahut and American John Isner at the 2010 Wimbledon Championships. It lasted 11 hours and five minutes over three days and consisted of 183 games. John Isner ended up being the winner.

220.   San Francisco uses pee repellent paint to protect public walls from bodily fluids. It causes urine to splash back at the offender. This was inspired by Hamburg, Germany, who painted all of their city walls with this repellent and saw public urination drop significantly.

221.   Alaska has the longest coastline in the United States at 6,640 miles long.

222.   The oldest octopus fossil was discovered in northeast Illinois U.S. It dates back approximately 296 million years.

223.   Ronald Reagan and Donald Trump are the only two divorced men to ever be elected president. That includes more than two centuries worth of U.S. presidential elections.

224.   Dwayne The Rock Johnson played football for the CFL's Calgary Stampeders back in 1995 before he went into wrestling and acting.

225.   47% of the world's mail volume is handled by the United States Postal Service.

226.   An Iowa artist named Patrick Acton built a complete model of Hogwarts out of six hundred and two thousand matchsticks held together by almost 60 liters of wood glue.

227.   Research conducted at the University of Stanford concluded that a racially diverse group has the ability to solve problems more effectively than a group with only one race in it.

228.   The Boeing Factory in Everett just north of Seattle is so massive that rain clouds began forming inside the facility until they were finally forced to install a state-of-the-art air circulation system.

229.   There's a waterfall that exists where nobody knows where the water goes. Minnesota's Devil's Kettle Falls dumps into a giant pothole with no seeable exit. Researchers have actually poured dye and logs into it, then watched the lake for any sign of them. So far, none have ever been found.

230.   In the 1960s in Nevada's Black Rock Desert, a power company accidentally created the Fly Geyser. They did this by drilling into a geothermic pocket that let loose a stream of oil, water and calcium deposits. Today, it's a vibrant, living sculpture that's always evolving due to the colorful algae in the water.

231.   A woman in Florida once spent six years sitting on a couch. She actually died during surgery, after doctors attempted to remove her after her skin grafted to the fabric.

232.   Research from the University of Chicago concluded that people think more rationally in their second language and make better choices.

233.   Actor Bradley Cooper begged his father to send him to Japan until he was 21 so that he could train to become a ninja.

234.   Jonah Hill was only paid $60,000 for his role in The Wolf of Wall Street due to the fact that he wanted it so bad. For that role, he received an Oscar nomination for Best Supporting Actor.

235.   The pink cherry blossoms in Washington DC were actually a gift from Japan in 1912 as a symbol of friendship between the two nations.

236.   Cornelius Mike Anderson helped rob a Burger King employee in 1999 and was ordered to serve 13 years in prison, but nobody ever came for him, so he went on living his life in Saint Louis and 12 years later, the prison was preparing for his release only to realize that they had never arrested him in the first place.

237.   Americans work 137 more hours per year than a Japanese worker, 260 more hours a year than a British worker, and 499 more hours a year than French workers.

238.   During the American Civil War, some soldiers' wounds actually glowed blue. These soldiers had a better survival rate so the glow was called Angel's Glow. The luminescence was actually due to bacteria that produce antibiotics that live inside Nematodes who have made homes in the soldiers' open wounds.

239.   2015 was the first year in over 40 years that McDonald's closed more stores than it opened in the United States.

240.   In 2013, a California elderly home went bankrupt leaving 16 residents with nowhere to go. Most of the staff moved on, but Maurice Roland, a cook, and Miguel Alvarez, a janitor, refused to leave their posts and took care of the residents at their own expense.

241.   There's such a thing as fainting goats. In fact, Tennessee holds a Fainting Goat Festival. These goats are born with a condition called myotonia congenital, which causes their muscles to tense up for 10 to 20 seconds whenever they're spooked, which can cause them to easily faint.

242.   Petaluma, California has been holding a world's ugliest dog contest since the 1970's. It's extremely competitive and the world's ugliest title is a fiercely coveted one.

243.   During World War II, because a lot of players were called to duty, the Pittsburgh Steelers and the Philadelphia Eagles were combined to make one team, the Steagles.

244.   The 60 acre Cool Patch Pumpkins Corn Maze in Dixon, California, is so big that people routinely call 911 for help getting out.

245.   There was an actual superhero movement in Seattle led by a mixed martial artist who went by the name Phoenix Jones, and they were pretty successful. They stopped multiple assaults and robberies until 2014.

246.   Michigan oncologist, Doctor Fareed Farah, was convicted and sentenced to 45 years in prison after it was discovered that he had billed 553 cancer patients for millions of dollars by overtreating, undertreating, misdiagnosing, and even administering treatment to people that never had cancer in the first place.

247.   By definition if you commit any crime at sea, you're considered a pirate.

248.   In Queens, New York in 2010, a 12 year old girl named Alexa Gonzalez was arrested, handcuffed, and detained at a police precinct for several hours just for doodling on her desk.

249.   America's first female self-made millionaire was a black woman named Sarah Breedlove or Madam Walker. She made her fortune by developing a tonic that could grow back hair faster.

250.   On January 15th, 1919, a storage tank burst on Boston's waterfront, releasing almost two million gallons of molasses in a 15 foot high, 160 foot wide wave. It rushed through the city's north end at 35 miles per hour, killing a 10 year old boy and injuring many others. It was so powerful that it even swept a train off its tracks and toppled electrical poles.

251.   According to U.S. soldier Sean O'Shea, who guarded Saddam Hussein after he was captured in '03, the only time Saddam ever looked defeated in prison was when they brought him the wrong cereal. "No Froot Loops!" he would scream out.

252.   70% of U.S. elite athletes were found to have a key heart gene variant, known as 'ACTN3' that makes them great sprinters. In fact, 75% of all Jamaicans have this gene.

253.   A 31-year-old man named Jason Willis from Waterford, Wisconsin was banned from the internet in 2014 after sending naked men to a neighbor's house through a Craigslist ad.

254.   In 1991, billionaire George Barber from Alabama had a bunch of life-size dinosaurs built and placed randomly in a 10,000-acre wooded area around his home.

255.   It is entirely possible to see the Milky Way, but light pollution has made that a rare occurrence. In fact, in the 1990s there was a massive power outage in California and the residents of Los Angeles actually began to worry about the strange clouds that they saw overhead. As it turns out, they were actually seeing the Milky Way for the first time.

256.   Even though Chicago has some of the toughest gun control laws in America, the total number of murders there is double the number of American forces that have died in Afghanistan in the last decade.

257.   A Nestle store in Japan sold Kit-Kats coated with edible gold. Limited to only 500, they were sold for the U.S. equivalent of 16 dollars each.

258.   Kyoto, Japan was originally at the top of the atomic bomb target list during World War II, but was personally removed by U.S. Secretary of War Henry L. Stimson because he had previously been to Kyoto on his honeymoon.

259.   In the U.S., being clean-shaven only became popular after troops returned home as heroes from World War I. This is because they had been required to shave so that gas masks could securely fit on their face.

260. Research conducted by Yale psychologist Oriana Aragon determined that tears of joy is your body's way of neutralizing your emotions and helps restore your emotional equilibrium.

261. There's a 39-year-old man named Dan Janssen from Maryland USA who has lived exclusively on pizza for the last 26 years.

262. In 1903, Massachusetts and Missouri were the first states to require a driver's license, although it wasn't necessary to pass a test to obtain one.

263. The first woman in the United States to receive a medical degree was Elizabeth Blackwell, back in 1849.

264. Wild pigs are one of the most destructive animals in America, causing more than $400 million in damage each year in Texas alone. They destroy crops, feast on livestock, terrorize tourists and force other wildlife to flee their homes.

265. In 2011 a third of all divorce filings recorded in the United States, contained the word Facebook. Divorce attorneys say social networking in divorce proceedings and child custody battles has been well on the rise.

266. In Brooklyn, New York entrepreneur Nina Keneally established a business called Need A Mom that you can call and literally rent a mom for $40. She listens to you, gives you advice, cooks, and helps you with chores.

267. At the Marine Mammal Studies Institute in Mississippi, dolphins were trained to turn in trash that fell into the pools in exchange for fish. One dolphin named Kelly was smart enough to hide pieces of paper under a rock, tearing off smaller pieces from the paper in order to get more fish out of it.

268. Fat Man was the codename for the atomic bomb that was detonated over the Japanese city of Nagasaki by the United States on August 9, 1945.

269. The candy-filled eggs Kinder Surprise made by Italian company Ferrero are actually illegal in the United States. The U.S. Food, Drug and Cosmetic Act bans all candies embedded with non-nutritive objects. If you bring one into the United States, you could actually be fined up to $1,200 per egg.

If you enjoyed this book and learned anything it would mean the world to me if you could please leave a review so others can easily find this book and itch their curiosity!

Bonus Facts

1.   The most expensive rose ever developed is the Juliet rose. Famed rose-breeder David Austin created it over the course of 15 years and it cost a whopping £3 million.

2.   Just days after the release of Eminem's 'The Marshall Mathers LP 2', his childhood home that is on the cover mysteriously caught fire and was left in ruins.

3.   On August 21st, 1986, Lake Nyos, a volcanic lake in Cameroon, Africa, suffocated over 1,746 people. The limnic eruption caused 1.2 cubic kilometers of CO_2 to be released in roughly 20 seconds. This massive wave of deadly gas swept over the countryside, killing people as far away as 15 miles (25 kilometers).

4.   The metal band that joins the eraser to a pencil is called a "ferrule". It is also the name of the metal band at the end of a cane.

5.   Three months after Charlie Chaplin died; his corpse was stolen by two auto mechanics who attempted to extort money from his family. They were eventually captured and Chaplin's body was found 11 weeks later. To prevent further attempts, his body was buried under concrete.

6.   Peladophobia is the fear of baldness.

7.   Fish have taste buds not just on their tongues but on their lips and bodies too. Taste buds need moisture to work and because fish are surrounded by water all the time, taste buds can survive on the exterior skin of their flanks and fins, as well as the inside of their mouths.

8.   A man named Luke Irwin inadvertently came across an amazing discovery buried under his newly-purchased property in Wiltshire, England. While an electrician that he hired was drilling into the ground, he hit a layer of intricate red, white and blue mosaic tiles. It turned out that the Irwin residence was built on one of the largest and best-preserved Roman villas ever found in Great Britain.

9.   There's such a thing as a museum dedicated to wax representations of disfiguring diseases. The Moulage Museum in Zurich, Switzerland, is one of them. Civilizations as old as the ancient Egyptians used wax to record how people looked when they died. By the early 1700's, Moulages were a well-known teaching method for medical students and doctors.

10.   The common housefly doesn't have a mouth. Instead, it has an eating tube through which it vomits a drop of fluid from its stomach onto its meal. It then sucks up the fluid along with the nutrients that it dissolved, leaving behind a huge amount of germs.

11. According to Universe Today, the distance between the surface and the center of the earth is about 21000 feet (6,378 kilometers).

12. In March of 1974, local farmers in the Shaanxi province of China were drilling for water when they discovered an underground chamber that contained over 8,000 life-sized warrior figures that were made out of terracotta clay. They were from China's first emperor, Qin Shi Huang, who ordered the construction of the figures back in 246 B.C. in readiness for his own burial; and he was only 13 years old at the time.

13. Singer Billy Joel has performed more concerts in Madison Square Garden than any other artist.

14. John Ratzenberger, known for his role as 'Cliff Clavin' in the hit TV sitcom 'Cheers', is the only actor to have voiced characters in every single Pixar movie.

15. The reason that tires are black and not another color is because of the chemical that's added to the tires called Carbon black. It's added to protect tires against ozone and UV damage, and it drastically prolongs the life of any tire, which is why all tire manufacturers use it.

16. Researchers from the UK's Manchester Metropolitan University found that mice don't really like cheese as much as we think. They much more prefer fruit and grains. The rumor of them liking cheese so much was spread via pop culture and cartoons.

17. Summer on the planet Uranus lasts 42 years long, followed by 42 years of winter. It's earth's tilt that gives us our seasons, but Uranus's is significantly more on its side in relation to its poles, hence the length of its seasons.

18. There's a place in Arizona called the boneyard that is the final resting place of about 3,000 military aircraft, some of them up to 60 years old. They literally just sit there and are gradually harvested for spare parts over time.

19. There's a very rare illness called Kleine-Levin syndrome or Sleeping Beauty syndrome, where those affected sleep for up to 20 hours per day for days, weeks, or even months at a time, only waking to use the washroom or eat.

20. In Victorian times, children as young as five years old were used as chimney sweeps. They were sent up the chimney, some of them as narrow as 12", to clean out soot and debris. And if they got stuck, the master chimney sweeper would light a fire to encourage them to continue working. But some of them just got stuck and died of suffocation.

21. Between 1347 and 1350, the Bubonic Plague, also known as Black Death, killed 20 million people in Europe. That was 30% of the continent's population at the time.

22.   Balut is a national delicacy in the Philippines. It's a fertilized duck egg or duck embryo that is boiled and eaten from the shell.

23.   The boot laced worm is the largest species of ribbon worm. They can grow up to 197 feet (60 meters) in length, which is longer than a blue whale.

24.   The proper medical term for burping or belching is eructation.

25.   On March 26, 1997, 39 members of the Heaven's Gate cult committed mass suicide because they believed that their souls would be transported to a spaceship that was following the Hale Bopp Comet.

26.   The Satere-Mawe Indians initiate their boys at the age of 13 by making them wear gloves made of bullet ants for 10 minutes. They are repeatedly bitten, which is incredibly painful, but must not cry out if they want to be declared a man.

27.   The Komodo dragon is the national animal of Indonesia.

28.   The baobab tree naturally hallows out after 1,000 years. In fact there's a 6,000 year old baobab tree in South Africa right now that is so large and hollow that it could enclose a small building.

29.   There's a website called Freerice.com that allows people to donate to charities by playing multiple choice quizzes. For every question correctly answered 10 grains of rice are donated through the World Food Programme.

30.   The Sagrada Familia is a large Roman Catholic church in Barcelona that has been in construction since 1882 and will not be completed till 2026.

31.   Dysania is the state of having a hard time waking up and getting out of bed in the morning.

If you enjoyed this book and learned anything it would mean the world to me if you could please leave a review so others can easily find this book and itch their curiosity.

Made in the USA
San Bernardino, CA
20 December 2019